陕西省非物质文化遗产（汉英对照）

Intangible Cultural Heritage of Shaanxi Province

（Chinese-English Edition）

田亚亚　杨　娇　廉　洁　编译

西北工业大学出版社

西　安

【内容简介】 本书按照民间文学，传统音乐，传统舞蹈，传统戏剧，曲艺，传统体育、游艺与杂技，传统美术，传统技艺，传统医药与民俗分类，系统性编选并翻译陕西省第一批到第四批颇具影响力的120项非物质文化遗产名录项目简介，简要介绍该120项非物质文化遗产项目的历史起源、基本内容、基本特征、独特价值、濒危状况等内容。本书内容丰富，图文并茂，旨在促进陕西省优秀传统文化的对外传播，推动陕西省非物质文化遗产的保护、传承与发展。

图书在版编目（CIP）数据

陕西省非物质文化遗产：汉英对照/田亚亚，杨娇，廉洁编译. —西安：西北工业大学出版社，2022.8
ISBN 978-7-5612-8338-7

Ⅰ.①陕… Ⅱ.①田… ②杨… ③廉… Ⅲ.①非物质文化遗产–陕西–汉、英 Ⅳ.①G127.41

中国版本图书馆CIP数据核字（2022）第149477号

SHANXI SHENG FEIWUZHI WENHUA YICHAN (HAN-YING DUIZHAO)

陕 西 省 非 物 质 文 化 遗 产（汉 英 对 照）
田亚亚　杨　娇　廉　洁　编译

责任编辑：李　欣		策划编辑：孙显章	
责任校对：隋秀娟		装帧设计：石小玲	
出版发行：西北工业大学出版社			
通信地址：西安市友谊西路127号		邮编：710072	
电　　话：（029）88491757，88493844			
网　　址：www.nwpup.com			
印 刷 者：西安五星印刷有限公司			
开　　本：720 mm×1020 mm		1/16	
印　　张：22.25			
字　　数：461千字			
版　　次：2022年8月第1版		2022年8月第1次印刷	
书　　号：ISBN 978-7-5612-8338-7			
定　　价：78.00元			

如有印装问题请与出版社联系调换

陕西省社会科学基金项目：
陕西省非物质文化遗产英译与国际传播
模式研究（立项号：2019M039）

前言 PREFACE

根据联合国教科文组织的定义可知,非物质文化遗产是指被各群体、团体,有时为个人,视为其文化遗产的各种实践、表演、表现形式、知识和技能,以及与其有关的工具、实物、工艺品和文化场所。它既是文化遗产的重要组成部分,又是历史文化的重要载体,展现了不同民族、不同群体的文化特性,反映了文化的多样性和人类的创造力,具有重要的历史、科学、教育、文化、审美、艺术和经济价值。

陕西省位于黄河中游,是中华民族重要的发祥地之一,有着5,000多年的辉煌历史,先后有周、秦、汉、唐等十几个朝代在西安建都。悠久的历史、深厚的文化积淀和独特的地理位置,孕育了陕西省丰富的非物质文化遗产资源。陕西省非物质文化遗产网(http://www.sxfycc.com)上的数据显示:陕西省已公示第一批到第六批非物质文化遗产名录,其中入选联合国教科文组织人类非物质文化遗产代表作名录的项目有3项,国家级非物质文化遗产名录项目87项、省级674项、市级2,000项、县级5,249项。

为了加深人们对非物质文化遗产的了解,增强民族自豪感、文化自信心和保护非物质文化遗产的责任感,2008年至2017年期间,陕西省文化厅(现陕西省文化和旅游厅)、陕西省非物质文化遗产保护中心精心编纂并出版了系列图书——《陕西省第一批非物质文化遗产名录图典》《陕西省第二批非物质文化遗产名录图典》《陕西省第三批非物质文化遗产名录图典》《陕西省第四批非物质文化遗产名录图典》(以下简称"《图典》系列图书"),系统、全面地介绍了陕西省世界级、国家级与省级非物质文化遗产名录项目的历史起源、基本内容、基本特征、独特价值、濒危状况等内容。《图典》系列图书内容丰富,具有较强的史料价值,为人们了解、研究陕西省非物质文化遗产提供了重要资料。

陕西省非物质文化遗产,是陕西的,也是中国的,亦是世界的,其英语译介有助于推动陕西省文化精粹走出国门，走向世界，助推陕西省非物质文化遗产在国际范围的保护、传承与发展，促进文化包容与互鉴。有鉴于此，我们先从《图典》系列图书中甄选了120项兼具传统性与时代性，富有生命力的非物质文化遗产代表项目；然后在该120项代表项目的汉语介绍文本的基础上，结合陕西省非物质文化遗产数据库（http://www.sxlib.org.cn）、中国非物质文化遗产网（https://www.ihchina.cn）等网站中的相关信息，对一小部分项目的汉语介绍文本进行了重新编辑，充实了内容；最后将编辑后的汉语介绍文本翻译成英语，以汉英对照、图文并茂的形式向国内外读者展示陕西省非物质文化遗产的绚丽多姿与独特魅力。

本书为田亚亚2019年承担的陕西省社会科学基金项目（立项号：2019M039）研究成果，田亚亚负责全书的统筹及审定。具体翻译分工：田亚亚翻译了民间文学、传统音乐、传统舞蹈、传统戏剧、曲艺、民俗等类别的58项非物质文化遗产代表项目；杨娇翻译了传统技艺类的32项非物质文化遗产代表项目；廉洁翻译了传统美术，传统医药，传统体育、游艺与杂技等类别的30项非物质文化遗产代表项目。在翻译的过程中，我们力求译文既能最大化地保留原文的韵味，最大限度地对外传播陕西文化，又能符合英语读者对中国文化的认知水平和语言阅读习惯，易于其理解接受。译文有待商榷之处，望读者不吝指正。

本书中非物质文化遗产代表项目的汉语介绍文本主要源于《图典》系列图书、陕西省非物质文化遗产数据库和中国非物质文化遗产网，图片主要源于陕西省非物质文化遗产网。在此，对汉语文本和图片的出处进行统一说明，书中将不再逐一标注。囿于版面限制，译文中的朝代起讫将不再详述。由于我们着手翻译之前，《陕西省第五批非物质文化遗产名录图典》尚未出版，陕西省第六批非物质文化遗产代表项目尚无系统、全面的官方介绍性文本，因此我们未翻译陕西省第五批与第六批非物质文化遗产代表项目，特此说明。

最后，我们向本书汉语原文本的编写者、图片拍摄者致以诚挚的感谢。本书在编译、出版的过程中得到了陕西省文化和旅游厅非物质文化遗产处领导以及西北工业大学出版社编辑的大力支持，在此也表示由衷的感谢。

田亚亚

2021年8月

Preface

According to the UNESCO, the Intangible Cultural Heritage refers to practices, performances, presentations, expressions, knowledge and skills recognized by groups, communities and in some cases, individuals as part of their cultural heritage, including the related tools, objects, crafts and cultural places. It is an essential component of cultural heritage, and an important carrier of history and culture, showing cultural characteristics of different nationalities and groups, reflecting cultural diversity and human creativity, and possessing important historical, scientific, educational, cultural, aesthetic, artistic and economic value.

Shaanxi Province is located in the middle reaches of the Yellow River and is one of the important cradles of the Chinese nation. It boasts more than 5,000-year brilliant history. Xi'an, the provincial capital of Shaanxi Province, used to be the capital of over ten dynasties, including Zhou, Qin, Han, Tang and so on. Shaanxi's long history, profound cultural accumulation and unique geographical location have given birth to rich and colorful intangible cultural heritage resources. According to relevant statistics on the website of Shaanxi's Intangible Cultural Heritage (http://www.sxfycc.com), Shaanxi Province has announced 6 batches of intangible cultural heritage representative items, among which 3 items have been included in the Representative List of Intangible Cultural Heritage of Humanity by UNESCO, 87 items included in national-level list, 674 items in provincial-level list, 2,000 items in city-level list and 5,249 items in county-level list.

In order to deepen people's understanding of intangible cultural heritage, enhance people's national pride, cultural confidence and sense of responsibility for protecting intangible cultural heritage, during 2008 and 2017, Shaanxi Provincial Department of Culture (the present Shaanxi Provincial Department of Culture and Tourism) compiled and published a series of books: *Illustrated Encyclopedia of the First (Second, Third, Fourth) Batch of Shaanxi's Intangible Cultural Heritage Items* (short for "the series of books" hereafter), which offer detailed introduction to Shaanxi's world-level, national-level and provincial-level intangible cultural heritage items, including their historical origin, basic content, basic characteristics, unique value, endangered status, etc. The series of books feature rich content and high historical value, which provide important data for people to understand and study the intangible cultural heritage of Shaanxi Province.

The intangible cultural heritage of Shaanxi Province is not only China's cultural treasure, but also the world's cultural wealth. Its English translation can promote the cultural essence of Shaanxi Province to go out of China and to the world, boost world-wide protection, inheritance and development of Shaanxi's intangible cultural heritage, and facilitate cultural tolerance and mutual learning. In view of this, we selected from the series of books 120 representative intangible cultural heritage items which feature both traditional and modern qualities and far-reaching influence. Then, on the basis of the introductory texts of the 120 representative items and relevant information in Shaanxi's Intangible Cultural Heritage Database (http://www.sxlib.org.cn) as well as on the website of China's Intangible Cultural Heritage (https://www.ihchina.cn), we edited a small part of the introductory texts of the 120 representative items to enrich their content. Finally we translated the Chinese introductory texts into English. This book, with Chinese-English bilingual texts and a large number of pictures, shows readers at home and abroad the great diversity and unique charm of Shaanxi's intangible cultural heritage.

This book is an important research achievement of the Shaanxi Social Science Foundation Project (No. 2019M039) undertaken by Tian Yaya in the year 2019. This book is organized and examined by Tian Yaya. The translation work is done by three translators: Tian Yaya, Yang Jiao and Lian Jie—all from Shangluo University. Tian Yaya translates the introductory texts of 58 representative intangible cultural heritage items which belong to 6 categories, including "Folk Literature", "Traditional Music", "Traditional Dances", "Traditional Operas", "*Quyi*, Folk Vocal Art Forms" as well as "Folk Customs". Yang Jiao translates introductory texts of 32 items from the category of "Traditional Craftsmanship". Lian Jie translates introductory texts of 30 items from categories of "Traditional Arts", "Traditional Medicine" as well as "Traditional Sports and Acrobatics". In the process of translation, we strive to make the translated texts maximize the charm of the original texts and spread Shaanxi's culture to the greatest extent. Meanwhile, we endeavor to make the translated texts meet English readers' cognitive levels and reading habits, and easy to be understood. However, due to limitation of our translating ability, the translated texts are far from perfect, and there is much room for improvement. Any corrections or suggestions from readers are warmly welcomed.

The Chinese introductory texts in this book mainly come from the series of books, Shaanxi's Intangible Cultural Heritage Database and the website of China's Intangible Cultural Heritage; the pictures in this book mainly come from the website of Shaanxi's Intangible Cultural Heritage. Here, we inform readers of the sources of the Chinese texts and pictures in this book, which will not be annotated hereafter. As limited by space, duration of the Chinese dynasties will not be annotated in detail in the English texts. In addition, this book doesn't cover the fifth and sixth batch of Shaanxi's intangible cultural heritage items for the reason that the *Illustrated Encyclopedia of the Fifth Batch of Shaanxi's Intangible Cultural Heritage Items* hadn't been published, and systematic and authoritative introductory texts of the sixth batch of Shaanxi's intangible cultural heritage representative items hadn't been available before we started the translation.

Finally, we would like to show our sincere thanks to the writers and editors of the original Chinese texts and the photographers who take the pictures. We also express our sincere gratitude to leaders of Intangible Cultural Heritage Division of Shaanxi Provincial Department of Culture and Tourism, as well as editors from Northwest Polytechnical University Publishing Press, who have done a lot in the process of editing and publishing this book.

Tian Yaya

August, 2021

目录 CONTENTS

一、民间文学 Folk Literature

- 003 黄帝传说故事 Legend of the Yellow Emperor
- 005 长安斗门石婆庙七夕传说 Legend of *Qixi* Festival in Doumen of Chang'an
- 008 孟姜女传说 Legend of Meng Jiangnü
- 011 农业始祖后稷传说 Legend of Houji, the Father of Agriculture
- 013 劈山救母传说 Legend of Chenxiang Rescuing His Mother
- 016 韩城古门楣题字 Gate-Lintel Inscriptions in Hancheng
- 018 花木兰传说 Legend of Hua Mulan
- 020 炎帝传说 Legend of Yan Emperor
- 022 仓颉传说 Legend of Cangjie
- 024 女娲的传说 Legend of Nüwa
- 027 鲤鱼跃龙门传说 Legend of Carps Leaping over the Dragon Gate

二、传统音乐 Traditional Music

- 033 西安鼓乐 Wind and Percussion Ensemble of Xi'an
- 036 蓝田普化水会音乐 *Shuihui* Music in Puhua of Lantian
- 038 白云山道教音乐 Taoist Music of Baiyun Mountain
- 042 紫阳民歌 Ziyang Folk Songs
- 044 陕北民歌 Folk Songs of Northern Shaanxi
- 047 绥米唢呐 *Suona* Music of Suimi
- 050 靖边信天游 *Xintianyou* Melody of Jingbian
- 052 神木酒曲 Drinking Songs of Shenmu
- 054 秦汉战鼓 Qin-Han Battle Drumming
- 056 埙乐艺术 Music of *Xun*

三、传统舞蹈 Traditional Dances

- 061 安塞腰鼓 Ansai Waist Drum Dance
- 064 陕北秧歌 *Yangge* Dance of Northern Shaanxi
- 067 洛川蹩鼓 *Bie* Drum Dance of Luochuan
- 070 周至牛斗虎 Dance of Bull Fighting Against Tiger of Zhouzhi
- 072 横山老腰鼓 Hengshan Waist Drum Dance
- 075 韩城行鼓 *Xing* Drum Dance of Hancheng
- 078 宜川胸鼓 Yichuan Chest Drum Dance
- 081 靖边跑驴 Jingbian Donkey Dance
- 084 吴起铁鞭舞 Wuqi Whip Dance
- 087 石泉火狮子 Shiquan Fire Lion Dance
- 090 周至龙灯 Zhouzhi Dragon Dance

四、传统戏剧 Traditional Operas

- 095 华阴老腔 Huayin *Laoqiang* Opera
- 097 华县皮影戏 Huaxian Shadow Play
- 100 秦腔 *Qinqiang* Opera
- 103 汉调二簧 Han Tune *Erhuang* Opera
- 106 汉调桄桄 Han Tune *Guangguang* Opera
- 109 商洛花鼓 Shangluo *Huagu* Opera
- 111 合阳提线木偶戏 Heyang Marionette Show
- 114 华阴迷胡 Huayin *Mihu* Opera
- 116 眉户曲子戏 *Meihu* Opera
- 118 府谷二人台 Fugu Song-and-Dance Duets

五、曲艺 *Quyi*, Folk Vocal Art Forms

- 123 陕北说书 Storytelling of Northern Shaanxi
- 126 榆林小曲 Yulin Ditties
- 129 陕北道情 *Daoqing* of Northern Shaanxi
- 131 洛南静板书 *Jingbanshu*, a Form of Storytelling and Singing in Luonan Dialect
- 133 陕西快板 Shaanxi Clapper Talk
- 135 眉县曲子 Meixian Tunes

六、传统体育、游艺与杂技 Traditional Sports and Acrobatics

- 139　甘水坊高空耍狮子 High-Altitude Lion Dance of Ganshuifang
- 142　吴东无底鸳鸯秋千 Swing Playing of Wudong
- 145　柳池芯子 *Xinzi* Acrobatic Performance of Liuchi
- 148　花样跳绳 Fancy Rope Skipping
- 150　少摩拳 *Shaomo* Boxing
- 152　周化一魔术 Zhou Huayi's Magic Shows

七、传统美术 Traditional Arts

- 157　安塞剪纸 Ansai Paper-Cutting
- 159　凤翔泥塑 Fengxiang Clay Sculptures
- 163　凤翔木版年画 Fengxiang Woodblock New Year Pictures
- 166　安塞民间绘画 Ansai Folk Painting
- 168　定边剪纸艺术 Dingbian Paper-Cutting
- 171　澄城刺绣 Chengcheng Embroidery
- 174　西秦刺绣 *Xiqin* Embroidery
- 177　黄陵面花 Huangling Dough Figurines
- 179　陕北匠艺丹青 *Danqing* Painting of Northern Shaanxi
- 182　澄城手绘门帘 Chengcheng Hand-Painted Door Curtains
- 185　洛川刺绣 Luochuan Embroidery
- 187　延川布堆画 Yanchuan Cloth-Paste Pictures
- 190　吴起油漆画 Wuqi Oil Painting
- 192　旬邑彩贴剪纸 Xunyi Colorful Paper-Cuts
- 195　汉中民间木版图画 Hanzhong Folk Woodblock Pictures
- 198　黄陵木雕 Huangling Woodcarving
- 200　东龙山狗娃咪泥哨 Donglongshan Animal-Shaped Clay Whistles
- 203　商州花灯 Shangzhou Lanterns

八、传统技艺 Traditional Craftsmanship

- 207　耀州窑陶瓷烧制技艺 Firing Technology of Yaozhou Kiln Porcelain
- 210　澄城尧头陶瓷烧制技艺 Yaotou Ceramic Firing Technology in Chengcheng
- 213　华县皮影制作技艺 Craftsmanship of Making Huaxian Shadow Puppets

216　中华老字号西凤酒酿造技艺 Brewing Technology of China's Time-Honored Brand *Xifeng* Liquor

218　甘泉豆腐和豆腐干制作技艺 Skill of Making Ganquan Fresh Tofu and Dried Tofu

222　岐山臊子面制作技艺 Skill of Making Qishan *Saozi* Noodles

226　岐山空心挂面制作技艺 Skill of Making Qishan Hollow Dried Noodles

229　秦镇米皮制作技艺 Skill of Making Qinzhen Rice Noodles

232　狄寨徐文岳泥哨制作技艺 Xu Wenyue's Craftsmanship of Making Clay Whistles

234　狄寨竹篾子灯笼编织技艺 Craftsmanship of Making Dizhai Bamboo Strip Lanterns

236　凤翔草编技艺 Craftsmanship of Fengxiang Straw Plaiting

238　阎良核雕技艺 Craftsmanship of Yanliang Peach Pit Carving

241　中华老字号德发长饺子制作技艺 Dumpling-Making Skill of China's Time-Honored Defachang Restaurant

243　中华老字号张记馄饨制作技艺 Skill of Making China's Time-Honored Zhang's Wontons

245　同盛祥牛羊肉泡馍制作技艺 Skill of Cooking Pita Bread Soaked in Beef or Mutton Soup of Tongshengxiang Restaurant

248　蒲城杆火技艺 Technology of Making Pucheng Pole Fireworks

251　太白酒酿造技艺 Brewing Technology of Taibai Liquor

254　陈仓传统银器制作技艺 Traditional Craftsmanship of Making Chencang Silverware

257　张氏风筝制作技艺 Zhang's Craftsmanship of Making Kites

260　武功手织布技艺 Hand-Weaving Craftsmanship of Wugong Cloth

262　普集烧鸡制作技艺 Skill of Cooking Puji Braised Chicken

264　咸阳琥珀糖制作技艺 Skill of Making Xianyang Amber Candy

266　陕北窑洞建造技艺 Architectural Craftsmanship of Cave Dwellings in Northern Shaanxi

269　岐山擀面皮制作技艺 Skill of Making Qishan *Ganmianpi*

272　渭南时辰包子制作技艺 Skill of Making Weinan *Shichen* Steamed Stuffed Buns

275　岐山农家醋制作技艺 Traditional Brewing Technology of Qishan Farmhouse Vinegar

278　丹凤葡萄酒酿造技艺 Traditional Brewing Technology of Danfeng Wine

280　神仙豆腐制作技艺 Skill of Making Fairy Leaf Tofu

283　紫阳毛尖传统手工制作技艺 Traditional Hand-Processing Skill of Ziyang *Maojian* Tea

286　商南草鞋制作技艺 Craftsmanship of Making Shangnan Hemp Shoes
288　传统乐器手工制作技艺 Craftsmanship of Making Traditional Musical Instruments
290　绥德石雕雕刻技艺 Craftsmanship of Suide Stone Carving

九、传统医药 Traditional Medicine

297　孙思邈养生文化 Sun Simiao's Health-Preservation Thoughts
300　华县杏林许氏正骨技艺 Xu's Bone-Setting Technique in Xinglin of Huaxian
303　杨氏一指诊脉技艺 Yang's Pulse-Feeling Diagnosis Technique
305　针挑治疗扁桃体炎 Acupuncture Therapy for Tonsillitis
307　郭氏中医正骨技艺 Guo's Bone-Setting Technique
310　马明仁膏药制作技艺 Technique of Making Mamingren Plaster

十、民俗 Folk Customs

315　黄帝陵祭典 Sacrificial Ceremonies at the Yellow Emperor's Mausoleum
318　宝鸡民间社火 Baoji Folk *Shehuo* Performance
321　白云山庙会 Temple Fair in Baiyun Mountain
323　谷雨祭祀文祖仓颉典礼 Ceremonies of Offering Sacrifices to Cangjie on the Day of Grain Rain
325　炎帝陵祭典 Sacrificial Ceremonies at the Yan Emperor's Mausoleum
327　药王山庙会 Temple Fair in Yaowang Mountain
329　楼观台祭祀老子礼仪 Ceremonies of Offering Sacrifices to Laozi in Louguantai
331　西安都城隍庙民俗 Folk Customs in the City God Temple of Xi'an
333　洛川婚俗 Luochuan Wedding Customs
336　上巳节风俗 *Shangsi* Festival Customs

339　主要参考文献　Main References

一

民间文学

Folk Literature

黄帝传说故事
Legend of the Yellow Emperor

黄帝传说故事普遍流传于陕西省延安市黄陵县的民间口头文学中，它的起源可以追溯到5,000年以前的原始社会末期。据司马迁的《史记·五帝本纪》记载，"黄帝者，少典之子，姓公孙，名曰轩辕"。黄帝是5,000年前华夏民族的一位英明无比的部落联盟领袖。在传说中，黄帝勤劳智慧，正义仁爱，有许多不朽的历史功绩与优秀的品德。

相传，黄帝与蚩尤经过数年交战，最终黄帝把蚩尤消灭在涿鹿之野；黄帝又与炎帝大战于阪泉，炎帝亦为黄帝所败。于是，黄帝成为雄踞中原辽阔土地上的部落联盟首领。他率领先民们在中

The legend of the Yellow Emperor which can be traced back to the end of primitive society 5,000 years ago is a kind of folk oral literature that has widely spread in Huangling County of Yan'an City. According to Sima Qian's *Historical Records: Biographical Sketches of Five Emperors*, the Yellow Emperor was the son of Shaodian, his family name was Gongsun and his given name was Xuanyuan. He was a wise leader of tribes of the Chinese nation 5,000 years ago. As the legend goes, the Yellow Emperor had many invaluable achievements and noble virtues like diligence, wisdom, justice and benevolence.

According to the legend, after several years of fighting between tribes led by the Yellow Emperor and tribes led by Chiyou, Chiyou's tribes were finally wiped out in the wilds of Zhuolu. The Yellow Emperor also fought against and finally defeated the Yan Emperor in Banquan, which made him win the leadership of all the tribes throughout the Central Plains. He led people to make a living on the land of the Central Plains, digging wells, demarcating regions and building palaces. Together with his wife Leizu and his subjects, he

华大地上繁衍生息，计亩设井，划野分州，营造宫室。他还同妻子嫘祖以及臣属们开始了养蚕、做衣帽鞋子、制造舟车、制作指南车、制陶，用火、酿酒、用药等，并创造了文字，开创了中华文明的先河。5,000年来黄帝得到了后世海内外中华儿女的一致崇敬，被奉为"人文初祖"。

黄帝的精神品质以及黄帝所引领的灿烂文化已深植于中华民族历史文化的沃土之中，黄帝传说故事也从他"驭龙升天"后一直流传至今。

2007年，黄帝传说故事被列入陕西省第一批非物质文化遗产名录。

introduced sericulture, medication, clothing making, fire using and wine making, invented boats, carts, southward pointing carts, pottery, characters, etc., which laid the foundation of the Chinese civilization. For the past 5,000 years, the Yellow Emperor has been widely respected by Chinese descendants home and abroad, and is regarded as the "Ancestor of Chinese Civilization".

The virtues of the Yellow Emperor and the brilliant culture led by him have been deeply rooted in Chinese history and culture. The legend of the Yellow Emperor has also been passed down up to now since his death.

In 2007, the legend was listed in the first batch of Shaanxi Provincial Intangible Cultural Heritage List.

长安斗门石婆庙七夕传说
Legend of *Qixi* Festival in Doumen of Chang'an

牛郎织女传说由来已久。其故事的雏形最早可溯源到3,000多年前的西周。西汉时,牛郎织女的故事已逐渐演变为动人的神话传说。千百年来,这个妇孺皆知、优美动人的民间传说一直在中华大地广为流传。

据《汉书·武帝纪》记载,元狩三年(公元前120年),汉武帝为讨伐西南诸国,在今长安斗门沣河东岸开凿昆明池,训练水军,并在池畔东西两侧分别

The legend of the Cow Herder and the Weaver Girl has a long history. The prototype of the story can be traced back to the Western Zhou Dynasty more than 3,000 years ago. In the Western Han Dynasty, the story of the Cow Herder and the Weaver Girl gradually evolved into a touching folktale, which has been widely circulated in China for thousands of years.

According to *The Book of Han: Emperor Wu*, in 120 BC, Emperor Wu of the Han Dynasty had Kunming Lake dug on the east bank of the Fenghe River near Doumen of

立牛郎、织女石像，使牛郎织女传说有了具体的承载空间。后来，当地群众分别为牛郎、织女建庙祭祀，将牛郎、织女石像放置在庙中。人们习惯把织女石像称为石婆，石婆庙由此而得名。唐宋时期，牛郎、织女成为上至朝廷下至平民百姓共同祭祀的神灵，并逐渐形成了七夕民俗活动。明清时期，七夕民俗活动除了沿袭历代流传下来的供五子、求灵巧、水浮针、拜魁星等以外，还上演《天河配》《长生殿》等节令戏，并形成了影响巨大的民俗盛会。

随着千百年的传承，七夕节已成为海内外华人祈求心灵手巧、爱情美满、家庭团圆、国泰民安的传统节日，形成了独特的"七夕文化"。同时，牛郎织

Chang'an City (the present Doumen neighborhood in Chang'an District of Xi'an City) and trained naval forces there in order to conquer the southwestern states. The stone statue of the Cow Herder was placed on the east side of the lake and the stone statue of the Weaver Girl on the west side—the statues serve as the specific carrier for the legend of the Cow Herder and the Weaver Girl. Later, local people built temples to worship the Cow Herder and the Weaver Girl, and placed stone statues of the Cow Herder and the Weaver Girl in their temples respectively. People were accustomed to call the stone statue of the Weaver Girl "Shipo", hence the name of Shipo Temple. During the Tang and Song dynasties, the Cow Herder and the Weaver Girl became deities who were worshiped by both the imperial court and the common people, and *Qixi* (the seventh day of the seventh lunar month) folk activities gradually formed. During the Ming and Qing dynasties, *Qixi* Festival retained traditional activities held in former dynasties, such as offering up five kinds of foods including longans, red dates,

女传说与七夕节习俗也流传到了韩国、日本以及东南亚地区。牛郎织女的爱情故事对我国文学、戏曲、美术、影视等文艺创作产生了巨大影响，成为永恒的创作母题。

2007年，长安斗门石婆庙七夕传说被列入陕西省第一批非物质文化遗产名录。

hazelnuts, peanuts and sunflower seeds, praying for ingenuity, floating needles on the surface of water, worshiping *kuixing* (the star at the tip of the bowl of the Big Dipper). In addition, love-themed operas such as *Goddess Marriage*, *Palace of Eternal Life,* were also performed. *Qixi* folk activities became more and more popular with great influence.

With thousands of years of inheritance, the *Qixi* Festival has become a traditional festival for Chinese people at home and abroad to pray for ingenuity, happy love, family reunion, and national peace, therefore the unique "*Qixi* culture" formed. At the same time, the legend of the Cow Herder and the Weaver Girl and the customs of the *Qixi* Festival also spread to South Korea, Japan and Southeast Asia. The love story of the Cow Herder and the Weaver Girl has become an eternal theme for Chinese literary and artistic creation, exerting a huge influence on Chinese literature, opera, fine arts, film and television, etc.

In 2007, the legend of *Qixi* Festival in Doumen of Chang'an was included in the first batch of Shaanxi Provincial Intangible Cultural Heritage List.

孟姜女传说
Legend of Meng Jiangnü

孟姜女传说以陕西省铜川市王益区黄堡镇孟家塬村为源起地，广泛流传于铜川王益区、印台区、耀州区和宜君县城乡。《大明一统志》云："孟姜女本陕之同官人。"同官即今之铜川。同官在历史上长期是长安的辖县。秦朝和明朝大修长城之时，关中一带为筑城的民夫、戍卒集结出发之地。同官则坐落在长安通往北部边塞的要道上，因而此处就上演了一幕幕无数开赴边关的民夫、征夫与其亲人之间悲欢离合的故事，孟姜女传说就这样在同官形成。

孟姜女传说最早见于唐代的一些史料与文学诗歌中，以主人公"孟姜女"

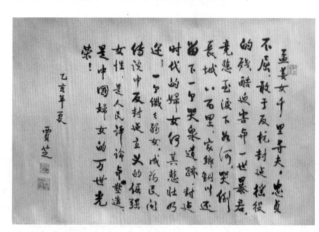

The legend of Meng Jiangnü originated in Mengjiayuan Village, Huangbao Town, Wangyi District of Tongchuan City, and is widely circulated in Wangyi District, Yintai District, Yaozhou District and Yijun County of Tongchuan City. According to historical records, Meng Jiangnü's hometown is Tongguan (the present Tongchuan) which was a county of ancient Chang'an for a long time in history. When the Great Wall was constructed in the Qin and Ming dynasties, Guanzhong area (the central part of Shaanxi) was a place where civilian workers and garrison soldiers who were ordered to build the Great Wall gathered and set off from. Tongguan was located in a strategic place connecting Chang'an (the present Xi'an) and the northern frontier. Therefore, here occurred tragic and touching stories between countless family and the civilian workers as well as garrison soldiers who were about to go to the border. The legend of Meng Jiangnü came into being under such background in Tongguan.

The legend of Meng Jiangnü was first seen in

为主线。它讲述了这样一个故事：孟姜女诞生；秦始皇"焚书坑儒"，万喜良逃到菜园与孟姜女相遇，二人结亲；万喜良被抓走服役，筑长城；孟姜女千里寻夫，哭倒长城，裹夫遗骸，逃奔故里，一路上遇到种种危难，屡现奇迹；最后，当孟姜女一路惊险逃回已近家乡的同官城北之金山崖下时，已是身衰力竭。她将丈夫遗骸安葬并祭烧了"寒衣"后，依然泪涌不止，最终哀伤而逝。一石匠遇此情景深为感动，凿以石室为其安葬。

这个传说故事美丽感人，颂扬了孟姜女的勤劳善良、坚贞勇敢，寄托着封建统治下劳动人民的思想感情，反映了历史行进过程中人民生活的又一个侧

some historical records and literary poems in the Tang Dynasty. The legend takes the protagonist Meng Jiangnü as the main storyline. The story tells the birth of Meng Jiangnü, Emperor Qin Shihuang's brutality of "burning books and burying Confucian scholars alive", Wan Xiliang's escape to the vegetable garden and his encounter with Meng Jiangnü as well as their marriage, sufferings and death. The major part of the legend goes as follows:

As Wan Xiliang was arrested to serve in the military to build the Great Wall, Meng Jiangnü trudged thousands of miles to look for him. When she knew her husband's death, she cried so desperately that the Great Wall fell down, then she wrapped her husband's dead body and tried to go back to her hometown. On her way home, she came across numerous difficulties and miracles. Finally, when Meng Jiangnü fled all the way to the foot of Jin

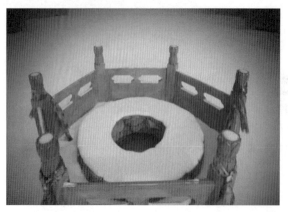

Mountain in the north of Tongguan, which was near her hometown, she was extremely exhausted. When she burried her husband's remains and burned sacrificial paper clothing for him, she was overwhelmed by agony and died of grief. A stonemason happened to see such a scene and he was so deeply moved that he carved a stone chamber to place her dead body.

The legendary story about Meng Jiangnü is touching and appealing. It sings highly of Meng Jiangnü's hardwork, kindness, steadfastness and bravery, reflects the thoughts and feelings of working people under the feudal rule, and shows another aspect of people's lives in the course of history. The legend of Meng Jiangnü has been circulated for more than 2,500 years, and its content has also evolved. The plot is related to Qiliang's wife Meng Jiangnü who lived in the Qi State in the Spring and Autumn Period, but her tragic fate is linked to Emperor Qin Shihuang and the Qin Great Wall.

At present, there still lies Meng Jiangnü Temple in Yintai District of Tongchuan City, and in Yijun County there are names of places such as Spring of Tears, Spring of Heroine, which are closely related to the legend of Meng Jiangnü.

In 2009, the legend was included in the second batch of Shaanxi Provincial Intangible Cultural Heritage List.

面。孟姜女传说流传2,500多年而不衰，内容上也多有演变，情节上和春秋齐国的杞梁妻（孟姜女）有关，但最终其悲剧的命运却与秦始皇和秦长城联系起来。

现今在铜川市印台区仍有孟姜女祠，宜君县有哭泉、泪泉、烈泉等与孟姜女传说紧密相关的地名。

2009年，孟姜女传说被列入陕西省第二批非物质文化遗产名录。

农业始祖后稷传说
Legend of Houji, the Father of Agriculture

陕西省咸阳市武功县古称有邰，据《诗经》《史记》记载，农业始祖后稷（名弃）在这里教民稼穑，开创了光辉灿烂的农耕文化。

4,000多年前，炎帝后裔有邰氏的女儿姜嫄，因踩巨人足迹而受孕生子，以为此婴是不祥之物，结果三弃不死，就又抱回养育，起名"弃"。弃从小就喜欢农艺，在母亲的教诲下，长大后遍尝百草，掌握了农业知识，就在教稼台讲学，指导人们种庄稼，传播农耕文

According to *The Book of Songs* and *The Historical Records*, Houji (given name Qi), the Father of Agriculture, taught people to cultivate crops in Youtai (the present Wugong County of Xianyang City) and created a brilliant farming culture.

About 4,000 years ago, the descendant surnamed Youtai of the Yan Emperor had a daughter called Jiang Yuan, who conceived and gave birth to a child because of stepping on the footsteps of a giant. The child was named Qi (meaning "discarding" in English) for he was discarded three times because his mother thought he was ominous; fortunately he survived every time, so his mother brought him back to raise. Qi was fond of agronomy since his childhood. Under the instruction of his mother, he tasted hundreds of plants and mastered agricultural knowledge. He gave lectures at Jiaojiatai (located in the present Wugong County), instructed people to grow crops and spread farming knowledge, hence was honored as Houji, the Father of Agriculture. People have commemorated Houji for thousands of years, and his story has been widely spread among people. For example, tales such as *The legend of Houji—The Father of Agriculture* and

化，因此被尊称为农业始祖后稷。千百年来，人们纪念后稷，后稷的故事在民间广泛流传。如《神农后稷传奇》《教稼台下赛蒸馍会》都是流传在当地的本乡本土的故事，表达了人们对农业始祖后稷的敬仰之情。

后稷的传说流传年代久远，不仅内容丰富，而且讲述人很多，历朝历代都有造诣颇深的代表人物，如明朝状元康海在编撰《武功县志》时，对后稷的故事就有详细描述。

2009年，农业始祖后稷传说被列入陕西省第二批非物质文化遗产名录。

Steamed Bun Competition at Jiaojiatai spread among the locals, expressing people's admiration for him.

The legend of Houji is rich in content and popular among the people. The legend has passed down from ancient times and many people told the story in the past dynasties. For example, Kang Hai who was a Number One Scholar in Ming Dynasty recorded the story of Houji in detail in *Wugong County Annals*.

In 2009, the legend of Houji was listed in the second batch of Shaanxi Provincial Intangible Cultural Heritage List.

劈山救母传说
Legend of Chenxiang Rescuing His Mother

西岳华山是中华民族文明的象征之一，数千年来与它有关的神话故事引人入胜，发人深思，形成了独具一格的华山神话。华山神话内容丰富，组成了一个异彩纷呈的文化宝库，家喻户晓的"劈山救母传说"就是华山神话中的一个优秀代表。

"劈山救母传说"也称"宝莲灯传说"。它是华山神话中最具有思想性和审美因素的口头文学作品。它依附于华山西峰岩罅的自然景观，是古代劳动人民触景生情、突发奇想而编织的人神结缘的爱情佳话。

故事的基本情节是：唐时，书生刘玺在一年进京应试，途经西岳庙于三圣母殿求神问卜，因见三圣母造像仪态

Huashan Mountain is one of the symbols of the civilization of Chinese nation. Rich in content, unique in style, the myths related to it are fascinating and thought-provoking, forming a grand cultural treasure. The legend of Chenxiang rescuing his mother is one of the outstanding representatives.

The household legend of Chenxiang rescuing his mother, also called the legend of Lotus Lantern (Baoliandeng), belongs to oral literature, which possesses great ideological significance and esthetic value. Based on the natural scenery of the west peak formation of Huashan Mountain, the legend that was created by ancient people is about a love story between a mortal and an immortal.

The story is as follows: In the Tang Dynasty, a young man called Liu Xi went to the capital city to take the national exam held by the imperial court. When he passed the Huashan Mountain, he visited the hall of a beautiful goddess called Sanshengmu in Xiyue Temple to ask his fortune. He couldn't help writing a poem on the wall of the hall to show his adoration to Sanshengmu when he saw the beauty of her sculpture. After the goddess returned,

端丽，偶萌春情，信笔题诗于壁。三圣母回宫后，见题诗羞愤不已，即驾云赶刘玺于途，欲施报复，却被刘玺翩翩风姿倾倒，遂施雨阻途，并化造仙庄一座，引刘玺投宿于此。二人两相倾慕，结为百年之好。不日，刘玺如期赴考，有幸金榜题名，赴任雒州，途中又几次得三圣母以宝莲灯相救。不料此事被三圣母之兄杨戬得知，杨戬以三圣母私配凡夫，有辱仙籍之由，施法将三圣母压于华山西峰。此时三圣母已怀有身孕，后于华山囚地产下一男婴，取名沉香，差侍女灵芝送之至刘玺府第。沉香年龄稍长，得知生母冤情，义愤填膺，遂走出家门，直奔华山营救生母，途中又蒙霹雳大仙传道授术，法力大增，降龙得斧登上西峰，打败杨戬，并持斧劈开山石，救出三圣母，母子重聚。

劈山救母传说通过曲折离奇的故事

she felt so ashamed and angry when she saw the poem that she rode on a cloud and ran after Liu, wanting to revenge on him. But when she saw Liu, she was attracted by Liu's impressive appearance and charm. So by using her magic power, she made it rain to stop Liu's journey and had a mansion built. She led Liu to shelter in the mansion and finally the two fell in love and got married.

Soon, Liu left to take the exam as scheduled, and was lucky enough to pass the exam. He was rescued several times on his way to Luozhou to take office by Sanshengmu with a magic lotus lantern called Baoliandeng. Unexpectedly, Yang Jian, the brother of Sanshengmu, also called God Er-lang, learned of this matter. He thought it was a great shame for an immortal to marry a mortal, so with his magic power, he imprisoned Sanshengmu who was pregnant under the west peak of Huashan Mountain, where Sanshengmu gave birth to a baby boy named Chenxiang and she sent her maid Ling Zhi to take the baby to Liu's mansion. With time going by, Chenxiang learned of his mother's suffering when he grew older and was so indignant that he left home alone to rescue his mother. On his way to Huashan Mountain, he was taught supernatural power by God Thunderbolt and became more powerful. He tamed a dragon and got an magical axe. After defeating his uncle God Er-lang, he cut open the rock with the axe, rescued his

情节和情感纠葛,成功地塑造了沉香不畏神权和暴力、矢志不渝地拯救生母的英雄形象,讴歌了纯真的人性和真挚的爱情,具有反对封建道统、追求个性解放的精神价值,发扬了扶正抑邪、安良除暴的人间正义和民族精神。

2009年,劈山救母传说被列入陕西省第二批非物质文化遗产名录。

mother, and finally the family reunited.

Through fascinating and mysterious story plot, the legend of Chenxiang rescuing his mother successfully shapes Chengxiang's heroic image of not fearing divine power or violence. It eulogizes innocent humanity and sincere human love, possesses spiritual value of opposing feudal orthodoxy and pursuing individual liberation, and shows human justice and national spirit of upholding righteousness, suppressing evil, and eliminating violence.

In 2009, the legend was listed in the second batch of Shaanxi Provincial Intangible Cultural Heritage List.

韩城古门楣题字
Gate-Lintel Inscriptions in Hancheng

陕西省韩城市历史悠久,民俗风情别具特色,素有"文史之乡"和"关中文物最韩城"之美誉。韩城民居建筑在明清时期繁荣发展,独具特色的四合院为韩城赢得了"小北京"的美称。韩城古门楣题字多见于金城区、党家村、东彭村、西庄镇等地,尤以党家村、东彭村的保存最为完好。这些村落的居民旧时多在外经商,家庭富有,房屋考究,门楣匾额制作精美,工艺精湛,内容丰富,是古门楣题字最具典型性的代表。

门楣题字在韩城由来已久,而且至今不衰。韩城古门楣题字的内容,言必称圣贤,语必出六经,均为警句格言,内容经典,用以教化后人,作为祖训代

Hancheng City features a long history and unique folk customs, and is well known for its rich culture relics. The residential buildings in Hancheng flourished during the Ming and Qing dynasties, and the unique quadrangle dwellings won Hancheng the reputation of "Little Beijing" as there are many quadrangle dwellings in Beijing. The inscriptions on the gate-lintels of the traditional houses are mainly found in Jincheng District, Dangjia Village, Dongpeng Village, Xizhuang Township, with those in Dangjia Village and Dongpeng Village being most well-preserved. In the past, residents of these villages were wealthy and owned exquisite houses for they did business and earned much money in other places. With beautiful design, excellent craftsmanship and rich content, gate-lintel inscriptions in these villages are the most typical and representative.

The gate-lintel inscriptions in Hancheng have a long history. The contents of inscriptions are from ancient Chinese classics, which are regarded as mottoes to guide later generations of the family and passed down from generation to generation. Most of the words were written by scholars and calligraphers. Vigorous, bold and graceful calligraphy together with exquisite carving skills make the inscriptions simple, elegant, classical and well matched with the Hancheng-style courtyard, hence they have great preservation value.

代相传。题字书法多出自文人墨客之手，风格浑厚雄逸，刚健秀美，潇洒传神，形成了古朴大方、浑厚规整的审美趋向。古门楣题字再配以精湛的雕刻技艺，古色古香，清雅大方，不落俗套，与韩城特色民居融为一体，相得益彰，极具保存价值。

2009年，韩城古门楣题字被列入陕西省第二批非物质文化遗产名录。

In 2009, the gate-lintel inscriptions in Hancheng were included in the second batch of Shaanxi Provincial Intangible Cultural Heritage List.

花木兰传说
Legend of Hua Mulan

花木兰传说普遍流传于全国的民间口头文学中。这一传说的起源可追溯到北魏时期。脍炙人口的北朝民歌《木兰辞》生动地刻画了花木兰代父从军的英雄形象。明代邹之麟的《侠女传》云："木兰，陕人也。代父戍边十二年，人不知其为女，归赋戍边诗一篇。"位于黄河西侧的延安万花山下的花源头村，被民众传为木兰故里之一。

传说木兰征战归来，不愿在朝廷为官，便引退归故乡，活到80岁，无疾而终，被朝廷赐葬于她的故里山前。人们缅怀这位传奇式的女英雄，有关花木兰的传说一直在民间广为流传。花木兰的传说主要围绕木兰热爱家乡、居功不骄、不谋官禄、顽强拼搏的故事展开，

The legend of Hua Mulan is a kind of folk oral literature that is widely spread in China. The origin of this legend can be traced back to the Northern Wei Dynasty. A popular folk song of the Northern Dynasty, *The Ballard of Mulan*, vividly portrays the heroic image of Hua Mulan who performed military service on behalf of her father. In the Ming Dynasty, Zou Zhilin wrote *Biographies of Chivalrous Girls*, which says "Mulan, a girl from Shaanxi, disguised herself as a man and garrisoned the frontier on behalf of her father for twelve years without revealing her identity. When she returned home from the army, a poem was written to praise her for her military service to the country." Huayuantou Village at the foot of Wanhua Mountain on the west side of the Yellow River in Yan'an City is regarded as one of Mulan's hometowns.

According to the legend, after Mulan returned home from the battle field, she did not want to be an official in the court, so she retired to her hometown and lived to 80 years old. After her passing, she was buried by the imperial court in front of a mountain in her hometown. As people want to remember this legendary heroine, legends about her have been widely circulated

有描述她种花的生活场景,有描述她以国事为重、代父出征的爱国情操,有描述她骑马的故事。这些故事大都有相应的遗迹作为依托,如当地有木兰跑马梁、木兰陵园、万花山等。

花木兰传说寄寓着亿万民众对花木兰的崇敬之情,是对花木兰热爱家国、壮志报国精神的最好的肯定和褒扬。挖掘、保护花木兰传说,对继承中华民族传统文化、弘扬爱国主义精神、增强民族自豪感和民族凝聚力具有积极意义。

2011年,花木兰传说被列入第三批国家级非物质文化遗产名录。

among the folks, which are mainly about stories of Mulan's love for her hometown, her humility, desirelessness, and tenacious efforts. In the stories, there are scenes in which she was planting flowers or riding a horse, and there are also descriptions of her patriotic sentiments. Most of these stories are illustrated by corresponding local remains, such as Mulan Racecourse, Mulan's Memorial Park, Wanhua Mountain and so on.

The legend of Hua Mulan indicates hundreds of millions of people's respect and admiration for her. It is the best affirmation and praise for her love for her homeland and her patriotic spirit of repaying her country. Exploration and protection of the legend has positive significance in inheriting traditional culture of the Chinese nation, promoting the spirit of patriotism, and enhancing national pride and national cohesion.

In 2011, the legend of Hua Mulan was included in the third batch of China's National Intangible Cultural Heritage List.

炎帝传说
Legend of Yan Emperor

炎帝，即神农氏，是中华农耕文化的创始者，世有农业之神之称谓。上古之时，人民皆吃禽兽肉；到了神农统治时，人民众多，禽兽不足，神农为此十分担忧，整天思谋着解决人民吃饭的问题。炎帝的诚心感动了天帝，于是天降了一场粟雨。炎帝将粟收拢起来，教人民耕种，人民才有了充足的食物，还把多余的粮食储存起来，以备缺粮时食用。

传说炎帝在天台山首创日中市，开创了市场交易活动，解决了部落之间物品交换的问题，因而被人们尊为"太阳神"。至今在天台山仍有日中市遗迹。

传说炎帝发现了草药，造福人民，被尊为医药之神。炎帝以秦岭为药园，尝

Yan Emperor, also known as Shennong (Divine Husbandman), is the Founder of Chinese Farming Culture and is known as the God of Agriculture. In ancient times, people all ate animal meat. In the reign of Yan Emperor, there were a large number of people but a shortage of animals. Yan Emperor was so worried that every day he thought about how to solve the problem of the shortage of food. His sincerity moved the Emperor of the Heaven, so a rain of millet fell from the sky. He gathered up the millet and taught his people to farm so that people had enough food and were free from hunger, and they also stored the surplus millet in case of food shortage.

Legend has it that Yan Emperor first held market trading activities on Tiantai Mountains at noon and solved the problem of exchange of goods between tribes, which won him the name "God of Sun". There are still remains of the market in Tiantai Mountains.

Legend also holds that Yan Emperor found herbal drugs and taught his people to use them, so he was venerated as the Father of Chinese Medicine. He tasted hundreds of herbs in Qinling Mountains to test their medical value. One day he ate by

遍百草。一天炎帝来到天台山的莲花山，不料误食火焰子（即断肠草），逝于莲花山的老君顶下。炎帝的妻子及其族人为了悼念炎帝，在天台山设祠祭祀长达十日。后来，人们就把放置炎帝尸体的地方叫作"神农骨台"。至今神农骨台寝殿遗址仍在，几千年来民间祭祀从未中断。

传说炎帝逝后，轩辕黄帝亲自立祠祭祀，并封炎帝殉身之地为"嘉陵"，开创了中国祭陵之先河。炎帝之女瑶姬每逢七月初七（炎帝忌日）在莲花山以蟠桃祭祀炎帝，因而此地又称蟠冢。由于炎帝逝于莲花山，后人为了纪念他的功德，便以九品石莲为氏，称炎黄子孙世代生息之地为中华（古代"华""花"相通），以示永志。

2011年，炎帝传说被列入陕西省第三批非物质文化遗产名录。

mistake a poisonous weed called gelsemium elegan in Lianhua Mountain of Tiantai Mountains and finally gave his life for humanity. His wife and his people set up a shrine in Tiantai Mountains and mourned him for 10 days. Later the place where Yan Emperor's corpse was placed was called "Shengnong Remains Platform". Since then, sacrificial activities have been held among the folks for thousands of years.

It is said that after Yan Emperor's death, the Yellow Emperor set up a memorial temple to worship him and named the place where Yan Emperor died as "Jialing Mausoleum", creating a precedent for mausoleum worship in China. On the seventh day of the seventh lunar month (the deathday of Yan Emperor), Yaoji, the daughter of Yan Emperor sacrificed *pantao* (flat peaches) to Yan Emperor in Lianhua Mountain, hence the mausoleum is also called "Pan Mausoleum". As Yan Emperor passed away in Lianhua Mountain, in order to commemorate his merits and virtues, the place where his descendants live and reproduce is called *Zhonghua*.

In 2011, the legend of the Yan Emperor was listed in the third batch of Shaanxi Provincial Intangible Cultural Heritage List.

仓颉传说
Legend of Cangjie

渭南市白水县是字圣仓颉的出生地，至今白水县的史官镇还有仓颉庙和仓颉墓。仓颉造字的传说在白水县流传广泛，妇孺皆知。《白水民间故事集成》《渭南民间故事集成》《民间故事集成（陕西卷）》等书均收录了仓颉造字的传说。

仓颉为上古黄帝时期人，任黄帝的史官，用结绳的老办法录史记事。但在黄帝与炎帝为边境之事谈判时，仓颉使用绳结提供的史实出了差错，致使谈判失败。为了创造简便易记的记事符号，他辞官远游，遍访智者。三年之后，回归故里，居于深沟土窑之中，苦心研究

Cangjie was born in Baishui County of Weinan City. Cangjie Temple and Cangjie Tomb can still be seen there nowadays. The legend of Cangjie's invention of Chinese characters is known to everyone in Baishui and is recorded in books such as *Collection of Baishui Folk Stories*, *Collection of Weinan Folk Stories*, *Collection of Folk Stories: Shaanxi*.

Cangjie was an official historian of the Yellow Emperor. He kept records of information and events by tying knots. However, when the Yellow Emperor and the Yan Emperor were negotiating on border matters, Cangjie made an error based on the historical information provided by the knots, which caused the negotiation failure. In order to invent symbols that were simple and easy to remember to record information, he resigned from his post and traveled far and wide to visit wise men. Three years later, he returned to his hometown, living in an earthen cave dwelling in a deep valley to study symbols to record events and information. He observed the celestial phenomena, surveyed the shapes and patterns of different things on the earth, captured the image characteristics as well as connotation and

记事符号。他仰观天象，俯察地脉，摄取万物影像之特点，悟得万象内涵之精神，依类象形，创造了象形文字。

在黄帝的支持下，仓颉云游四方，给民众教字，遂使人间有了记录语言行为的统一符号。据说他创造的文字的数量有一斗油菜籽的数量那么多。博学的孔子只学得七升，所余三升无用，撒向海外，遂使外国人也有了文字。

仓颉传说歌颂了仓颉创造文字的执着精神和惊人毅力，具有重要的历史和文化价值。

2014年，仓颉传说被列入第四批国家级非物质文化遗产名录。

spirit of the things he had observed, and finally created hieroglyphs according to the shapes and connotations of different things.

With the support of the Yellow Emperor, Cangjie traveled around to teach people the characters he had created so that people had unified symbols for recording information. It is said that the characters he created are as many as a bucket of rapeseed. The erudite Confucius only learned seventy percent of the characters, and the other thirty percent of characters were scattered overseas so that foreigners also had written words.

The legend of Cangjie shows Cangjie's great determination and perseverance in creating characters, which has important historical and cultural values.

In 2014, the legend was included in the fourth batch of China's National Intangible Cultural Heritage List.

女娲的传说
Legend of Nüwa

平利女娲山位于安康市平利县西北部。在当地女娲山一带，长期流传着女娲造人和女娲补天等美丽的传说。

女娲造人传说的主要内容是：女娲在造人之前，从正月初一至初六分别造出了鸡、狗、羊、猪、牛、马，供随后造的人饲养。初七这一天，女娲用水把黄土和成泥，仿照自己的样子造出了一个个小泥人。她造了一批又一批，觉得太慢，于是用一根藤条沾满泥浆，挥舞起来，一点一点的泥浆洒在地上，都变成了人。为了让人类永远繁衍下去，她创造了嫁娶之礼，让人们凭自己的力量传宗接代。

Nüwa Mountain is located in the northwest of Pingli County of Ankang City. Legends about Nüwa's creation of mankind and patching the sky have been circulated for a long time in Nüwa Mountain area.

Legend of Nüwa's creation of mankind goes like this. Before creating humans, Nüwa created chickens, dogs, sheep, pigs, cows, and horses from the first day to the sixth day of the first lunar month, which were raised by the people she created later. On the seventh day, Nüwa mixed the loess with water into mud, and made small clay figures one after another based on her own appearance. But she thought it was too slow to make figures this way. Instead of hand crafting each figure, she dipped a rattan into the mud and flicked it, so mud blobs scattered everywhere and each of these blobs became a person. In order to allow humans to reproduce from generation to generation, she created marriage ritual so that human could carry on the family line by themselves.

Another legend holds that Nüwa and Fuxi were brother and sister. At the beginning of the world, they were the only original

另一种说法是：女娲与伏羲为兄妹。当宇宙初开时，天地之间只有他们兄妹二人，他们住在昆仑山下。为了繁衍后代，他们想结为夫妻，又自觉羞耻。于是兄妹二人登上昆仑山，对天说道："天若同意我兄妹二人为夫妻，请将天上的云都聚成一团，要不然就把云散了吧。"说完只见天上的云立即聚合在一起，他们就按上天的旨意结为夫妻。

女娲补天的传说是：在洪荒时代，水神共工和火神祝融因故吵架而大打出手，最后祝融打败了共工。共工恼羞成怒，朝西方的不周山撞去。不周山是撑天的柱子，被共工撞断后天塌下去半边，出现了一个大窟窿。洪水铺天盖地而来，毒蛇猛兽也出来吞食人民，人类面临着空前大灾难。女娲目睹人类遭遇如此奇祸，决心补天，以终止这场灾难。她选用五色石，架起火把它们熔成浆，用石浆把窟窿补好。随后又斩下一只大龟的四脚，当作四根

human beings who lived at the foot of the mythological Kunlun Mountain. They wanted to get married in order to reproduce offspring but felt ashamed of doing so. So they climbed up to Kunlun Mountain and said to the heaven, "If the heaven agrees my brother and me to get married, please gather all the clouds in the sky into one, otherwise let the clouds scatter." The clouds immediately gathered together, and they got married according to the will of the heaven.

The legend of Nüwa patching the sky goes that: there was a quarrel between the Water God Gonggong and the Fire God Zhurong, and they decided to settle it with fists. When Gonggong was beaten by Zhurong, he was ashamed into anger so that he knocked his head against Buzhou Mountain, a pillar supporting the sky. The pillar toppled, therefore the sky was broken, which gave rise to great calamities, such as terrible floods and the appearance of fierce man-eating beasts. Nüwa witnessed the occurrence of such a miraculous disaster that threatened the survival of mankind and determined to mend the sky to end the disaster. She melted the five-colored stones into liquid and used the liquid to mend the

柱子把倒塌的半边天支起来。女娲还擒杀了残害人民的黑龙，又收集了大量芦草，把它们烧成灰，堵住了向四处泛滥的洪水。女娲补天后，人们又重新过上了安居乐业的生活。但是这场灾祸还是留下了痕迹：从此天还是有些向西北倾斜，因此太阳、月亮和星星都很自然地归向西方；又因为地向东南倾斜，所以江河都向东南汇流。天空出现的彩虹，就是女娲的补天石发出的光彩。

2013年，女娲的传说被列入陕西省第四批非物质文化遗产名录。

broken sky, and cut off the legs of a giant tortoise and used them to serve as pillars to support the sky. She killed a black dragon that was killing people, collected a large amount of reeds and blocked the fatal flood with the ashes burned from the reeds. After Nüwa repaired the sky, the people were able to live and work in peace and contentment again. But after all this disaster left some trace: from then on the sky tilts to the northwest and the ground slopes to the southeast, which explains the phenomenon that the sun, the moon, and the stars move towards the west, and that rivers in China flow southeast into the Pacific Ocean. It is said that the rainbow in the sky is the brilliance of Nüwa's sky-filling stones.

In 2013, the legend of Nüwa was listed in the fourth batch of Shaanxi Provincial Intangible Cultural Heritage List.

鲤鱼跃龙门传说
Legend of Carps Leaping over the Dragon Gate

鲤鱼跃龙门传说起源于陕西省韩城市龙门镇。相传，大禹治水凿开龙门后，眼望着龙门两岸悬崖峭壁相对如门的奇景，便取"唯神龙可越"之意，把此地命名为龙门。龙门，亦称禹门渡、禹门口。

鲤鱼跃龙门传说有两种说法。

一种说法是，从远古大禹时期开始，在每年三四月份，众鲤鱼成群结队逆流而上，奋力争相跳跃龙门。跳上龙门的鲤鱼由大禹在其头顶点红，瞬间鱼变化为龙，冉冉腾空而起。鲤鱼跃龙门遂成为招考天下英才的象征，有青云得路、变化飞腾之意。民间把考中状元叫

The legend of carps leaping over the Dragon Gate originated in Longmen Town of Hancheng City. According to the legend, after Yu the Great (a legendary ruler in ancient China famed for flood control) controlled the flood by chiseling a mountain ridge apart to let water flow away, he looked at the grand cliffs on both sides of the river which seemed like a gate and thought that only dragons can leap over it, hence this place is named the Dragon Gate, which is also called Yumendu, or Yumenkou.

There are two versions of the legend of carps leaping over the Dragon Gate.

One goes that since the time of Yu the Great, in the third and fourth lunar month every year, carps swam up against

the current, struggling to leap over the Dragon Gate. Carps that jumped over the Gate were painted a red spot on the head by Yu the Great, and immediately turned into dragons and flied into the sky. Thereafter the saying "carps leaping over the Dragon Gate" becomes a metaphor of recruiting talents from all walks of life or dramatic promotion in one's career or life. Among the folks, "carps leaping over the Dragon Gate" means people change their fate and raise their social position by passing the college entrance examination, as well as a leap to a happy life or career success.

作"鲤鱼跃龙门",老百姓把幸福生活的飞跃或事业的成功亦称为"鲤鱼跃龙门"。

另一种说法是,居住在黄河里的鲤鱼听说龙门风光好,都想去观光。它们从黄河孟津段出发,来到龙门,但龙门山上无水路,上不去,众鲤鱼只好聚在龙门的北山脚下。一条大红鲤鱼建议大家跳过龙门山,但伙伴们心里胆怯,拿不定主意。大红鲤鱼自告奋勇从半里外就使出全身力量,纵身一跃,一下子跳到半天云里。这时,一团天火从身后追来,烧掉了它的尾巴。它忍着疼痛,继续朝前飞跃,终于越过龙门山,落到山南的湖水中。山北的鲤鱼见大红鲤鱼的尾巴被天火烧掉,吓得缩在一起,不敢

Another saying goes that the carps living in the Yellow River heard that the Dragon Gate had beautiful scenery and wanted to see it. They set off from Mengjin of Henan Province and arrived at the northern foot of the mountain where the Dragon Gate located. But they couldn't climb up the mountain for there was no river for them to swim across. A big red carp suggested that everyone jump over the Dragon Gate, but the rest were timid and could not make up their minds. The big red carp volunteered to jump with all its strength from half a mile away, and suddenly jumped into the cloud. At that moment, a fire in the sky chased it from behind and burned its tail. Enduring the pain, it continued to leap forward, and finally leapt over the gate and fell into the lake in the south. The rest carps saw the tail of the big red carp being burned by the sky

再去冒险。这时，忽见天上降下一条巨龙，说："我就是你们的伙伴大红鲤鱼，因为我跳过了龙门，就变成了龙。你们也要勇敢地跳。"其他鲤鱼受到鼓舞，开始跳龙门山，可是除了个别的跳过去化为龙以外，大多数都过不去。凡是跳不过去从空中掉下去的，额头上都落下一个黑疤。直到今天，这个黑疤还长在黄河鲤鱼的额头上。唐朝诗人李白专门为这个故事写了首诗，其前两句为："黄河二尺鲤，本在孟津居。点额不成龙，归来伴凡鱼。"

2013年，鲤鱼跃龙门传说被列入陕西省第四批非物质文化遗产名录。

fire, shrank together in fright, and did not dare to take risks anymore. Suddenly, a giant dragon appeared in the sky and said, "I am your partner, the big red carp. I turned into a dragon because I had jumped over the Dragon Gate. You must try bravely." The other carps were encouraged and started to jump. Most of them couldn't make it except for a few who jumped over and turned into dragons. Those carps that didn't jump over and fell down from the air had a black scar on the forehead. Now people can still see Yellow River carps with black scars on their foreheads. Li Bai, a brilliant poet of the Tang Dynasty, wrote a poem specifically for this story. The first two sentences of the poem read, "The carps in the Yellow River, originally lived in waters in Mengjin. As they failed to jumped over the Dragon Gate, they could do nothing but to be common fish."

In 2013, the legend of carps leaping over the Dragon Gate was listed in the fourth batch of Shaanxi Provincial Intangible Cultural Heritage List.

二

传统音乐

Traditional Music

西安鼓乐
Wind and Percussion Ensemble of Xi'an

西安鼓乐起源于隋唐,历经宋、元、明、清,流传至今。它是一种以打击乐和吹奏乐混合演奏的大型鼓乐艺术形式,流行于陕西西安(古长安)及其周边地区,尤其是秦岭北麓的众多寺庙和道观。

西安鼓乐内容丰富,乐队庞大,曲目众多,曲调优美,风格典雅。曲与鼓、铙混声交响,相映生辉,鼓曲并作,气势磅礴。

西安鼓乐的演奏形式主要有坐乐和行乐两种。坐乐是乐手在室内围绕桌案坐着演奏的,有严格、固定的曲式结

Wind and percussion ensemble of Xi'an originated in the Sui and Tang dynasties, which went through the Song, Yuan, Ming and Qing dynasties. It is still popular nowadays. It is a large-scale production of percussion music and wind music that has been prevailing in Xi'an (ancient Chang'an) and its surrounding areas, especially in the Buddhist and Taoist temples along the north side of Qinling Mountains.

Wind and percussion ensemble of Xi'an is characterized by its rich content, grand performing band, various tunes, beautiful melody and elegant style. During the performance, the music and sounds of drums and cymbals blend together, producing a magnificent effect.

构，较为精致。全曲由头（又称帽）、正身、尾（又称靴）三部分组成。坐乐常出现在艺人们比赛技艺的场合，称为"斗乐""对垒"。行乐比坐乐简单，是乐手在行走中或站立着演奏的，演奏以曲调为主，节奏乐器只起伴奏、击拍作用，多见于街头表演和庙会等场合。

西安鼓乐乐器分旋律乐器与节奏乐器两大类。旋律乐器有笛、笙、管、双云锣等，其中笛为主奏乐器；节奏乐器有鼓、铙、木鱼等。

西安鼓乐至今仍然相当完整地保留着传统的演奏形式、结构、乐器、曲牌、谱式等，仍保留着唐宋以来中国音乐的许多元素，是中国古代传统音乐的重要遗存，是迄今为止在中国境内发现并保存得最完整的大型民间乐种之一。

According to performing forms, the wind and percussion ensemble of Xi'an can be divided into two categories: one is the "sitting-type" and the other is the "walking-type". The sitting-type music, played by performers sitting together around a table in a hall, follows a strict and fixed musical pattern and it is very delicate. The whole melody consists of head (also called cap), body and tail (also called shoe). It is often performed for skill competition among artists, which is called *douyue* or *duilei*, meaning competition or confrontation. While the walking-type music is a simpler type played by performers who stand or walk while playing musical instruments. The walking-type performance focuses on melodies with rhythm instruments playing the roles of accompanying and beating the rhythm. It is usually played on public occasions such as street performances and temple fairs.

The instruments of wind and percussion ensemble of Xi'an are divided into two categories: melody instruments and rhythm instruments. Melody instruments include bamboo flute, *sheng* (a reed-pipe wind instrument), *guan* (a pipe-shaped wind instrument), Chinese gong chime, etc. Among them, bamboo flute is the main instrument. Rhythm instruments include drum, cymbal, wooden fish, etc.

The wind and percussion ensemble of Xi'an has still kept intact all its traditional characteristics concerning the form and structure of the performance, the instruments, the names of tunes, the patterns of music score, etc. Besides it is an important relic of Chinese traditional music, retaining many Chinese musical elements of the Tang, Song and later dynasties. It is one of the most complete genres of large-scale folk music that has been found in China.

The wind and percussion ensemble of Xi'an is a key to many mysteries in the history of ancient Chinese music. It has important historical value and practical significance for the study, inheritance and development of traditional music in China, hence the fame "the living fossil of ancient Chinese music".

In 2006, Xi'an wind and percussion ensemble was included in the first batch of China's National Intangible Cultural Heritage List. And in 2009, it was included in the Representative List of the Intangible Cultural Heritage of Humanity by UNESCO.

西安鼓乐是破解中国古代音乐史上众多谜团的一把钥匙，对于研究、继承和发展我国传统音乐有着重要的历史价值和现实意义，因此被誉为"中国古代音乐的活化石"。

2006年，西安鼓乐被列入第一批国家级非物质文化遗产名录。2009年，它被联合国教科文组织列入人类非物质文化遗产代表作名录。

蓝田普化水会音乐
Shuihui Music in Puhua of Lantian

蓝田普化水会音乐始于隋，盛于唐，迄今已有1,300多年历史，多见于陕西省西安市蓝田县普化镇的全家岭村和楸树庙村一带。水会音乐是唐代宫廷音乐传入民间并与民间音乐融合后形成的具有地方特色的民间乐种。蓝田普化水会音乐主要用于民间庙会、大型祭祀活动、水陆道场等，后来每年过年时演奏者也在村中神庙前吹奏。其演奏的传统乐器有吹奏乐器和打击乐器两大类。

普化水会音乐手抄传谱有80多种曲牌，使用的是唐代燕乐半字记谱法。其

Shuihui music in Puhua Town of Lantian County, which has a history of more than 1,300 years, dates back to the Sui Dynasty and flourishes in the Tang Dynasty. It mainly prevails in Quanjialing Village and Qiushumiao Village in Puhua Town, Lantian County, Xi'an City. *Shuihui* music, a kind of folk music with local characteristics, took shape after the royal music of the Tang Dynasty spread among the people and merged with folk music. The music is mainly played at folk temple fairs, rain-praying activities, large-scale sacrificial activities, Buddhist ceremonies, etc. Later, it is also played in front of the village temples during the Spring Festival. The traditional musical instruments played include wind instruments and percussion instruments.

The handwritten music scores of *Shuihui* music in Puhua involves more than 80 names of tunes and they adopt the half-word notation of *yanyue* in the Tang Dynasty. The form of performance is divided into two categories: walking-type music (playing while performers are walking) and sitting-type music (playing while performers are chanting indoors). The music is played for serious and solemn occasions, never played for festive wedding

演奏形式分为行乐（行进中演奏）和坐乐（室内诵经时演奏）两大类。因演奏所涉事由严肃、庄重，故从不用于喜庆婚俗场合。水会音乐旋律委婉，清雅细腻，悦耳动听，俗称细乐，具有明显的唐朝传统民族音乐风格和浓厚的佛教文化色彩。水会乐班一般有十到四十多人，每遇大型活动还有仪仗队配合，阵容可超100人，有时也有锣鼓队配合壮势。

蓝田普化水会音乐在乐队乐器构成、曲目、记谱法等方面具有很高的历史价值和学术研究价值，抢救、保护这一民间特有的音乐形式，对于丰富人们的文化生活、继承和发扬我国民族音乐文化具有重要意义。

二十世纪六七十年代，蓝田普化水会音乐遭受重创后，多年来一直处于濒危状态，抢救、传承工作刻不容缓。

2006年，蓝田普化水会音乐被列入第一批国家级非物质文化遗产名录。

occasions. The music is melodious, elegant, smooth, pleasant to the ears, and is commonly known as *xiyue* (fine music), which features obvious traditional folk music style of the Tang Dynasty and strong Buddhist cultural color. The music band ranges from 10 people to more than 40 people. During the large-scale activities, the music band is accompanied by the guards of honor, and the number of people of the whole performing team can reach more than 100. Sometimes there are also gong and drum teams to enhance atmosphere.

Shuihui music of Puhua has high historical value and academic research value in terms of musical instruments, repertoire, notation, etc. Rescuing and protecting this unique folk music form is significant not only for enriching people's cultural life, but also for inheriting and developing Chinese national music culture.

In the 1960s and 1970s, *Shuihui* music of Puhua suffered severe damage, and it has been in an endangered state for many years, therefore the rescue and inheritance work is urgent.

In 2006, the music was included in the first batch of China's National Intangible Cultural Heritage List.

白云山道教音乐
Taoist Music of Baiyun Mountain

白云山上的白云观是西北地区最大的道观，地处陕西省榆林市佳县城南5公里外的崇山峻岭之中。白云山道教音乐是白云山道教活动的主要内容之一，常配合白云山庙会举行。

白云山道教音乐被誉为"白云神韵""圣境仙乐"。明万历三十六年（1608年），北京白云观道士王真寿、张真仪等人来白云山总理教务，首次把北京白云观的道教音乐传到白云山，从而使白云山道教音乐具有古典音乐和宫廷音乐的双重特点，既古朴典雅，又庄重肃穆。清康熙年间，白云山道士苗太稔云游江南各地，广集名山道乐，并使之融入白云山道教音乐。于是，白云山道教音乐又具有婉转优美、清新秀丽的江

Baiyun Temple is the largest Taoist temple in the northwestern region of China. It is located on Baiyun Mountain, five kilometers south of Jiaxian County of Yulin City. The Taoist music of Baiyun Mountain, often played during Baiyun Mountain temple fair, is indispensable to the Taoist activities held in Baiyun Mountain.

The Taoist music of Baiyun Mountain is known as "Baiyun Sacred Music" and "Holy Music in the Wonderland". In the thirty-sixth year during the Wanli Period in the Ming Dynasty (1608 AD), Wang Zhenshou and Zhang Zhenyi, the Taoist priests in Baiyun Temple in Beijing, came to Baiyun Mountain in Jiaxian to preside over religious affairs. They brought the Taoist music of Baiyun Temple in Beijing to Baiyun Mountain in Jiaxian for the first time. Due to their efforts, the Taoist music of Baiyun Mountain combines the features of both classical music and court music, simple and elegant, dignified and solemn. During the Kangxi Period of the Qing Dynasty, the Taoist priest Miao Tairen from Baiyun Mountain travelled all over places in the south of the Yangtze River, collecting famous Taoist music and integrating different music into the Taoist music of

南风格。在长期的演奏过程中，道士们又吸收佛教音乐、晋剧、唢呐、陕北民歌等曲调的精髓和演奏技巧，创作了独具特色的白云山道教音乐。

白云山道教音乐由经韵曲调、笙管音乐和打击乐三部分组成。

经韵曲调是道士诵经时唱的曲调，又称经歌。其内容有赞美道教教义、祈福保安、消灾免难、超度亡魂、劝人行善、孝顺父母、忠君爱国等多种。经文多是古体诗以及对仗工整的骈文，韵律性强，便于歌唱。

笙管音乐因主要乐器为笙和管子而得名，是白云山道教音乐中十分重要的

Baiyun Mountain so that the music became graceful and fresh, featuring Jiangnan (regions in the south of the Yangtze River) music style. In its long-term performing process, Taoist priests have taken in the essence of tunes and performance skills of other music, such as Buddhism music, *jin* Opera, *suona* music, and northern Shaanxi folk songs, which endow the Taoist music of Baiyun Mountain with unique style and feature.

The Taoist music of Baiyun Mountain falls into three categories: the scripture tunes, *sheng* and *guan* music, and the percussion music.

The scripture tunes, also known as the scripture songs, are the tunes sung by Taoist priests when they chant scriptures. They cover a wide range of subjects, including

部分。它除为演唱经韵曲调伴奏外，还可单独演奏笙管曲牌，几乎用于一切道教活动仪式。由于笙管音乐的重要乐器笙、管子、海笛的音色清脆明亮，曲牌古老典雅，再加上特殊的演奏环境，这种音乐听起来庄重肃穆、清心悦耳、委婉细腻、文静优美，是具有浓郁宗教气氛的神韵仙乐。

白云山道教音乐的打击乐属于道教科仪音乐。它的乐器有大鼓、小镲、大铙、铛铛、手铃、大小木鱼等，在特定情况下还使用大小钟、铜鼓、磬等乐器。打击乐乐器特别，音色清脆，音量宏大，击法奇妙，既可在各项科仪活动程序的转换、连接时单独演奏，又可在演唱或演奏经韵曲调、笙管音乐的过程中作为引子、间奏和尾声使用，起着加

praise for Taoism, prayers for good luck, health and safety, expiation for the dead, persuasion of people to do good deeds, filial piety to parents, loyalty to the emperor and the country, etc. The scripture tunes are mostly in the form of Chinese ancient poetry and rhythmical prose and are easy to sing.

Sheng and *guan* music is named after its main instruments *sheng* (a reed-pipe wind instrument) and *guan* (a pipe-shaped wind instrument), and it is an essential component of the Taoist music of Baiyun Mountain. Apart from serving as the accompaniment for singing scripture tunes, it can also be played separately, so it is used in almost all Taoist activities and ceremonies. Due to the clear and bright sound produced by instruments like *sheng*, *guan* and *haidi* trumpet, the ancient and elegant tunes, and the special playing environment, this kind of music is dignified and solemn, soothing and pure, smooth and delicate, gentle and pleasant. It is known as a kind of sacred music full of religious charm.

The percussion music of Baiyun Mountain Taoist music belongs to Taoist religious rite music. The musical instruments include big drums, small cymbals, big cymbals, *dangdang* (a kind of Buddhist and Taoist percussion musical instrument), hand bells, big and small wooden fish, etc. Under certain circumstances, large and small bells, bronze drums, chimes and other musical instruments are also used. Percussion instruments are special, featuring crisp timbre,

强节奏、渲染情绪、烘托宗教气氛的作用。

经韵曲调、笙管音乐、打击乐在道教活动中常穿插、配合使用。这三部分既是独立的，又是不可分割的。演奏时，一名道士常"身兼数职"，该唱时则唱，该吹时则吹，该打时则打。

白云山道教音乐中的大部分几乎是原生态地传承下来的，是古老的、少见的道教音乐和民族民间音乐遗存。它影响着历代人们的信仰和行为，影响着整个社会生活，并对中国传统音乐具有深远的影响。白云山道教音乐是历史文化名城佳县的重要标志性文化，是道教"道法自然，清静无为"理念的形象体现，是道教文化的生动展示。

2006年，白云山道教音乐被列入第一批国家级非物质文化遗产名录。

high sound volume, and unique playing methods. The percussion music can be played individually during the transition and connection of various ceremonial activities, and can also be played as introduction, interlude and epilogue in the singing and performance of scripture tunes as well as *Sheng* and *Guan* music, playing a role of strengthening the rhythm, rendering emotions and highlighting religious atmosphere.

The above three kinds of music are both independent and inseparable, which are often played cooperatively in Taoist activities. During the performance, a priest often plays several roles, singing tunes and playing wind and percussion instruments according to practical need.

Most of Baiyun Mountain Taoist music is inherited in its original form, and is the remains of ancient and rare Taoist music and folk music. It affects the beliefs and behaviors of people throughout the ages, influences the social life, and has a profound impact on traditional Chinese music. It is an important cultural symbol of Jiaxian County, a historical and cultural county, and is a vivid manifestation of Taoist concept of following nature's course and keeping inner peace.

In 2006, the Taoist music of Baiyun Mountain was included in the first batch of China's National Intangible Cultural Heritage List.

紫阳民歌
Ziyang Folk Songs

紫阳民歌是流传在陕西省安康市紫阳县的民间歌曲的总称，是陕南地区最具代表性的民歌之一。

紫阳民歌是紫阳人民在长期的生产、生活、劳动中创作的，无论是词或曲都能体现当地的风俗，明白晓畅，通俗易懂。紫阳民歌分为劳动号子、山歌、小调、风俗歌曲和新民歌等十几个种类。劳动号子是紫阳民歌的基础，而船工号子是劳动号子的内核，在紫阳民歌中占有重要地位。劳动号子的风格粗犷豪迈，音调、节奏复杂多变，具有较强的生活气息。山歌指劳动号子以外的各种山野歌曲，是最能代表山区特点的民歌。山歌的歌词有很多是人们在劳动中即兴创作的，演唱者见景生情，随编

Ziyang folk songs, a generic name of all the folk songs prevailing in Ziyang County of Ankang city, are a kind of the most representative folk songs in southern Shaanxi.

Ziyang folk songs are created by local people in their daily life and work. Both the lyrics and tunes are clear and easy to understand, which can well reflect the local traditions and customs. Ziyang folk songs can be classified into more than ten categories, including work songs, mountain songs, ditties, custom songs, new folk songs, etc. Work songs are the basis of Ziyang folk songs, and boatmen songs are the essence of work songs, playing an important role in Ziyang folk songs. The work songs are bold and unrestrained, featuring complex and changeable tone and rhythm as well as strong life flavor. Mountain songs, referring to all kinds of songs (work songs excluded) sung on the mountains, in the fields, etc., can well embody the characteristics of people in mountainous areas. A large part of the lyrics of mountain songs are improvised in local people's work and show love between men and women. When singers are touched by what they see, they will improvise songs and sing them simultaneously.

随唱，大多是表现男女情爱的内容。小调和山歌一样量大面广，歌词较为固定，曲调细腻流畅，旋律优美动听，节奏平稳细碎，具有较强的叙事性和个人感情色彩。风俗歌曲是紫阳民间举行婚丧嫁娶等各种仪式时所唱的歌曲。新民歌是1949年以后编创的具有鲜明时代特征的新创紫阳民歌。

紫阳民歌的歌词鲜活生动，风趣幽默，有较高的文学价值；所用方言独具韵味；其旋律优美婉转，悦耳动听。紫阳民歌的代表作品有《郎在对门唱山歌》《洗衣裳》《唱山歌》《南山竹子》等。

紫阳民歌对于丰富中华民族音乐宝库、弘扬中华民族音乐文化有不可低估的作用。

2003年，紫阳县被文化部命名为"中国民歌艺术之乡"。2006年，紫阳民歌被列入第一批国家级非物质文化遗产名录。

Like mountain songs, ditties are also characterized by large quantity and abundant themes. Furthermore, they have fixed lyrics, fine and smooth tunes, exquisite and pleasant melodies as well as steady rhythm. They are usually narrative and can well express personal feelings. Custom songs are sung at folk ceremonies including weddings, funerals and so on. New folk songs refer to the songs composed after 1949, which boast distinct characteristics of the times.

The lyrics of Ziyang folk songs are lively and humorous, having high literary value. The dialect in which the folk songs are sung has special flavor; the melody is beautiful and pleasant to ears. The representative songs include *A Young Man Sings Songs on the Opposite Side*, *Washing Clothes*, *Singing Folk Songs*, *Bamboos in the Southern Mountain* and so on.

Ziyang folk songs play a significant role in enriching and promoting the music of the Chinese nation.

In 2003, Ziyang County was named by the Ministry of Culture of China as "Hometown of Chinese Folk Song Art". In 2006, Ziyang folk songs were included in the first batch of China's National Intangible Cultural Heritage List.

陕北民歌
Folk Songs of Northern Shaanxi

陕北民歌是流传于陕北及山西、宁夏、甘肃、内蒙古、河北等陕北周边地区的地域性民歌，是人民群众在长期的生产和生活实践中口头创作的诗歌式民间艺术形式。

陕北民歌是陕北人民的伟大创造，是劳动人民集体智慧的艺术结晶。它最真实、最直接、最深刻地表达了人民的意志、精神、愿望和心声，是劳动人民思想感情的自然表露。人们在生产劳动中为振奋精神而唱；赶牲畜的脚夫们在那偏僻崎岖的山路上为解闷而唱；男人们在劳动休息时，为得到精神上的放松、解除疲劳而唱；婆姨们在纺线织布干活时，为抒发内心情感而唱；少男少女们为爱情而唱……因此，陕北民歌所

The folk songs of Northern Shaanxi are prevailing in Northern Shaanxi and its peripheral areas, including Shanxi, Ningxia, Gansu, Inner Mongolia and Hebei, etc. The songs are a folk artistic form of oral creation in the poetic style that are formed in the masses' work and life.

The folk songs of Northern Shaanxi are great creation of the local people and artistic crystallization of the collective wisdom of the working people. They express people's will, spirit, desires and aspirations in the most authentic, direct and profound way. People sing the songs to lift their spirits while working; porters who drive draught animals sing to relieve boredom on the remote and rugged mountain roads; men sing to get spiritual relaxation and relieve fatigue during work breaks; women sing to express their inner thoughts in the work like spinning and weaving; boys and girls sing to express their love for each other .... The feelings contained in the folk songs are sincere and simple, reflecting the tenacious, generous and rigid character of people in Northern Shaanxi.

The folk songs fall into two major categories: *Xintianyou* melody and the

蕴含的感情真挚、朴实，反映了陕北人民顽强、憨厚、刚直的性格特点。

陕北民歌的形式以信天游、小调为主，此外还有风俗歌（秧歌、酒曲、叫卖歌、婚嫁歌、丧葬歌、祈雨歌）、劳动歌、宗教歌等，约27,000首，其中革命历史民歌约1,400首。

信天游是即兴而作的，歌声粗犷、豪放、高亢、舒展、跌宕起伏，蕴含着浓郁的陕北地域风情、韵味。它的语言生动，情感真切，多用重词、叠字突出歌词的节奏美、音律美与修辞美，并结合比兴、夸张、排比、白描等多种艺术手法使歌词言简意赅，扣人心弦，引人入胜。

小调是人们在日常生活中经常哼唱的歌曲。它的题材面广，内容广泛，曲调丰富多彩，有大量"土生土长"的曲调，也有众多由外地传来但被"陕北化"的曲调，内容涉及陕北人民生活的各个方面，生动地反映了陕北各个历史时期人民群众

ditty. Besides, there are also custom songs (including *yangge* songs, drinking songs, peddling songs, wedding songs, funeral songs, rain-praying songs and so on), labour songs, religious songs, etc. There are about 27,000 songs, among which about 1,400 are revolutionary folk songs.

Xintianyou melody is often improvised, and it is bold, unrestrained, high-pitched and sonorous, featuring a strong regional flavor of Northern Shaanxi. Its language is vivid and expressive, often employing repetitive words to show the rhythmic, sound and rhetoric beauty of the lyrics. And it also makes use of various techniques such as metaphor, exaggeration, parallelism, and traditional delineation to make lyrics concise and fascinating.

The ditty is a kind of song that people often hum in daily life. It boasts a variety of themes, a wide range of content, and various tunes. A large number of tunes are native, and quite a few tunes come from other places and have been assimilated into the local tunes. The content involves various aspects of people's life, vividly reflecting the life events, folk customs, thoughts, emotions and pursuits of the people in different historical periods in Northern Shaanxi. In a word, the ditty is just like an encyclopedia which can showcase all aspects of local people's life.

The folk songs of Northern Shaanxi cover various aspects of life in Northern Shaanxi and are closely related to the

的生活事件、民情乡俗、思想情感、理想追求，犹如陕北的百科全书。

陕北民歌的内容涉及陕北生活的方方面面，与陕北人民的语音腔调、性格特征、生存环境、生活情感有密切联系，展现了陕北黄土高原民歌的地域风采和特色（如信天游、山曲等）。有的源于历史传承，可追溯至古代占卜巫术或先秦时乡俗遗风等；有的源于周边各地并受到蒙古族、回族民歌的影响，形成了多元化、综合化的民歌风格。陕北民歌的代表作品有《东方红》《兰花花》《三十里铺》《走西口》《黄河船夫曲》等。

由于陕北长期处于相对封闭的状态，陕北民歌这一古老的艺术形式至今保留着民族早期文化的诸多特征，具有很高的历史价值和艺术价值。

2008年，陕北民歌被列入第二批国家级非物质文化遗产名录。

local people's accent, character traits, living environment as well as feelings and emotions. The songs such as *Xintianyou* melody and mountain songs can embody the regional flavor of the Loess Plateau folk songs. Some songs originated from the historical inheritance and can be traced back to the ancient divination and witchcraft or the customs in the pre-Qin period. Meanwhile, there are also folk songs which originate from Northern Shaanxi's peripheral regions and are deeply influenced by the folk songs of Mongol and Hui nationalities. Therefore, the diversified and comprehensive folk song style has formed. The representative songs include *The East is Red, Lan Huahua: A Miserable Girl, Thirty-mile Village, Struggling to Xikou for Wealth, Yellow River Boatmen's Song* and so on.

Up to now, due to Northern Shaanxi's long-term relative seclusion from the outside, the folk songs of Northern Shaanxi still retain many characteristics of the Chinese nation's ancient culture and they have very high historical and artistic value.

In 2008, the songs were included in the second batch of China's National Intangible Cultural Heritage List.

绥米唢呐
Suona Music of Suimi

唢呐是一种外来乐器，金元之际从波斯、阿拉伯一带传入我国，成为一种宫廷器乐演奏形式，明朝以后传入民间。陕北绥米唢呐经过历代唢呐手的吹奏，在传承中完成了发展、完善的漫长过程。改革开放后，绥米唢呐进入高速发展期，民间唢呐手遍布各地，吹奏唢呐成为婚丧嫁娶、喜乐庆典中最主要的演奏形式之一。

绥米唢呐在陕北人的生、死、婚嫁、娱神娱人等社会生活的方方面面都是不可或缺的。按用途分类，唢呐可分为喜庆唢呐、娱神祭祀唢呐与哀悼唢呐。喜庆唢呐主要用于寿辰、婚礼、节日、娱乐、开业庆典等场合，娱神祭祀

Suona horn, originally a kind of foreign musical instrument, was introduced into China from Persia and Arabia in the Jin Dynasty and Yuan Dynasty. *Suona* music first served as palace music and hadn't spread among the folks until the Ming Dynasty. *Suona* music of Suimi (referring to Suide County and Mizhi County in Northern Shaanxi) was inherited, developed and perfected by *suona* players with the development of history. Since China's Reform and Opening-up policy, it has developed rapidly and a large number of folk *suona* players have sprung up. Playing *suona* becomes one of the most important performing forms at weddings, funerals and on other celebration occasions.

Suona music of Suimi has indispensable links with all aspects of local people's social life such as birth, death, marriage and entertainment. According to its use, it can be divided into festive *suona*, entertaining-god and sacrificial *suona* as well as mourning *suona*. Festive *suona* is mainly played for birthdays, weddings, festivals, entertainment, opening ceremonies and so on; entertaining-god and sacrificial *suona* is mainly played for temple fairs, temple worship, etc.; mourning *suona* is mainly

唢呐主要用于庙会、谒庙请神等场合，哀悼唢呐主要在殡葬仪式上吹奏。

绥米唢呐的音乐曲牌丰富，种类繁多，风格各异。除了传统唢呐专用曲牌，还有与民族音乐和民歌小调嫁接产生的新曲牌、取材于戏剧音乐的曲牌、吸收宗教音乐形成的曲牌、作曲家创作的曲牌等。绥米唢呐的吹奏形式主要有"大吹""小吹"两种。大吹由五件乐器和五人组成。两个唢呐手各吹一个唢呐，鼓手、镲手、锣手分别击打牛皮鼓、小镲、钩锣。另有两把长号，由唢呐手和鼓手吹奏。小吹有小海笛一把，笙一把，管子一支，再配上小铰子、小铜锣等乐器，吹奏风格委婉清丽。另外，也有100余人的集体表演，场面恢宏，气势磅礴。

绥米唢呐的吹奏形式还可分为"动态"与"静态"两种。动态吹奏一般随迎亲队伍、出殡队伍、秧歌队伍、谒庙队伍、请神队伍在行进中吹奏。吹奏时间不一，若遇村村相连路段，要在行进中连续不断吹奏二十多里路。静态吹奏在各种吹奏场合都能见到，鼓乐班在厅堂围坐吹奏，吹奏时间以活动仪式时间为准，长则2~3小时，短则数分钟。

played at funeral ceremonies.

Suona music of Suimi boasts rich and different styles of names of tunes. In addition to traditional exclusive names of tunes, there are names of tunes which developed from folk music, ditties, drama music, religious music, etc. In addition, there are also names of tunes created by composers. The playing forms of Suimi *suona* can be classified into "the large-scale playing" and "the small-scale playing". The large-scale playing team is composed of five players with five instruments. Two performers play *suona* horns respectively, and the other three people play the cowhide drum, small cymbal and gong respectively. Meanwhile, the drummer and one of the two *suona* players also need to play trombones. The small-scale playing, gentle and fresh, is played with several instruments including the flute, *sheng* (a reed pipe wind instrument), *guan* (a pipe-shaped wind instrument), cymbal, gong, etc. In addition, there is also "collective playing" with over 100 players, which is magnificent and grand.

The playing form of Suimi *suona* can also be divided into "dynamic *suona* playing" and "static *suona* playing". The dynamic playing team usually follows the guards of honour to play *suona* on the move. The playing time varies according to the concrete situation. On the road connecting several villages, players continuously play for more than 10 kilometers' distance. Static *suona* playing can be seen on all kinds of occasions. In

绥米唢呐用途多样,特征鲜明。唢呐传入我国后,先为宫廷器乐,后明戚继光用于军乐,现在陕北唢呐中的一些曲牌体现了铿锵有力的军乐特征。绥米唢呐既保留了传统曲牌,又借鉴了秧歌、民歌小调、戏剧曲牌,曲目具有多元化特征。由于乐班人数少,便于组队出行,加之收费不高,老百姓在婚丧嫁娶、生日庆典等场合都乐于邀请乐班表演,所以绥米唢呐具有广泛的群众性。

绥米唢呐是传播黄土地优秀民间音乐的重要工具之一,具有很高的实用价值和学术价值。

2008年,绥米唢呐被列入第二批国家级非物质文化遗产名录。

this kind of performance, *suona* players sit together and perform in the courtyard and the playing time depends on the duration of the activities, ranging from a few minutes to 2-3 hours.

Suona music of Suimi features various usages and unique characteristics. After *suona* was introduced into China, it was first used as court music and later as military music via Qi Jiguang (a Chinese hero in the Ming Dynasty who was famous for fighting against Japanese pirates). Hence some tune names of Northern Shaanxi *suona* embody strong military music characteristics. *Suona* music of Suimi not only retains traditional names of the tunes, but also takes in names of the tunes of *yangge* (a typical form of collective folk dance of the Chinese Han nationality), folk songs, ditties, and dramas, so its names of tunes feature multiple characteristics. Because a *suona* music band only needs a small number of players, it can travel easily and the performing expense is relatively low. Therefore *suona* players are always invited to perform at weddings, funerals and birthdays or on other important occasions, hence the music has a solid mass base.

Suona music of Suimi, as an important art form that spreads the brilliant folk music of Northern Shaanxi, possesses very high practical and academic value.

In 2008, it was included in the second batch of China's National Intangible Cultural Heritage List.

靖边信天游
Xintianyou Melody of Jingbian

信天游是以驰名中外的草原丝绸之路的交通枢纽古夏州——陕西省榆林市靖边县一带为发祥地，并流行于我国西北地区的一种民间音乐艺术形式。广泛流传在靖边这块土地上的信天游被当地群众称为"山曲儿"。它以质朴的语言、浓郁的乡土特色和优美动听的曲调受到人民群众的喜爱和赞赏，世代传唱，经久不衰。

信天游有即兴演唱、无拘无束、信天而游的特点。当地人称信天游是"土

Xintianyou melody is a kind of folk music that is popular in the northwestern region of China, and its birthplace is the ancient Xiazhou (the present Jingbian County of Yulin City, Shaanxi Province), the transportation hub of the well-known grassland Silk Road. *Xintianyou* melody that is widely circulated on the land of Jingbian County is called "Mountain Tune" by the local people. It has been deeply loved and appreciated by local people and sung from generation to generation as it features simple language, strong local characteristics as well as beautiful and moving tunes.

Xintianyou melody is characterized by its impromptu and unrestrained singing. The locals think it comes and develops from local people's life, and features local dialect. The content of the melody is concerned with the life of the working people, which is narrative, lyrical, funny, humorous, etc. The tunes of *Xintianyou* melody of Jingbian can be roughly divided into two types. One is mountain tunes with high pitch, free rhythm and melodious music; the other is tunes with gentle tone and more complete rhythm, somewhat similar to ditties. Both types of the tunes

生土长土里料，土言土语土腔调"。歌中所唱内容都是劳动人民自己的生活，叙事、抒情、逗趣、调侃无所不有。靖边信天游的曲调大致分为两种类型。一种是音调高亢、节奏自由、气息悠长、空间感很强的山野之歌，另一种是音调委婉、节奏较完整、略带小调性质的曲调。它们都以上下两句组成的单元段为基本结构形式，上句比兴，下句陈述要反映的真实内容。歌词以七字句"一二、三四、五六七"为基本结构，也有五字句"一、二、三四、五"和十字句"一二三、四五六、七八九十"的句式。

靖边信天游以清唱为主，不受舞台、伴奏等条件限制。它贴近生活，易学易唱，不分男女老少，张口就唱，便于流传。歌者以大自然为舞台，兴之所至，尽情抒发。靖边信天游的主要曲目有《卖草鞋》《上一道坡坡下一道梁》《沙梁梁上站个俏妹妹》《哪达达也不如咱山沟沟好》等。

2009年，靖边信天游被列入陕西省第二批非物质文化遗产名录。

are composed of basic unit segments of two sentences. The first sentence is a metaphor, and the second sentence states the implied meaning contained in the metaphor. The lyrics are mainly in the form of seven-character sentences, and there are also five-character sentences and ten-character sentences.

Xintianyou melody features acappella singing, and is not restricted by the stage or accompaniment. It is close to life, easy to learn, thus easy to spread. Nearly everyone can sing it, no matter men or women, the young or the old. Singers take many places in nature as the stage to fully express their feelings. The repertoires of Jingbian *Xintianyou* melody include *Selling the Straw Shoes*, *Climbing up a Slope and down a Ridge*, *A Pretty Girl Stands on a Sand Dune*, *Nowhere Is as Good as Our Mountainous Village* and so on.

In 2009, *Xintianyou* melody of Jingbian was included in the second batch of Shaanxi Provincial Intangible Cultural Heritage List.

神木酒曲
Drinking Songs of Shenmu

流行于陕西省榆林市神木市的神木酒曲是当地广大群众喜闻乐唱的一种民间歌曲，流传广泛，影响深远。从歌词内容来看，酒曲可分为敬酒曲和对酒曲两种，广泛应用于亲朋聚会或喜庆酒宴。

神木酒曲形成的原因有以下几点。一是这里气候寒冷，人们常常用酒来御寒，所以饮酒的习俗就流行起来。家里来了客人或是亲友相聚，都少不了几盅酒。二是神木在古代属于边塞军事重镇，战乱频繁，为抵御外敌、鼓舞斗志，人们喝酒壮行，所以喝酒之风遍及神木。三是神木地处晋陕蒙三地交汇处，各地群众经常到神木进行农副产品贸易，在交往中，特别是内蒙古人喜欢饮酒的豪爽性格对神木人影响极大。在

The drinking songs of Shenmu, circulated in Shenmu City of Yulin City, are a kind of folk songs deeply preferred by the local people. They have spread widely and have far-reaching influence. According to the content of the lyrics, the drinking songs of Shenmu can be divided into toasting songs and antiphonal songs, which are widely sung in family and friends gatherings or at festive banquets.

There are several reasons for the birth of Shenmu drinking songs. First, the climate in Shenmu is cold, and people often drink liquor to keep out the cold, so the custom of drinking liquor has formed and spread. When guests come to the host's house or relatives or friends get together, liquor must be served and people present will drink a few cups. Second, Shenmu used to be a place of strategic importance in military in ancient times, and wars were frequent here. In order to resist enemies and lift fighting spirit, people drank to boost their courage, so drinking is popular all over Shenmu. Third, since Shenmu is located at the intersection of the three areas of Shanxi, Shaanxi, and Inner Mongolia. People from other places often come to Shenmu to trade agricultural and sideline products. In their contacts and communication, people

长期饮酒的过程中，人们除了用语言交流外，也开始吟唱，边饮酒边唱酒曲，把想说的话、想表达的感情都用酒曲唱出来。饮酒唱酒曲便成为当地的文化特色之一。

神木酒曲的主要艺术特征有三个。一是曲调自由活泼。歌者可根据想表达的内容选择曲调，主要曲调有山曲调、民歌调、信天游和传统酒曲调。二是句式灵活多变。根据内容和曲调，酒曲可以是二句段、三句段或四句段，也有叙事性长段。三是即兴编唱。歌者可根据眼前的具体环境和人物情景随编随唱。

神木酒曲饱含当地人民群众生活的酸甜苦辣和思想感情，对促进人们之间的交流、提升人的精神文化品位、构建和谐社会有着积极的作用。

2009年，神木酒曲被列入陕西省第二批非物质文化遗产名录。

in Shenmu are greatly influenced by the bold and forthright drinking manner and outgoing personality of Inner Mongolians. When people drink, in addition to talking, they also sing songs to express their feelings and ideas. Therefore singing songs while drinking becomes one of the local traditions.

There are three main artistic characteristics of Shenmu drinking songs. First, the tune is free and lively. Singers can choose the tune according to what they want to express. The main tunes are mountain tune, folk song tune, *Xintianyou* melody (a kind of local melody in Northern Shaanxi), traditional drinking tune and so on. Second, the sentence structure of the lyrics is flexible and changeable. According to the content and tune, one paragraph of the lyrics can be made up of two sentences, three sentences or four sentences, and there are also narrative long paragraphs. Third, the songs are impromptu creation. Singers can compose and sing according to the specific environment and scenes that they see.

The drinking songs of Shenmu express the happiness, sorrows, thoughts and feelings of the local people. They play a positive role in promoting communication between people, enhancing people's spiritual and cultural taste, and building harmonious society.

In 2009, the drinking songs of Shenmu were included in the second batch of Shaanxi Provincial Intangible Cultural Heritage List.

秦汉战鼓
Qin-Han Battle Drumming

秦汉战鼓流传于陕西省咸阳市渭城区正阳镇掌旗寨。传说秦朝时该村有人在军中掌管战旗，故此村名为掌旗寨。后来掌管战旗的人将行军作战的鼓调带回该村，流传至今。据传秦王横扫六合、统一天下，汉王刘邦东征西战、建立大汉基业，都用过此鼓调，故称为秦汉战鼓。

秦汉战鼓的阵容壮观，少则三五十人，多则数百人。他们全都穿着古代将士服装。秦汉战鼓在表演时分为三部分。第一部分是出征曲。出征曲悠扬动听，威武庄严，好似部队在调兵遣将，扎营布阵，磨刀擦枪，时刻准备取胜于千里之外。第二部分是交战曲。交战曲紧凑激烈，刚猛高亢，汹涌澎湃，震撼

The Qin-Han battle drumming is spread in Zhangqi Village, Zhengyang Town, Weicheng District of Xianyang City. According to the legend, a villager took charge of the battle flag in the army during the Qin Dynasty, so the village was named Zhangqi Village ("Zhangqi" means "taking charge of the battle flag" in English). Later, the villager brought back to the village the drumming tunes played during the soldiers' march and fighting in battles, and the tunes have been passed down until now. It is said that these drumming tunes were used when the King of the Qin defeated other six states and united the whole country, and they were also used by the King Liu Bang when he battled to establish the Han Dynasty. So the tunes are called "Qin-Han Battle Drumming".

The lineup of Qin-Han battle drumming performance is spectacular, ranging from 30-people performance to hundreds-of-people performance, and the drummers are all in ancient soldier-costumes. The performance is divided into three parts. The first part is characterized by the expedition tune, which is melodious, forceful and solemn, sounding as if the troops are being deployed, stationed and

人心，鼓舞士气，有战马的奔跑声，有刀枪的撞击声，有将士们勇往直前、浴血奋战的厮杀声。此曲助军威，让人精神倍增，充满必胜的信心。第三部分是凯旋曲。凯旋曲铿锵有力，豪情激昂，同时又轻松快乐，奔放喜悦，好似将士们克敌制胜、满载而归，体现出将士们胜利后的兴奋心情和向往和平、渴望幸福的强烈愿望。

秦汉战鼓通过出征、交战、凯旋曲调及各种阵法和指挥作战的槌法，完整地展现了秦汉时期作战时的鼓乐文化特色。

2009年，秦汉战鼓被列入陕西省第二批非物质文化遗产名录。

arrayed, and the weapons being cleaned and sharpened to fight off the enemy. The second part features the battle tune, which is intense, fierce, high-pitched, passionate, overwhelming, and encouraging. In this part, the audience seem to hear the clatters of horses' running, the clashes of weapons, and the shouting and screaming of fighting soldiers. The tune can cheer the army, make soldiers more energetic and full of confidence in winning. The third part features the triumph tune. It is sonorous, powerful, vigorous and exhilarating, and at the same time relaxing, unrestrained and joyful, sounding as if soldiers have defeated the enemy and returned with fruitful results. The triumph tune can reflect soldiers' excitement after victory and their strong desire for peace and longing for happiness.

Through the tunes, including the expedition tune, battle tune and triumph tune, as well as various battle formations and battle-commanding drumming techniques, the Qin-Han battle drumming fully embodies the cultural characteristics of battle drum music in the Qin and Han dynasties.

In 2009, Qin-Han battle drumming was included in the second batch of Shaanxi Provincial Intangible Cultural Heritage List.

埙乐艺术
Music of *Xun*

埙是先民在长期的生产和生活实践中创造出来的乐器。目前所知的年代最古老的埙是浙江河姆渡遗址出土的陶埙，只有吹孔，没有音孔，距今大约7,000年。1957年，在西安半坡遗址出土的两枚陶哨（埙），一个只有吹孔，另一个有一个吹孔和一个音孔，距今大约6,700年。

埙在历史上广泛见于中国各地城乡，近代以来集中保存在少数大中城

Xun is a musical instrument invented by primitive people in their long-term production and living practice. The oldest *xun* known so far are the pottery *xun* unearthed at Hemudu Ruins in Zhejiang Province, which have only blow holes but no sound holes and have a history of about 7,000 years. In 1957, two pottery *xun* were unearthed at the Banpo Ruins in Xi'an City. One only has a blow hole, the other has a blow hole and a sound hole. And they have a history of about 6,700 years.

Xun have been discovered widely in urban and rural areas throughout China in history, and have been concentrated in a few large and medium cities in modern times. In recent decades, the music of *xun* has recovered and developed throughout the whole country. In Shaanxi Province, the music of *xun* mainly prevails in cities such as Xi'an, Xianyang, and Baoji. *Xun* have various shapes, like oval-shape, fish-shape, rod-shape, gourd-shape, bull-head-shape, etc., and the oval-shape are the most common. *Xun* were originally made of clay, animal bones, jade, wood and even synthetic materials, but the most frequently used material is clay. In the past twenty years, standardized professional *xun*

市。近几十年来，全国埙乐艺术有所恢复和发展，陕西省的埙乐多见于西安、咸阳、宝鸡等城市。埙的形状有卵形、鱼形、棒形、葫芦形、牛头形等，但为数众多的是卵形埙。埙的制作材料初始时为泥土，也有兽骨、玉石、木材，甚至合成材料，但使用最多的材料还是泥土。近20年来，标准化的专业制埙工艺以树脂、砂、黏土等材料按一定比例搭配制作埙。

埙的体积可大可小，腔体大的发音的频率低。指孔的多少和大小不等，打开的面积越大，发音的频率越高。一般靠指孔的开合可以吹出的音域大概有十度，称为指孔音。指孔全部闭合后，可以改变吹气的角度和力度，还可以向下吹出五度甚至八度音，音越低时音量越小，称为俯吹音。俯吹音的音量虽稍小，但在音色上有独特的魅力。

埙乐艺术传承数千年，有众多的名

production has been developed, which uses a certain proportion of resin, sand, clay and other materials to produce *xun*.

The volume of *xun* can be large or small. The frequency of sound of a large cavity is low. The number and size of the finger holes are different. The larger the opened area, the higher the frequency of sound. The sound produced by covering and uncovering finger holes is called the finger hole sound. When the finger holes are all covered, by changing the angle and strength of the blowing, the player can also blow a quint or even an octave, which is called downward blowing sound. Although the volume of the downward blowing sound is a little lower, it has a unique charm in the tone colour.

The music of *xun* has been passed down for thousands of years, and many masterpieces have been handed down from ancient times. Famous tunes often played by *xun* musicians include *Songs of Chu*, *Thoughts at the Dressing Table in Autumn*, *Bamboo in the Wind*, *Sorrowful Farewell*, *Deep Valley*, *Su Wu Herds Sheep*, *Parting at Yangguan Pass*, *Tang Music*, *Wind*,

曲传世。《楚歌》《妆台秋思》《风竹》《伤别离》《幽谷》《苏武牧羊》《阳关三叠》《唐乐》《风》《悲风》《月下海棠》《寒江残雪》等都是埙乐演奏家经常吹奏的名曲。近年来,也有新创作的曲目结集出版,如《刘宽忍笛埙独奏辑》《埙的世界》等。

埙所独具的古雅深沉、浑润醇厚、幽静深邃的音色风格体现了中华民族传统文化所追求的"形神兼顾,养神为先,虚静养神"的气韵和特征。

2011年,埙乐艺术被列入陕西省第三批非物质文化遗产名录。

Bleak Wind, *Begonia in the Moonlight*, *Remnant Snow by the Cold River*, etc. In recent years, collections of new compositions have also been published, such as *Collections of Liu Kuanren's Flute and Xun Solo* and *Xun's World*.

Xun's elegant, deep, mellow, and quiet music style embodies the charm and characteristics of the traditional culture of the Chinese nation, which can be interpreted as "considering both form and spirit, cultivating the mind first, and nurturing the soul in tranquility".

In 2011, the music of *xun* was included in the third batch of Shaanxi Provincial Intangible Cultural Heritage List.

三

传统舞蹈

Traditional Dances

安塞腰鼓
Ansai Waist Drum Dance

安塞腰鼓是流传于陕西省延安市安塞区及其周边地区的一种民间鼓舞艺术形式。它是从古代作战时鼓舞士气、威慑敌人的战鼓演变而来的。据说早在秦汉时期，腰鼓就是将士们不可或缺的装备。遇到敌人突袭，就击鼓报警，传递讯息；两军交锋，则击鼓助威；征战取得胜利，士兵们又击鼓庆贺。到了宋代，安塞腰鼓发展成为一种民间的娱乐活动。20世纪80年代，安塞腰鼓的表演与扭秧歌、舞彩绸、转九曲等融为一体。此后，又逐渐将舞蹈、武术、体操等融入腰鼓表演，发展成为当地老百姓祈求神灵、祝愿丰收、欢度佳节的一种民俗性舞蹈。

Ansai waist drum dance is a unique, large-scale folk drum dance, which is popular in Ansai District of Yan'an City and its sounding areas. It originates and develops from the war drums in ancient times that were beaten to enhance soldiers' morale and frighten enemies. According to the local people, waist drums were used as indispensable armaments for soldiers as early as the Qin and Han dynasties. The drums were beaten to send alarm messages when the army was attacked by surprise, to boost soldiers' morale in battlefields, and to celebrate victories. In the Song Dynasty, beating waist drums developed into a kind of folk entertainment activity, and in the 1980s, waist drum dance combined with the *yangge* (a typical form of collective folk dance of the Chinese Han nationality), waving colorful silk ribbons and other forms of performances. Later it integrated with the performing form of dances, martial arts, gymnastics, etc., and finally developed into a folk dance of the local people for the purposes of worshiping the deity, praying for good harvest and celebrating festivals.

According to the beating methods, Ansai waist drum dance is divided into two categories: the *wen* drum dance

and the *wu* drum dance, with the former focusing on dancing rather than beating the drum and the latter focusing on beating the drum rather than dancing. In the *wen* drum dance, relatively gentle and mild, the performers express their joy and happiness through their dancing to the lively *suona* music, which can make the audience feel relaxed and cheerful. In the *wu* drum dance, relatively vigorous and powerful, performers beat the drums and dance vigorously, passionately and powerfully.

According to the performing form, Ansai waist drum dance falls into three categories: road drum dance, square drum dance and stage drum dance. Road drum dance is also called "marching drum dance" or "street drum dance", in which performers dance while marching forward, doing major motions like cross step, backward kicking, hopping and so on. Square drum dance, usually performed on squares or in specified places, is the main form of Ansai waist drum dance, which features rich content and various performing forms. When a large number of performers participate in the performance, it is fairly grand and stunning. Stage drum dance is performed on a stage with a small number of performers ranging from 8 to 12 and it has high requirement for performing skills.

Ansai waist drum dance, full of Chinese national characteristic and regional flavor, is an important component of the Chinese culture of the Yellow River

从打法上安塞腰鼓可分为文鼓和武鼓两种。文鼓以扭为主，扭中伴舞，舞中含扭，伴着欢快的唢呐声，将内心的喜悦之情用"能劲"抒发出来，使人心旷神怡。武鼓以打踢为主，重打轻扭，动作刚劲激昂、彪悍豪放、铿锵有力、威猛刚烈。

从表演形式上安塞腰鼓可分为路鼓、场地鼓和舞台鼓三种。路鼓也叫"行进鼓""过街鼓"，是腰鼓队在行进过程中的表演形式，动作主要有十字步、倒踢腿、跑步跳等。场地鼓多在广场或指定的地点表演，是安塞腰鼓表演的主要形式。场地鼓内容丰富，形式多

样,表演人数众多时,势如排山倒海,极为壮观。舞台鼓是少数鼓手在台上集中表演的形式,表演的人数为8~12人,技术要求比较高。

安塞腰鼓是黄河流域文化的重要组成部分,体现了黄土高原人民憨厚、实在、乐观、开朗的性格,极具民族风格和地域特色。

1996年11月,安塞县被文化部命名为"腰鼓之乡"。2006年,安塞腰鼓被列入第一批国家级非物质文化遗产名录。

Valley, which embodies the personalities of people living on the Loess Plateau, such as innocence, honesty, optimism and open-mindedness.

In November of 1996, Ansai County was named as the "Hometown of Waist Drum Dance" by the Ministry of Culture of China. In 2006, Ansai waist drum dance was included in the first batch of China's National Intangible Cultural Heritage List.

陕北秧歌
Yangge Dance of Northern Shaanxi

陕北秧歌是流行于陕北高原的一种具有广泛群众性和代表性的传统舞蹈艺术形式,又称"闹红火""闹秧歌""闹社火""闹阳歌"等,一般在春节期间在广场、场院、街道等场地演出,多见于陕北地区的榆林(绥德、米脂)、延安等地,其中尤以绥德秧歌最具代表性。

陕北秧歌历史悠久,经历了宋代中期的孕育期、明代中期的转型期,繁盛于清代中期,从清末民初起进入低潮期。1942年,在延安兴起的新秧歌运动中,陕北秧歌被赋予了新的精神风貌和时代内容,并随着时代的发展而传遍

The *yangge* dance of Northern Shaanxi, a typical and traditional artistic form popular among the masses in Northern Shaanxi, is often performed on squares, in courtyards or on streets during the Spring Festival. This kind of artistic form is widespread in the northern areas of Shaanxi Province like Yulin City (mainly in Suide County and Mizhi County), Yan'an City and so on, with that in Suide County most typical.

The *yangge* dance of Northern Shaanxi incubated in the middle of the Song Dynasty, reformed in the middle of the Ming Dynasty, flourished in the middle of the Qing Dynasty and declined in the late Qing Dynasty and the early period of the Republic of China. In 1942, in the new *Yangge* Movement in Yan'an, it flourished again with new spirits and epoch themes and spread across China with the development of the times. Since China's Opening-up and Reform, it has gained more attention and developed more quickly. A large number of texts, pictures, videos related to

it have been collected, and relevant books and audio-visual materials have been published.

Yangge performance usually involves dozens of performers, sometimes more than 100 performers. Under the guidance of the team leader and to the sonorous music of gongs, drums and *suona* horns, performers fully enjoy themselves, performing motions like twisting, swaying, walking, hopping and turning. The *yangge* dance is usually divided into two categories as the large-scale performance and small-scale performance. In the large-scale performance, guided and directed by the leading dancer, the whole team ranging from 20 to 200 dancers change performing patterns from time to time. There are hundreds of performing patterns, such as "the dragon sways its tale" "two dragons spout water" "twelve lotus lanterns". The small-scale performance includes performing forms like "boating" "driving donkeys" "walking on stilts"

全国。改革开放以来，陕北秧歌更加受到重视，大批有关陕北秧歌的文字、图片、录像资料已编撰成书或刻制成光碟。

秧歌表演者常有数十人，有的多达百余人，在伞头的率领下，踏着铿锵的锣鼓节奏，和着嘹亮的唢呐音乐，表演者做出扭、摆、走、跳、转的动作，尽情欢舞。秧歌一般分为"大场"和"小场"两种。大场表演时整个舞队在伞头的统一指挥和带领下扭出变化丰富的队形，有"龙摆尾""二龙吐水""十二莲灯"等数百种队形，参加表演的人数少则二三十

三、传统舞蹈　Traditional Dances

人，多则一二百人。小场表演包括"水船""跑驴""高跷""霸王鞭"等。也可以根据动作风格和内容将秧歌分为"文场子""武场子""丑场子""踢场子"等。其中踢场子为表现男女爱情生活的双人舞，有许多较高难度的动作。

陕北秧歌表现了陕北人民质朴、憨厚、乐观的特点，具有突出的历史文化价值。

2006年，陕北秧歌被列入第一批国家级非物质文化遗产名录。

"playing with colorful sticks" and so on. The *yangge* dance can also be divided into different categories like passionate dance, gentle dance, comic dance and double dance according to the dancing style and theme, among which the double dance features a lot of difficult motions and shows romance between men and women.

The *yangge* dance of Northern Shaanxi showcases the simple, honest and optimistic characters of people in Northern Shaanxi, and possesses outstanding historical and cultural value.

In 2006, the dance was included in the first batch of China's National Intangible Cultural Heritage List.

洛川蹩鼓
Bie Drum Dance of Luochuan

陕西省延安市洛川县在春秋战国时期一直是秦、晋、魏的争夺之地。军队遇到敌人袭击时，要击鼓报警；军队出征时，要击鼓助威；军队得胜回营时，要击鼓迎接。蹩鼓就是适应这种军事需要而产生的一种军中用鼓。后来蹩鼓传入民间，成为民间祭祀和祈雨时表演的一种舞蹈形式，并得以流传。

洛川蹩鼓的表演者均为男性，士卒装扮，头包战巾，身穿对襟彩服，背插战旗，腰系战裙，腿扎裹带。道具以鼓为主，表演时鼓、锣、钹同时演奏。蹩鼓表演的基本动作有单跳、双跳、搓步、拧摆等。单跳稳健潇洒，大起大落，灵活自如；双跳即双脚同时起跳下

Luochuan County of Yan'an City was a battleground between states of Qin, Jin and Wei during the Spring and Autumn Period and the Warring States Period. When the enemy was waging an attack, drums were beaten to give an alarm; when the army was going to a battle, drums were beaten to boost soldiers' morale; when the army was returning with victory, drums were beaten to welcome the army. In such background, beating *bie* drum became popular in the army to meet the above military needs. Later, beating *bie* drum was introduced into the folks and became a form of dance performed during folk sacrifice and praying for the rain, and it continued to develop with time going on.

Bie drum dance of Luochuan is performed by men attired as soldiers who wrap headcloth and puttees, wear colorful tops and martial skirts, and carry flags on their backs. Drums serve as the main props, and the sound of drums, gongs, and cymbals blend together in the performance. The basic motions of the dance include single-leg hop, double-leg jump, *cuobu*, twisting and swaying, etc. Single-leg hop is steady and unrestrained, with big ups and downs and flexible postures. Double-leg

jump is bold and powerful, which means that both feet of the performer jump up and fall on the floor at the same time with his body leaning back. The motion *cuobu* is vigorous while twisting and swaying is graceful. To the sonorous drum and gong sound, performers dance, hop and jump in various styles with rough, powerful and vigorous body movements, just like ancient soldiers fighting fiercely, bringing audience a feeling of presenting at the ancient battlefield.

Because the major movements of *bie* drum dance are jumping and hopping, and "jump and hop" is called "*bie*" in Luochuan dialect, hence the name *bie* drum dance. When it is performed, eight drummers, six cymbal players and four gong players compose a *bie* dance team which is led by two leading dancers, either of whom wears a skullcap and a blue robe, holding a blue cloth umbrella in the left hand and a whip in the right hand. Moreover, a *bie* drum team can also be composed of four drummers, four cymbal players and four gong players. The gong players are usually 14-year-old or 15-year-old teenagers, who perform in the rear of the team. In some performances, the *bie* drum team is followed by a *yangge* (a typical form of collective folk dance of the Chinese Han nationality) team composed of young women and men, which makes the *bie* drum performance much livelier.

Bie drum dance of Luochuan has three styles. The first is "Xiantou style"

落，上身后仰，动作粗犷有力；搓步刚健；拧摆柔美。锣鼓齐鸣，表演者在舞、蹦、跳中做出各种造型，动作粗犷，剽悍豪放，如古代士卒拼搏冲杀，给人一种置身古战场的感觉。

由于蹩鼓的舞蹈动作在跳蹦中产生，而洛川当地方言称跳蹦为"蹩"，蹩鼓以此得名。蹩鼓表演时，在两个头戴瓜皮帽、身穿蓝布长袍、左手执蓝布伞、右手持一蝇甩的伞头率领下，由八名鼓手、六名镲手、四名锣手组成蹩鼓队，也有的按四鼓手、四镲手、四锣手组成。锣手一般由十四五岁的少年担任，跟在队尾表演。有的蹩鼓表演队后

还跟随着由男女青年组成的秧歌队,以烘托蹩鼓表演的热烈气氛。

洛川蹩鼓有三种风格流派:以黄章乡现头村为代表的"现头派",强调舞者双脚同时起跳,突出弹跳性和舞者的狂劲,动作粗犷有力;以旧县镇洛生村为代表的"洛生派",突出表演时的整体性和统一性,鼓点较缓;以永乡镇阿寺村为代表的"阿寺派",表演时突出拧脚扭腰,突出"拧摆",动作潇洒、稳健。

洛川蹩鼓在陕北民间舞蹈中占有重要地位,其丰富的内容和独具特色的艺术形式在中国鼓舞中实属罕见。

2006年,洛川蹩鼓被列入第一批国家级非物质文化遗产名录。

represented by Xiantou Village of Huangzhang Township, which emphasizes the dancers, lifting up both feet at the same time, the bouncing nature of the dance and the dancers' enthusiasm as well as their wild and powerful movements. The second is "Luosheng style" represented by Luosheng Village of Jiuxian Town, which highlights the integrity and unity of the performance and slow drumming rhythm. The third style is "A'si style" represented by A'si Village of Yongxiang Town, which is characterized by the smart and steady movements, highlighting the twisting of the feet and waist.

Bie drum dance of Luochuan plays an important role in Northern Shaanxi folk dances. Its rich content and unique artistic form are rare among Chinese drum dances.

In 2006, it was included in the first batch of China's National Intangible Cultural Heritage List.

周至牛斗虎
Dance of Bull Fighting Against Tiger of Zhouzhi

牛斗虎是流行在陕西省西安市周至县楼观镇八家庄村的民间传统舞蹈节目，早年庄东的什字井庙内的木匾上就有"乾隆年间八家庄耍牛斗虎"的字样。相传，当地有位叫杜困的画匠在进山打柴的时候，惊见一头凶猛的豹子欲袭击放牧的小童，正在吃草的牛见此情景用蹄子奋力一蹬，将豹子蹬得翻了个跟头，倒在山坡上。勃然大怒的豹子返身猛扑向牛，而牛却越斗越猛，最后斗得豹子落荒而逃。受到这件事的启发，杜困便与庄里的民间艺人创编了一个舞蹈，并把豹子改成了虎，起名"牛斗虎"。后经不断丰富和完善，这一具

"Bull fighting against tiger" is a traditional folk dance in Bajiazhuang Village, Louguan Town, Zhouzhi County of Xi'an City. In the early years, the wooden plaque in Shizijing Temple in the east of the village recorded "Bajiazhuang performed the dance of bull fighting against tiger during the Qianlong Period in the Qing Dynasty". According to the legend, when a local painter named Du Kun went to the mountain to collect firewood, he was surprised to see the scene: a fierce leopard was about to attack a shepherd boy, but the leopard was kicked to a somersault by the grazing bull and fell down on the hillside. The furious leopard turned back and pounced on the bull, but the bull fought more and more bravely, and finally the leopard fled. Inspired by this story, Du Kun created a dance with folk artists in the village. They replaced the leopard in the story with the image of tiger and named the dance "bull fighting against tiger". After continuous enrichment and improvement, this folk dance art with local

有地方特色的民间舞蹈艺术形式逐渐形成。

牛斗虎表演由五人组成，其中两人演牛头、虎头，两人演牛尾、虎尾，一人扮演牧童。虎势有四大势八小势，二十四个平阳势。四大势有趄虎势、搜山势、望山势、捕食势，八小势有立、卧、坐、缩、滚、上山、下山、跳涧，二十四个平阳势贯穿每个动作。牛势也有回头望月、舔背、吃草、挖耳等动作。牛斗虎表演时舞者动作粗犷勇武，舞蹈气氛紧张激烈。虎有虎势，牛有牛劲，互不相让，最后牛取得了胜利。

周至牛斗虎是一种土生土长的民间舞蹈，源于生活，贴近生活。发掘、保护、抢救牛斗虎对于丰富民间舞蹈和发展舞蹈事业都有特殊意义。

2007年，周至牛斗虎被列入陕西省第一批非物质文化遗产名录。

characteristics has gradually formed.

The performance consists of five people, two of whom act as the bull (one as bull's head and the other as the bull's tail), two act as the tiger (one as tiger's head and the other as the tiger's tail), and one acts as a shepherd boy. The tiger can perform four major motions, eight minor motions, and twenty-four common motions. The four major motions are staggering, searching, gazing, and preying; the eight minor motions include standing, lying, sitting, curling up, rolling, going uphill, going downhill, and jumping over the valley; the other twenty-four common motions run through the whole performance. The bull can perform movements such as looking back at the moon, licking the back, eating grass, picking the ear. The movements of the performers are bold and unconstrained, creating tense and exciting atmosphere. During the performance, the bull and tiger fight fiercely and the performance ends up with the bull's victory.

The dance of bull fighting against tiger was born and developed in the local area. It comes from life and is close to life. The protection, rescue and promotion of the dance have special significance for enriching Chinese folk dances and promoting dance development.

In 2007, the dance was included in the first batch of Shaanxi Provincial Intangible Cultural Heritage List.

横山老腰鼓
Hengshan Waist Drum Dance

横山老腰鼓可追溯至明代中期,是流传在陕北地区的一种独特的民间舞蹈艺术形式,多见于陕西省榆林市横山区的乡镇与村落。

横山老腰鼓的表演形式多样,通常以舞队的形式出现,有单人打、双人对打、四人对打、八人对打等。舞队由伞头、鼓子手、腊花、杂色丑角组成。鼓子手动作幅度大、力度强,节奏快速多变,舞姿优美,情绪亢奋,有时会达到情不自禁的程度;腊花含嗔带羞,舞步轻盈,与鼓子手成双配对,眉目传情,使整个舞队表演更加生动活泼、情趣盎然、富有艺术感染力。

2019年10月1日晚,庆祝中华人民共和国成立70周年的联欢活动在北京天

Hengshan waist drum dance can be dated back to the middle of the Ming Dynasty. It is a unique folk dance art form that spreads in Northern Shaanxi, mainly in towns and villages of Hengshan District of Yulin City.

Hengshan waist drum dance is characterized by various performing forms, usually in the form of team dance. According to the number of performers, the performance can be divided into several categories including one-performer drumming, two-performer drumming, four-performer drumming, eight-performer drumming and so on. The performance team consists of a team leader who holds an umbrella in his/her hand, drummers, *lahua* and different kinds of clowns. The drummers dance elegantly and rhythmically in high spirit with powerful, vigorous and graceful motions, and sometimes they dance so feverishly that they can not control their feelings and motions. The *lahua*, shy, light-footed, join into pairs with and make eyes at the drummers, making the entire dance performance more lively, interesting, and artistic.

On the evening of October 1, 2019, a gala celebrating the 70th anniversary

安门广场举行，来自横山的54名老腰鼓表演队员集体亮相天安门。在一个小时三十分钟的联欢活动中，横山老腰鼓表演队多次出现在荧屏，完美呈现了中华儿女的精神风貌。身挂红腰鼓，头系羊肚白毛巾，腾空、摆头、舞臂、跳转、走翻等舞蹈动作，无不表达着劳动人民对美好生活的向往和憧憬。

横山老腰鼓在服装、道具、扮相、

of the founding of the People's Republic of China was held in Beijing Tian'anmen Square. Hengshan waist drum dance team composed of 54 members performed on the special stage, Tian'anmen Square. During the one-hour and thirty-minute gala, the dance team appeared on the screen many times, perfectly presenting the spirit of the Chinese people. The red waist drums, the white towels on the performers' heads, and various motions such as rising high into the air, shaking heads, waving arms, flipping, turning somersaults, etc., fully express the working people's yearning and longing for a better life.

Hengshan waist drum dance, very distinctive in costumes, props, appearance, dance movements, etc., has maintained the original drumming techniques and its traditional characteristics of robustness,

三、传统舞蹈　Traditional Dances

舞蹈动作等方面极具特点，始终保持着原生态打鼓技法，保持着粗狂、豪放、激越、诙谐的特点。横山老腰鼓是劳动人民特有的调剂精神生活、表达思想情感的民间舞蹈之一，是古代文化与现代文化融合的产物，具有重要的历史文化价值和艺术研究价值。

2008年，横山老腰鼓被列入第二批国家级非物质文化遗产名录。

boldness, exaltation and humor. As one of the characteristic folk dances of the working people, it helps people to enrich their spiritual life and express their thoughts and emotions. It is the product of the integration of ancient and modern culture, and has important historical, cultural and artistic value.

In 2008, Hengshan waist drum dance was listed in the second batch of China's National Intangible Cultural Heritage List.

韩城行鼓
Xing Drum Dance of Hancheng

韩城行鼓，俗称"挎鼓子"，在陕西省韩城市传布极广。韩城行鼓历史悠久。据传，元灭金后，蒙古骑兵在韩城敲锣打鼓，欢庆胜利。韩城群众研习模仿，韩城行鼓遂成为民间鼓乐。

韩城行鼓在保留原有军鼓乐艺术风格的同时与时俱进，特别是在表演的艺术效果上进行了深加工，增强了宏伟气势。随着激昂的鼓声，身着鲜艳服饰的黄河汉子以骑马蹲裆之势摆开阵势，

Xing drum dance of Hancheng, also called *kuaguzi*, is widely spread in Hancheng City. The dance has a long history and it is said that after the Yuan army defeated the Jin army, the Mongolian cavalry in Hancheng beat drums and gongs to celebrate the victory. People in Hancheng learned and imitated the cavalry's drumming behavior and thus *xing* drum dance of Hancheng came into being.

Xing drum dance of Hancheng keeps pace with the times while preserving the original artistic style of military drumming, with more attention paid to improving the artistic effects of the performance, such as the magnificent effect. To the exciting drumming sound, the performers in bright costumes start the performance with postures of squatting and riding the horse. Flags are waved, drums and gongs are beaten, creating thunderous sound. The whole spectacle is like the Yellow River roaring and thousands of horses galloping, which is quite magnificent and thrilling. When performers are completely immersed in the performance, they dance in an unrestrained and wild manner and beat drums and cymbals boldly with ecstasy as if they are drunken, fully showing

令旗挥舞，锣鼓齐鸣，击声如雷，吼声震天，似黄河咆哮，如万马奔腾，气势恢宏，扣人心弦。敲到得意时，舞者狂跳狂舞，如痴如醉，醉鼓醉镲，狂敲狂拍，酣畅淋漓，身处忘我之境界，狂放不羁，野味十足，尽显黄河汉子热情、粗犷、豪爽、彪悍之英气。

在表演时，韩城行鼓总离不了"绕杆子"，其目的是更好地渲染气氛，增强视觉效果。身着艳服的姑娘，手执饰有彩绸花束和串串银铃的长绕杆，婀娜多姿。绕杆的阵营与锣鼓队的阵营相互呼应，鼓声激越，铙钹声飞扬，几十杆

the enthusiastic, rough, bold and valiant character of men living near the Yellow River Valley.

"Waving colorful poles" is an indispensable part of the drum dance. The purpose is to better render the atmosphere and enhance the visual effect. The girls in colorful clothes dance gracefully and charmingly with long poles decorated with colorful silk bouquets and strings of bells in their hands. During the performance, the colorful pole team echoes the gong and drum team. In the thrilling and sonorous music of drums, cymbals and gongs, dozens of even over a hundred colorful poles wave up and down among the drummers, which inspires the gong and drum players perform so vigorously and breathtakingly that the

甚至上百杆花杆合着鼓点上下翻飞，使锣鼓队越敲越起劲、越神气，让观者目不暇接、心情激荡。

韩城行鼓已日趋成熟，几支突出的锣鼓队已受邀走出韩城赴全国各地演出，并广受赞誉。

韩城行鼓是韩城传统文化的一张闪亮名片，2008年被列入第二批国家级非物质文化遗产名录。

audience completely lose themselves in the exciting atmosphere.

Xing drum dance of Hancheng has become more and more mature, and several outstanding gong and drum teams have been invited to perform all over the country and have won wide praise.

In 2008, *xing* drum dance of Hancheng, a name card of Hancheng's traditional culture, was listed in the second batch of China's National Intangible Cultural Heritage List.

宜川胸鼓
Yichuan Chest Drum Dance

宜川胸鼓是以鼓、舞为基础的一种传统民间舞蹈形式。它由古代战争中人们擂鼓助战、传递信号、击鼓庆捷的形式演变而来。宜川胸鼓主要流行于宜川、洛川和定边一带。

宜川胸鼓属集体群打式。表演时，男女鼓手各半，旁设打击乐队，舞者均身穿短服，头扎英雄巾，佩戴武士缨，前额上插五彩纸蝶，胸前扎红绸英雄结，身背英雄花，腰系彩色绸，手腕紧袖口，下腿扎裹缠，脚穿登云鞋，英俊威武，洒脱不俗。男子胸前斜挂扁圆形小鼓，左手握木制硬鼓槌，右手持牛皮软鞭，轮换击鼓作舞。女子有的手持霸王鞭，有的胸挎条形鼓，有的手握彩扇，有的手击小锣、小镲伴舞。

Yichuan chest drum dance is a traditional folk dance based on drumming and dancing. It evolves from the form of drumming to assist fighting, transmitting signals and celebrating victory in ancient wars. Yichuan chest drum performance mainly prevails in Yichuan County, Luochuan County and Dingbian County.

Yichuan chest drum dance is a kind of group dance. In the performance, male performers and female performers, with the same number, drum and dance together to the music played by the percussion band. All performers wear short jackets, heroic scarves and *dengyun*-brand shoes, 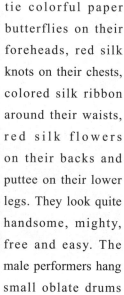 tie colorful paper butterflies on their foreheads, red silk knots on their chests, colored silk ribbon around their waists, red silk flowers on their backs and puttee on their lower legs. They look quite handsome, mighty, free and easy. The male performers hang small oblate drums

宜川胸鼓表演的主要特点是鼓点花而不乱，动作小巧，衔接变换流畅，节奏起伏对比强烈，鼓声清脆欢快，表演风趣幽默。"双手击鼓稳准狠，颤步摆头眼传神"概括了宜川胸鼓的表演技法。舞蹈姿态力求舒展大方，更重要的是舞者在击鼓过程中，重视情绪和神韵的表现，不仅要求手、眼、身、法、步的紧密配合，还要注意击鼓节奏与舞蹈变化的配合一致。特别是有些艺人打至高潮时，情不自禁地摆头、抖肩，使表演更突出了夸张的情绪和动人的风采。

before their chests, hold wooden drumsticks in their left hands and soft leather whips in their right hands, beating the drum with the drumsticks and whips alternatively. The female performers dance to accompany the male performers. Some of them beat small drums on their chests, some hold short colored sticks in their hands, some wave colored fans, and others strike small gongs or cymbals.

Yichuan chest drum dance is characterized by variable and rhythmic drumbeats, small and elegant dance movements, smooth movement transitions, strong rhythmic contrasts, crisp and cheerful drumming music, and humorous atmosphere. "Drumming steadily, accurately and fiercely, vibrating legs, turning heads, and speaking with eyes" well summarize the performing techniques of the Yichuan chest drum dance. The performers dance in an unrestrained manner, and more importantly, they pay attention to the expression of their emotions and charms

表演刚柔并济、声情并茂，给观众留下深刻的印象。

宜川胸鼓具有明快、活泼、诙谐、风趣的艺术特色。舞者以丰富的舞蹈队形变化，烘托热烈的表演气氛，展现娴熟高超的技艺。整个表演气势磅礴、绚丽多彩，具有浓郁的生活气息和强烈的艺术感染力。

2008年，宜川胸鼓被列入第二批国家级非物质文化遗产名录。

during the drumming process, which not only requires close cooperation of hands, eyes, body, and feet, but also requires coordination of drumming rhythm and dancing movements. At the climax of the performance, some performers can't help shaking their heads and shoulders, making the performance more fascinating. The performance couples hardness with softness, beautiful singing with rich feelings, leaving audience a deep impression.

Yichuan chest drum dance features bright, lively, humorous and funny artistic characteristics. The performers create lively atmosphere and demonstrate adroit performing skills through various team formation patterns. The performance is magnificent and colorful, characterized by its strong life flavor and artistic appeal.

In 2008, Yichuan chest drum dance was included in the the second batch of China's National Intangible Cultural Heritage List.

靖边跑驴
Jingbian Donkey Dance

靖边跑驴在清代就已盛行，是靖边县民俗社火中的一种歌舞表演形式，流行于陕西省榆林市靖边县的一些村镇。靖边跑驴源于生活，艺人在日常生活中巧妙利用感人的驴趣和人与驴交流的情

Jingbian donkey dance is a kind of singing and dancing folk performance which was very popular in the Qing Dynasty. It is prevailing in some towns and villages of Jingbian County, Yulin City. Jingbian donkey dance comes from life. In the daily life, the artists artistically adapt the touching and joyful scenes about contact and communication between people and donkeys into interesting performances. The dance performance is expressive, attractive, lifelike, humorous, and funny, making people realize the beauty of life in fun.

Usually, the donkey dance performers follow *yangge* (a typical form of collective folk dance of the Chinese Han nationality) team to put on impromptu performances—the donkey dance performers can perform flexibly, without being restricted by the *yangge* team and drumming rhythm. In the folk comprehensive performance *shehuo* during the Spring Festival, donkey dance will be first performed to attract audience. To the exalting and cheerful percussion sound, performers dance spontaneously. Their exaggerating and vivid movements, humorous postures, funny tricks as well as witty songs and narrations, which well

景，编排成趣味盎然的表演。整个表演传神、传情、诙谐、幽默，让人们在乐趣中体会生活的美。

一般情况下，靖边跑驴尾随秧歌队在行进间即兴表演，不受秧歌队及鼓乐节奏的约束。春节闹社火时先"打场子"，就是要靠跑驴。在激越欢快的锣鼓声中，表演者即兴起舞，常以夸张的动作、风趣的舞姿、滑稽的嬉逗、幽默的演唱及道白抒发对美好生活的追求和向往，引逗观众发出阵阵笑声。

靖边跑驴在表演形式上有一人跑驴、双人跑驴、多人跑驴。多数情况下，跑驴表演为双人表演。其中一人手执驴形道具，扮作骑驴人；另外一人则扮作赶驴人，配合表现"夫妻探亲""回娘家""赶集路上""爷孙

express people's aspiration and pursuit of a good and happy life, always make the audience burst into daughters.

Jingbian donkey dance performance can be classified into three categories: one-person performance, two-person performance and many-person performance, among which the two-person performance is most popular. In the two-person performance, one performer is holding the donkey-shaped prop, pretending as a donkey rider, and the other pretends as the person who drives the donkey. The two performers cooperate with each other to act out common life scenes like "a couple are visiting their relatives" "visiting the wife's parental home" "on the way to the market" "the grandpa and grandson are going to the market", etc. The basic motions of the donkey dance include uphill steps, downhill steps, crossing-river steps, trotting steps, running steps, galloping steps, etc, and more complex motions include "fighting

赶集"等传统生活场景。跑驴的基本动作有"上坡步""下坡步""过河步""小跑步""大跑步""撒欢跳"等。组合动作有"惊驴打斗""陷泥救驴""双人骑驴""太平跳跃"等。

1976年,靖边县文化馆与民间艺人合作,编创了跑驴新节目《探亲路上》。这个节目的演出使靖边跑驴由广场表演走上了舞台,并于1982年参加了农业电影制片厂的电影《泥土的芳香》的拍摄,后又赴法国、瑞士等国进行文化交流,在国内外产生了较大的影响。

近年来,靖边跑驴已蜚声国内外,以耐人寻味的乡土风情与浓郁质朴的生活气息为艺术百花园中增添了土香土色、清新瑰丽的色彩。

2008年,靖边跑驴被列入第二批国家级非物质文化遗产名录。

between panic donkeys" "rescuing the donkey from mud" "two performers riding a donkey" and so on.

In 1976, Jingbian County Cultural Center cooperated with folk artists and composed a donkey dance short play *On the Way Home*, which was a breakthrough achievement that led Jingbian donkey dance to the stage. In 1982, Jingbian donkey dance was shown in the film *Aromatic Soil* filmed by the Agricultural Film Studio. Later, it was performed in France, Switzerland and other countries, achieving great success.

In recent years, Jingbian donkey dance has become famous both at home and abroad. With intriguing local flavor as well as strong and simple life atmosphere, it has added earthy fragrance as well as fresh and magnificent colors to the Chinese art garden.

In 2008, Jingbian donkey dance was included in the second batch of China's National Intangible Cultural Heritage List.

吴起铁鞭舞
Wuqi Whip Dance

吴起铁鞭舞是陕西省延安市吴起县的一种民间节日喜庆舞蹈。自战国时期传入民间以来，吴起铁鞭舞已有2,000多年的历史。吴起县名源自战国时期驻边魏国大将吴起。当时那里人烟稀少，大将吴起所率兵力不足，为扩充兵源抵御秦兵，采用了"选卒制"。在这种背景下产生的吴起铁鞭舞是吴起操演军队、抵御外敌、促进生产的缩影。

吴起铁鞭舞动作简单，易学好记，

Wuqi whip dance is a folk festival dance in Wuqi County of Yan'an City. It was introduced to folks during the Warring States Period and has a history of more than two thousand years. The name of Wuqi County originated from Wu Qi, a general of the Wei State who stationed the frontier in the Warring States Period. At that time, as Wuqi was sparsely populated, general Wu Qi had inadequate troops. In order to expand the troops to resist Qin soldiers, the "soldier selection system" was adopted. The whip dance that came into being in such context is the epitome of general Wu Qi's

人数可多可少，场地可大可小，不论是在山坡还是平原，均可表演。此舞动作、节奏和伴奏虽然简单，但通过演员反复表演、变换使用，能够给观众留下鲜明的舞步印象及深刻的节奏印象。吴起铁鞭舞是在全面继承古代"将士舞"基本动作的基础上扬长避短形成的，既有粗犷豪放的大动作，又有轻柔慢步的小步舞，刚柔兼济，跌宕起伏。在伴奏方面仍然采用武乐器参演，悦耳动听，气势宏大。吴起铁鞭舞共分"出兵""布阵""格斗""收兵"四部分，表现了军队将士出征应战、英勇杀敌、凯旋的全部过程，描绘了一幅精彩

military exercises, defense against foreign enemies and promotion of production.

Wuqi whip dance features simple movements, so it is easy to learn. The number of performers can be large or small, and it is not restricted by the performing place—it can be performed on the hillside, on the flat land, etc. Although the movements, rhythm and accompaniment of the dance are simple, they are repeatedly and alternately used in the performance, leaving audience a clear and deep impression on the dance steps and rhythm. Wuqi whip dance has developed on the basis of fully inheriting the basic movements of the ancient "soldier dance". There are both wild and bold movements as well as gentle and slow movements, which make the performance both rigorous and soft, full of

的战斗画卷。吴起铁鞭舞的表演均由大鼓指挥，舞蹈以八个动作、八种节奏交替表演，简单大方，纯朴自然。

2009年，吴起铁鞭舞被列入陕西省第二批非物质文化遗产名录。

ups and downs. In terms of accompaniment, martial-type instruments are played in the performance, creating melodious and magnificent music effect. The dance is divided into four parts: "entering", "arraying", "fighting" and "returning", which fully display the whole process of soldiers' going out to fight, standing in ranks, fighting heroically, and returning in triumph, depicting a vivid battle picture. Directed by drums, eight kinds of movements and rhythms are alternately shown in the performance, which make the performance simple, elegant, and natural.

In 2009, Wuqi whip dance was included in the second batch of Shaanxi Provincial Intangible Cultural Heritage List.

石泉火狮子
Shiquan Fire Lion Dance

陕西省安康市石泉县群山环绕，山大沟深，因此古时当地人民在劳动生活中必须依靠强健的体魄和巨大的勇气同自然抗争，在强大的自然面前，兽中之王狮子便成为一种图腾崇拜。

相传火狮是天上的神灵图腾，神灵下凡赐予人类神奇的力量，能给人们带来吉祥如意，辟邪、降魔的美好愿望和幸福美好的生活。据说这种神灵在夜间降临，人们就用"堆火"来迎接神灵。这个狮子只能用"火"烧才能显示其灵气，人们称它为"火狮子"。后来烟花爆竹产生，人们就用烟花爆竹烧火狮，火狮与烟花爆竹交融，呈现火红吉祥的

Shiquan County of Ankang City is surrounded by high mountains and deep valleys. Therefore, the local people had to rely on strong physique and great courage to fight against nature in their work and life in ancient times. In the face of powerful nature, the lion, the king of beasts, became a totem worshiped by the local people.

According to the legend, the fire lion is embodiment of the god in the heaven. The god came to the man's world to give humans magical power and good wishes to ward off evil spirits and to live a happy life. It is said that when the lion descended at night, the local people used "fire" to welcome it as the lion can only be burnt with fire to show its anima, so people call the lion "fire lion". Later, when fireworks and firecrackers were produced, people used fireworks and firecrackers to burn the fire lion. The blending of fire lions, fireworks and firecrackers presents a warm and auspicious scene. With time going by, people perfected the performance of the fire lion dance in various celebrations, and gradually the current fire lion dance came into being.

场面。后来人们在各种庆典活动中，不断地完善火狮子舞的表演动作和表演形式，逐步演变成现在的火狮子舞。

火狮子的狮子头用竹篾和铁丝扎成，纸糊涂色。狮子嘴可张可合，狮子皮用兰麻或龙须草编结而成。狮子的身体由山上野生的棕叶编织而成，能耐火烧。每逢节日和庆典活动，表演者便顶着狮子头，披着狮子皮，模仿狮子的动作舞蹈狂欢，以祈福求祥。

火狮子的表演分文耍、武耍两类。文耍表演时，引狮郎手执绣球，武士打扮，侧翻入场，以绣球逗引狮子。舞蹈动作以模拟狮子生活习惯为主，如表演舔毛、搔痒、打滚、翻动、欢跳亲昵、护抚幼狮、与幼狮逗趣玩耍等动作，以表现狮子灵巧、温顺的性格。武耍主要表现狮子威风八面、气大势雄的特点，

The head of the fire lion is framed with bamboo strips and iron wire, pasted with paper and then painted in color. The lion's mouth can be opened or closed; the lion's hide is braided with hemp or Chinese alpine rush; and the lion's body is woven from wild palm leaves, which can withstand fire. During festivals and celebrations, people wear handmade lion heads and hides, and imitate the movements of lions to dance and revel, praying for good luck.

The performance of the fire lion can be divided into two types: *wen* performance and *wu* performance. In the *wen* performance, the man who is dressed up as a warrior holds in his hand an embroidered ball to lead the lion and enters the venue by turning somersaults. He teases the lion with the embroidered ball and the lion performs motions that mainly display the living habits of the real lion, such as licking the fur, scratching, rolling, jumping, playing with cubs, stroking cubs, which can show the lion's dexterity and docile character. The *wu* performance mainly shows the lion's majestic and powerful characteristics, in which the lion performs vigorous motions like jumping, climbing, fighting, etc. In the *wu* performance, the warrior holds an embroidered ball in his hand, turns a somersault and leaps onto the lion's back before it swings its body, and

如表演跳跃、登高、搏斗等动作。武耍表演时,引狮郎手执绣球,不等狮子摆身就耍一个鹞子翻身,纵身跃上狮背,然后做各种翻滚动作,犹如武士和狮子进行一场恶斗。

石泉火狮子表演既热闹、喜庆、幽默、风趣,又惊险刺激,是集舞蹈、杂技于一体的艺术形式。

2009年,石泉火狮子被列入陕西省第二批非物质文化遗产名录。

then performs various motions, creating a fascinating scene in which the warrior and the lion fights fiercely.

Shiquan fire lion dance, an art form that integrates dance and acrobatics, is lively, festive, humorous and thrilling.

In 2009, it was listed in the second batch of Shaanxi Provincial Intangible Cultural Heritage List.

周至龙灯
Zhouzhi Dragon Dance

周至龙灯是流传于西安市周至县的一种独特的民间艺术形式。关于周至龙灯的起源有两种说法：一种认为始于东汉初年，另一种认为始于明末。两种说法都认为周至龙灯与祭祀白色神龙有关。

周至龙灯活动仪式有请龙神、舞龙灯、送龙神等。舞龙时，锣鼓队在前，四对排灯、高六米宽五米的龙门以及高五米的龙柱紧随其后，接下来是鸡灯、鱼灯、虾灯、蝉灯、花鼓灯、五角星灯等。在浩浩荡荡的表演队伍中，巨龙摇头摆尾，畅游于街头巷尾，时而昂首腾空，时而扭头翻身，时而抱柱缠绕。场内时而云雾缭绕，时而火光冲天，时而星光点点。周至舞龙有"金龙

Zhouzhi dragon dance is a unique folk art form prevailing in Zhouzhi County of Xi'an City. There are two views about the origin of Zhouzhi dragon dance: one is that it began in the early years of the Eastern Han Dynasty, and the other is that it originated in the late Ming Dynasty. According to both views, the dragon dance is related to offering sacrifices to the White Dragon.

The dragon dance ceremonies include inviting the Dragon God, performing dragon dance, and seeing off the Dragon God. In the dragon dance, the gong and drum team is in the front, followed by four pairs of bank lights, a six-meter-high and five-meter-wide dragon gate and several five-meter-high dragon pillars; then followed by chicken-shaped lanterns, fish-shaped lanterns, shrimp-shaped lanterns, cicada-shaped lanterns, flower-drum lanterns, star-shaped lanterns, etc. In the grand performance team, the huge dragon shakes its head and tail, flying over the streets and alleys. The dragon sometimes lifts its head into the air, sometimes turns its head over, and sometimes winds around a pillar. Sometimes smoke fills the venue, sometimes fireworks illumine the sky,

出龙门""三抬头（放烟火）""金龙腾云""赐福天下""金龙嬉水""钻四柱""缠单柱"等十三个套路。

周至龙灯表演者为青壮年，他们身穿古装，头裹黄巾，腰系串铃，分三组轮换。每组11人，2人执龙头，2人执龙尾，7人执龙身。另有龙珠人、灯笼人、排灯人、龙门人、烟火人、锣鼓队员等30人参加表演。舞龙灯表演中用锣鼓伴奏，并燃烟火助兴，气氛热烈，异彩纷呈，场面壮观，赏心悦目。

2011年，周至龙灯被列入陕西省第三批非物质文化遗产名录。

and sometimes light-spots twinkle in the darkness. The dragon dance has 13 kinds of fixed dancing patterns, such as "golden dragon going out from the dragon gate", "golden dragon flying on clouds", "dragon delivering blessing", "golden dragon playing in the water", "dragon winding around a pillar" and so on.

The performers of Zhouzhi dragon dance are young and middle-aged persons who wear ancient costumes, with yellow scarves on their heads and strings of bells around their waists. They are divided into three groups, which perform alternatively. Each group involves eleven persons, and in each group two persons lift the dragon head, two persons lift the dragon tail, and seven persons lift the dragon body. In addition, there are another thirty performers including those who hold the dragon ball, lanterns and bank lights; those who carry the dragon gate; those who set off fireworks; and those who play gongs and drums, etc. The dragon dance performance is accompanied by gongs and drums, and fireworks are let off to add the excitement. The atmosphere is festive, and the scene is spectacular, pleasing both the eye and the mind.

In 2011, Zhouzhi dragon dance was included in the third batch of Shaanxi Provincial Intangible Cultural Heritage List.

四

传统戏剧

Traditional Operas

华阴老腔
Huayin *Laoqiang* Opera

华阴老腔系明末清初以当地民间说书艺术为基础发展形成的一个皮影戏曲剧种，发源于陕西省渭南市华阴县泉店村，并久为该村张家户族的家族戏（只传本姓本族，不传外人）。据《华县志》记载，老腔皮影又名拍板调，清乾隆元年至十年（1736—1745年）就已盛行于华州。因该剧种与当地流行的其他剧种相比出现的时间较早，尤其是其音乐风格古朴悲壮、沉稳浑厚、粗犷豪放，为古老之遗响，所以被称为老腔。

华阴老腔擅长表演以古代战争为内容的历史剧，剧目大都取材于《封神演义》《东周列国志》以及汉唐历史演义小说。华阴老腔的腔调粗犷豪放、

Huayin *laoqiang* opera is a kind of shadow puppetry opera developed from local folk storytelling in the late Ming and early Qing dynasties. It originates from Quandian Village in Huayin County of Weinan City, and has long been the family opera of the Zhang's family (the opera is only passed onto people whose surname is Zhang, not onto outsiders). According to the *Huaxian County Annals*, *laoqiang* opera is also known as "clapper tune", and it was already popular in Huazhou, from the first year to the tenth year of the Qianlong Period (1736–1745) in the Qing Dynasty. As this opera appears earlier than other popular local operas and is characterized by Chinese ancient music style of being simple and unsophisticated, solemn and stirring, as well as bold and unrestrained, hence its name *laoqiang* ("lao" means old or ancient in English, "qiang" means tune in English).

Huayin *laoqiang* opera is famous for historical operas themed on ancient wars. Most works of the repertoires are based on *The Creation of the Gods*, *The History of Romance of the States in the Eastern Zhou Dynasty* and historical novels of the Han and Tang dynasties. The tune of *laoqiang*

高亢激昂，地方色彩明显。在表演过程中有三个鲜明的特点：一是"惊木"配合，增加了剧情的激昂气氛。二是"拉坡"，即在更换场景时，由一人在唱到最后两句时唱起拖腔，全台所有人都帮和拖腔，音调激昂雄壮，能把剧情推向连续性的高潮。三是不用唢呐伴奏，独设檀板的拍板节奏。

华阴老腔最大的特点就在于它的原生态。老腔的语言性很强，呈现出由说唱向戏曲过渡的明显痕迹。事实上，在剧史的本源性、传承的封闭性、剧种的独存性、风格的张扬性等方面，老腔都有其独特的艺术价值和史学价值。

2006年，华阴老腔被列入第一批国家级非物质文化遗产名录。

opera is bold, vigorous, high-pitched and intense, full of local characteristics. The performance is characterized by three distinct features. The first one is the use of *jingmu* (wooden benches), which increases the passionate atmosphere of the performance. The second is *lapo*, that is, when the scene changes, one person prolongs his tone when singing the last two sentences. All the others on the stage join him, also prolonging their tones, which produces exciting and powerful atmosphere and pushes the plot to climax from time to time. The third is that clappers rather than *suona* horn are used as accompaniment musical instruments to beat the rhythm.

The prominent feature of Huayin *laoqiang* opera lies in its originality. It's language shows obvious trace of transition from talking and singing to opera. In fact, in terms of the origin of its history, the limitation of its inheritance, the singularity of its genre, and the boldness of its style, *laoqiang* possess unique artistic and historical value.

In 2006, Huayin *laoqiang* opera was included in the first batch of China's National Intangible Cultural Heritage List.

华县皮影戏
Huaxian Shadow Play

华县皮影戏形成于清朝初叶，流行于陕西省渭南市华州区、大荔县一带。

华县皮影造型以人物为主，兼有景物和道具。人物高约1尺，大头突额，色彩艳丽，图案精细，玲珑剔透，造型优美，个性特征明显，形象夸张诙谐。

皮影的制作相当复杂，主要依靠手工工艺。目前制作皮影所用的材料以牛皮为主。首先把皮影的造型画在纸上，然后把纸铺在牛皮的下面，在透明的牛皮上用针按照图案镂刻轮廓，之后把这个轮廓剪下来用刀进行雕刻，然后着色、涂漆。最后的工序是装订，用线将影人的手、臂、身体和双腿等十个关节缀在一起。经过这些程序，本来硬邦邦

Huaxian shadow play which came into being in the early Qing Dynasty is popular in Huazhou District and Dali County in Weinan City.

The leather-silhouette patterns are dominated by character figures, and there are also some scenery and prop patterns. The character figures are about 33 centimeters tall, with big heads, protruding foreheads, bright colors, exquisite patterns, beautiful design, distinct personality characteristics as well as exaggerated and funny images.

The manufacture of the shadow puppet is a highly complicated process, mainly relying on hands. At the present time the major material is cowhide. First, the shape of a shadow puppet is drawn on a piece of paper. Then the paper is put underneath a piece of leather and the outline of the puppet is carved on the transparent leather. Then the outline of the puppet is cut off from the piece of leather for engraving, coloring and painting. The last procedure is to bind together the ten joints on the hands, arms, body, legs and other parts of the puppet. Through such procedures, a cute puppet comes to life.

Wanwan tune is mainly employed

的皮影就变得栩栩如生了。

华县皮影戏的唱腔多为碗碗腔，唱腔细腻悠扬、婉转缠绵，长于表现人物的思想感情和内心活动，具有很大的艺术魅力。伴奏的乐手司掌琴、弦、钹、鼓以及铜制的打击乐器"碗碗"等。皮影班子一般为五至七人，一盏明灯，一个屏幕，两张方桌，几块木板就可搭台表演。演出时艺人在亮子（即屏幕）后，靠手中的签子操纵影人，表演出各种复杂的动作。

要学会制作皮影和表演皮影戏，至少需要四五年时间。一个娴熟的皮影艺

in Huaxian shadow play. It is fine and smooth, melodious and lingering, and can well expresses the characters' thoughts, feelings and inner activities, thus has a strong artistic charm. Musicians play accompaniment musical instruments *qin* (a plucked seven-stringed Chinese musical instrument), cymbal, drum, and percussion instrument like the *wanwan* (brass bowl) to intensify artistic appealing of the play. The shadow play team usually includes five to seven people. A light, a screen, two square tables and a few wooden boards can constitute the stage. During the performance, when the screen is lighted, performers will manipulate the leather-made puppets via bamboo sticks and strings

人，可以用两只手牵动十几根皮影的关节线杆，一人控制三四个皮影的动作。皮影艺人手指灵活，表演至高潮时，影人枪来剑往、上下翻腾，常使观众眼花缭乱、目不暇接。

华县皮影不仅是中国乃至世界最古老的艺术品种之一，同时也是国内外皮影界公认的世界皮影艺术之集大成者。因其最精粹、最成熟、最完美、最经典，它代表了中外皮影艺术的最高水平。

2006年，华县皮影戏被列入第一批国家级非物质文化遗产名录。

to perform various motions.

It takes a person at least four to five years to learn to make shadow puppets and perform shadow play. A skilled artist is able to control more than ten sticks at the same time with his/her two hands and manipulate the movements of three to four puppets. Under the nimble fingers of the artist, the puppets wield lances, jump up and down at the climax of the show, forming a picture too dazzling for the audience to feast on.

Huaxian shadow play is not only one of China's and even the world's oldest arts, but is also acknowledged as the most classic, exquisite and finest shadow play in the world, which represents the highest level of shadow play art.

In 2006, Huaxian shadow play was included in the first batch of China's National Intangible Cultural Heritage List.

秦腔
Qinqiang Opera

秦腔是中国最古老的戏曲剧种之一，主要流行于陕西、甘肃、宁夏、青海、新疆等西北部地区。明清之际，秦腔由陕西传入其他地区，在清初已发展成为全国有重大影响的戏剧曲种。

现已发现的秦腔传统剧目有3,000多种，大多取材于历史故事、神话和民间传说，代表性剧目有《长坂坡》《和氏璧》《玉虎坠》《荆轲刺秦》《三娘教子》《赵氏孤儿》《苏武牧羊》《孟姜女》《王宝钏》《法门寺》《白蛇传》《三滴血》《西安事变》等。秦腔剧目剧本基本上涵盖了中华五千年文明史，上至盘古开天辟地的神话传说，下至现当代各个阶段的历史故事和知名人物，从古代伦理到当代社会道德，包罗万象。

Qinqiang opera is one of the oldest operas in China, which is very popular in Shaanxi, Gansu, Ningxia, Qinghai, Xinjiang and other northwestern regions of China. During the Ming and Qing dynasties, *qinqiang* opera was introduced from Shaanxi and into other areas, and in the early Qing Dynasty it developed into a dramatic genre with great influence across the country.

So far a wide repertoires of more than 3,000 pieces of traditional *qinqiang works* have been discovered, most of which originate from historical stories, myths and folk tales. The representative works includes *A Battle at Changbanpo, A Priceless Gem, Jade Tiger Pendant, The Emperor and the Assassin, A Mother Educates Her Son, The Orphan of Zhao, Su Wu: the Shepherd, Lady Meng Jiangnü, Lady Precious Stream, Famen Temple, The Legend of the White Snake, Three Drops of Blood, Xi'an Incident* and so on. *Qinqiang* repertoires are inclusive, basically covering 5,000-year history of Chinese civilization, including the myths and legends about Pangu's creation of the world, historical stories and well-known figures in all stages of the modern and contemporary times,

秦腔剧本题材广泛，内容纷繁。剧本或歌颂普通人反抗封建统治阶级的壮烈行为，表现他们不屈不挠的斗争意志；或歌颂传奇式英雄的爱国主义、崇高的民族精神、高尚的民族气节；或揭露和批判封建社会的腐败、官场的黑暗、社会道德的沦丧、科场舞弊，控诉了封建统治阶级的罪恶与腐朽的本质；或颂扬人民群众的正直善良、勤劳勇敢、舍己为人、重承诺、守信义的传统美德；或揭露和批判封建婚姻制度的罪恶，歌颂了不同社会阶层女性追求幸福的勇敢精神；或鼓励和感召人民群众反帝反封建，鼓舞人民群众积极投身于民族解放和建设新生活的伟大斗争。

秦腔伴奏乐队分为文场和武场。文场以板胡为主，辅以笛、三弦、月琴、唢呐等；武场基本使用打击乐器，包括干鼓、战鼓、暴鼓、钩锣、手锣等。秦腔的角色行当传统上分为四生、六旦、

from ancient ethics to contemporary social morals.

Qinqiang scripts have a wide range of themes and various contents. Some scripts praise ordinary people's heroic behavior against the feudal ruling class, showing their indomitable will to fight against injustice; or sing high praise of patriotism and lofty national spirit of legendary heroes. Some scripts disclose and criticize the corruption of feudal society, the darkness of officialdom, the loss of social morality, and fraud in imperial examinations, accusing the evil and rotten nature of the feudal ruling class. Some scripts extol the traditional virtues of integrity, goodness, diligence, courage, self-sacrifice, commitment and honesty. Some scripts expose and condemn the evil of the feudal marriage system and praise the courageous spirit of women of different social classes who bravely pursued their happiness. There are also scripts that encourage and appeal to people to fight against imperialism and feudalism, and to actively participate in the great struggle for national liberation as well as a new and promising life.

The accompaniment band of *qinqiang* opera is classified into *wen* band and *wu* band. The *wen* band is dominated by *banhu* (a bowed two-stringed instrument with a thin wooden soundboard), supplemented by flute, *sanxian* (a three-stringed plucking instrument), *yueqin* (a four-stringed plucking instrument), *suona* horn, etc. The

二净、一丑，各有自己完整的唱腔和表现程式。秦腔的生、净唱腔高亢激越、慷慨悲凉、雄迈豪放，旦角唱腔委婉细腻、优美典雅。秦腔演员还极重工架和特技，在长期的舞台实践中形成了趟马、拉架子、担柴、梢子功、喷火等富有特点的表演程式。

秦腔是西北人民共同拥有的精神财富，也是三秦文化的典型代表，有着广泛的群众基础。20世纪80年代以后，秦腔和其他地方戏曲剧种一样受到了巨大的冲击，专业演出团队生存艰难，优秀演艺人才缺乏，观众流失严重。秦腔这一传统戏曲艺术处于举步维艰的境地，急需采取有效措施加以保护。

2006年，秦腔被列入第一批国家级非物质文化遗产名录。

wu band features percussion instruments, including different kinds of drums and gongs, etc. Traditionally, *qinqiang* opera involves four male roles, six female roles, two painted-face roles, and one comic role, each having his or her own complete singing tune and performing pattern. The singing tune of the male roles and painted-face roles are vehement and exhilarating, sad and dreary, bold and unconstrained. The singing tune of the female roles is melodious and smooth, beautiful and elegant. In addition, actors and actresses in *qinqiang* opera attach great importance to postures and stunts and they have developed a variety of characteristic performing patterns in practice, such as riding the horse, pulling the handcart, carrying the firewood, swaying the hair, breathing fire.

Qinqiang opera, which has a broad mass base, is a kind of spiritual wealth shared by people living in the Northwest China and a typical representative of Shaanxi culture. Since the 1980s, *qinqiang* opera, like other local operas in China, has suffered huge impacts. As a result, there is a shortage of excellent actors and actresses and the number of audience is becoming smaller, so professional performance groups can hardly survive. Now it is in a difficult situation and effective measures are urgently needed to protect it.

In 2006, *qinqiang* opera was included in the first batch of China's National Intangible Cultural Heritage List.

汉调二簧
Han Tune *Erhuang* Opera

汉调二簧是陕南地方戏曲剧种之一，流传于陕西的安康、汉中、商洛、西安，及四川、甘肃、湖北的部分地区。它源自汉水流域的山歌、民歌、小调，清朝初叶受秦腔影响，吸收昆曲、吹腔、高拨子等曲调，糅合当地方言，形成了独立的声腔剧种。原来用双笛伴奏，笛以竹作"簧"，故称"二簧"。为与"京二簧"区别，又称"土二簧"。此后全国各地出现的声腔剧种包括清末形成的京剧声腔都与其有着深厚的历史渊源。在历史上，汉调二簧曾有安康、汉中、商洛、关中四大流派，班

Han tune *erhuang* is one of the local operas in Southern Shaanxi, which enjoys popularity in Ankang City, Hanzhong City, Shangluo City, Xi'an City of Shaanxi Province, and parts of Sichuan, Gansu and Hubei Provinces. It originated from the mountain songs, folk songs and ditties of the Hanshui River Basin. In the early Qing Dynasty, it was influenced by *qinqiang* opera and formed its own style by absorbing the tunes of *kunqu* opera and some other operas, and by blending local dialects. At the beginning, the opera was accompanied by two flutes which used bamboo as *huang* (reed), hence the name *erhuang* (*er* means two in English, *huang* means reed in English). To distinguish it from "Beijing *erhuang*", it is also called "native *erhuang*". Later different types of tunes, which have appeared across the country including the Peking opera that came into being in the late Qing Dynasty, have close relationship with it. In history, Han tune *erhuang* once developed into four schools, respectively schools of Ankang, Hanzhong, Shangluo, and Guanzhong, and there used to be a large number of troupes as well as famous actors and actresses.

The roles of this opera fall into ten

categories including *mo* (the role of middle aged man), *jing* (the painted-face role), *sheng* (the male role), *dan* (the female role), *chou* (the comic role), etc. The performance stresses smoothness and exquisiteness. The combination of natural voices and falsetto makes the singing melodious and pleasant. Male roles and aged female roles usually sing in their natural voices, other female roles sing in falsetto, and painted-face roles sing in *huyin* (literally tiger voice, which is high, clear and strong). The opera is mainly performed in the musical styles of *erhuang* and *xipi*. The tunes of *erhuang* are used to express sorrowful, miserable and resentful emotions, while tunes of *xipi* express happy, bright and unrestrained emotions. As to the accompanying instruments, stringed and wind instruments include *huqin*, *erhu* (both are two-stringed bowed musical instruments), *yueqin* (a four-stringed plucking instrument with short neck and large round soundboard), *sanxian* (a three-stringed plucking instrument), *suona* horn, bamboo flute, trumpet and so on; percussion instruments include clappers, drums, gongs, cymbals, etc. Most works of Han Tune *erhuang* opera are based on historical tales and folklore from Chinese classic books like *Romance of the States in Eastern Zhou Dynasty*, *Romance of the Three Kingdoms*, *The Creation of*

社众多，名角层出不穷。

汉调二簧的角色共分末、净、生、旦、丑、外、小、贴、夫、杂十个行当，表演讲究细腻精到，唱腔方面真假嗓并用，悠扬婉转。生和老旦一般用真声演唱，旦用假声演唱，净则使用虎音。其唱腔以二簧、西皮为主。二簧多用于表现悲怆、凄凉、愤慨的情绪，西皮多表现舒畅、明快、豪放的情绪。伴奏乐队的文场使用胡琴、二胡、月琴、三弦、阮、唢呐、笛子、喇叭等乐器，武场则使用牙板、梆子、暴鼓、尖鼓、锣、铙钹等。其剧目多取材于《东周列

国志》《三国演义》《封神演义》及其他历史故事和民间传说,代表性剧目有《胡笳十八拍》《清风亭》《二度梅》《打龙棚》《梁红玉》等。

近年来,安康市实施了汉调二簧剧种保护工程,编印了有关资料,成立了汉剧(汉调二簧)研究会,对专业团体进行扶持。他们创作了一批新剧目,保护取得了一定效果。

2006年,汉调二簧被列入第一批国家级非物质文化遗产名录。

the Gods, etc. The representative works of the opera include *Qinfeng Pavilion*, *The Second Bloom*, *Liang Hongyu*, etc.

In recent years, Ankang City has implemented the protection project of Han tune *erhuang* opera which has achieved certain effects. Relevant materials have been compiled and printed. Han Tune *erhuang* Opera Research Association has been established. Professional opera groups have been supported, and a number of new works have been composed.

In 2006, Han tune *erhuang* opera was included in the first batch of China's National Intangible Cultural Heritage List.

汉调桄桄
Han Tune *Guangguang* Opera

汉调桄桄为关中秦腔南传汉中后，与当地民俗、民间音乐、方言融汇、整合而形成的具有汉水上游文化特色的梆子声腔剧种。汉调桄桄的前身是发源于西秦旧地（以陕西省凤翔区为中心）及其周边地区的"西秦腔"。明成化、正德年间，西秦腔传入洋县、南郑等地，在吸收当地方言，配以说唱歌调及其他民间音乐的基础上逐步演变为地方声腔，再经过艺人们的不断创新，其唱腔、表演和伴奏都有了鲜明的地方特色，形成了以洋县、城固县为中心的东路桄桄和以南郑区、汉台区为中心的西路桄桄。

新中国成立后，东路桄桄、西路桄桄被正式命名为汉调桄桄。汉调桄桄

Han tune *guangguang* opera is a kind of *bangzi* opera with cultural characteristics of the upper Hanjiang River. It was formed by the integration of *qinqiang* opera in the Guanzhong area with local folklore, folk music as well as local dialects when *qinqiang* opera spread southward to Hanzhong City. The predecessor of Han tune *guangguang* opera was the "Western Qin Opera" that was born in the previous Western Qin area (centered in Fengxiang District of Shaanxi Province) and its surrounding areas. During the Chenghua Period and Zhengde Period in the Ming Dynasty, "Western Qin Opera" was introduced to Yangxian County, Nanzheng County and other places, and gradually evolved into a local tune on the basis of absorbing the local dialects and supplementing talking and singing tunes as well as folk music. Then through the continuous innovation of artists, the singing tunes, performing form, and accompaniment have distinctive local characteristics. And finally it developed into two schools: the East *guangguang* opera with Yang Xian County and Chenggu County as the center and the West *guangguang* opera with Nanzheng District and Hantai District as the center.

After the founding of the People's Republic of China, the East *guangguang* opera and the West *guangguang* opera were officially named Han tune *guangguang* opera. During the long course of its development, the opera has taken in artistic elements from Sichuan opera and Han tune *erhuang* opera, so that it not only maintains the high-pitched and passionate characteristics of *qinqiang* opera, but also integrates the soft and graceful artistic style of Sichuan opera and Han tune *erhuang* opera. The opera involves joyous and bitter tunes with various types of meter which can be categorized into "slow meter" "media meter" "fast meter", etc. The lyric patterns include ten-character sentence, seven-character sentence, five-character sentence, prose sentence, etc., of which the ten-character sentence pattern and seven-character sentence pattern are most typical. In addition to a great deal of monophonic singing, there are also singing without accompaniment, singing with accompaniment, duet singing, chorus and other forms of singing.

The names of the tunes of Han tune *guangguang* opera are mostly from

在其发展的漫长历程中不断与川剧和汉调二簧进行了艺术上的交流，使汉调桄桄既保持了秦腔高亢激越的特点，又融入了川剧和汉调二簧柔和婉转的艺术风格。汉调桄桄的唱腔有欢音、苦音之别，有慢、中、快、散不同板眼、不同速度的板式，包括慢板、二六板、川板、二倒板、箭板、滚板六类。唱腔词格有十字句、七字句、五字句、散句等句式，以十字句、七字句为主。演唱除大量运用单声唱外，还使用干唱、伴唱、轮唱、对唱、合唱等形式。

汉调桄桄曲牌的来源多见于唐宋大曲、宋金诸宫调、南北曲、昆曲和明清小曲、近代民歌、民间器乐曲以及眉户、京剧、晋剧的曲牌。汉调桄桄体裁多样，有正剧、喜剧、悲剧、悲喜剧、耍戏等；表现形式齐备，有文戏、武戏、唱工戏、做工戏和唱做并重、文武兼备的全行当戏。汉调桄桄的传统剧目有1,500多个，代表性剧目有《孔雀胆》《帝王珠》《刘高磨刀》《镔铁剑》《夕阳山》等。

历史悠久的汉调桄桄对研究我国戏曲剧种的源流走向、演变规律等具有重要的学术价值，对研究汉水上游文化交流及变迁、文化整合及文化特质、大众审美等亦有重要的价值。

2006年，汉调桄桄被列入第一批国家级非物质文化遗产名录。

daqu (a kind of Chinese traditional music used in large-scale dancing and singing performance) in the Tang and Song dynasties, *zhugongdiao* (a kind of Chinese ancient singing and saying literature form) in the Song and Jin dynasties, Southern and Northern Drama Music in the Song and Yuan dynasties, ditties in the Ming and Qing dynasties, modern folk songs, folk instrumental music, *kunqu* opera, *meihu* opera, Peking opera, and Jin opera. The opera can be classified into various genres, including serious opera, comedy, tragedy, tragicomedy, martial opera, opera characterized by singing and acting, opera featuring singing, opera boasting performing, as well as opera featuring both singing and performing. The opera repertoires cover more than 1,500 traditional works, and representative works include *Peacock Gall*, *Imperial Pearl*, *Liu Gao Sharpens the Knife*, *Wrought Iron Sword*, *Mountain at the Sunset* and so on.

Han tune *guangguang* opera has important academic value for studying the origin, trend and evolution of Chinese operas; it is also significant for studying cultural exchanges, cultural integration, cultural characteristics and populace aesthetic in the upper reaches of Hanjiang River.

In 2006, the opera was included in the first batch of China's National Intangible Cultural Heritage List.

商洛花鼓

Shangluo *Huagu* Opera

商洛花鼓，在民间通称花鼓子、地蹦子，是一种在"跳"和"舞"中说唱的民间艺术形式，流行于陕西省商洛市。商洛花鼓跳法多样，舞姿刚健优美，有蹦跳、闪跳、弹跳、扭跳、踏跳、兔子跳、麻雀跳、侧身跳、单腿跳、双蹬跳、十字跳、之字跳等。跳的名目虽然很多，但表演起来却没有固定程式，由演员自由发挥。商洛花鼓以"三小戏"演出为主，小生、小旦、小丑是其主要角色，表演生动活泼，富于民间色彩。花鼓小调或单独使用，或将几首曲调有机地连缀起来，构成具体的花鼓唱腔。

商洛花鼓的内容主要反映当地群众的生产、生活、爱情、婚姻、伦理道德等。其代表性剧目有《夫妻观灯》《打铁》《打草鞋》《绣荷包》《送香茶》《山伯访友》等。新创作的剧

Shangluo *huagu* opera, commonly known as *huaguzi* or *dibengzi*, is popular in Shangluo City. It is a folk art form that performers talk and sing while dancing. The *huagu* opera features various dance styles as well as vigorous and graceful postures, including jumping, bouncing, rabbit-style jumping, sparrow-style jumping, sideways jumping, hopping, cross-step jumping and so on. Despite the different styles of dance movements, the performance is not confined to fixed performing pattern—actors and actresses can perform freely. The opera involves three majors roles, namely, *xiaosheng* (the young male role), *xiaodan* (the young female role) and *xiaochou* (the comic role). The performances are lively and vivid, full of folk features. In the performance, tunes can be either sung separately, or several tunes are harmoniously combined to form a specific *huagu* singing tune.

The content of the opera mainly reflects the production, life, love, marriage, ethics, etc., of the

目有《屠夫状元》《六斤县长》《山魂》《大云寺》《月亮光光》《带灯》等。

由于传播地域的不同,商洛花鼓戏可分为商丹路花鼓与镇柞路花鼓两种。商丹路花鼓音乐曲调优美柔和,语言音调上多用关中语音和当地土语。镇柞路花鼓音乐高亢、明亮、欢快,语言音调上一般采用当地语音(当地称下河语)。

商洛花鼓的传统唱腔音乐结构形式单一,历史久远,是研究戏曲音乐发展演变史的"活化石"。目前,由于群众文化活动形式丰富多样,加之后继乏人,商洛花鼓已处于濒危状态,急需抢救和保护。

2006年,商洛花鼓被列入第一批国家级非物质文化遗产名录。

local people. Representative works of the opera includes *A Couple Watch Lanterns*, *Forging Ironware*, *Making Straw Sandals*, *Embroidering the Pouch*, *Presenting Fragrant Tea*, *Shanbo Visits Friends* and so on. Newly created works are represented by *A Butcher Becomes an High Official*, *County Mayor Liujin*, *Mountain Soul*, *Dayun Temple*, *The Shinning Moon*, *Lantern Bearer*, etc.

According to the dissemination regions, Shangluo *huagu* opera can be divided into Shang-Dan (Shangzhou District and Danfeng County) school and Zhen-Zha (Zhan'an County and Zhashui County) school. The former features beautiful and soft tune as well as intonation of people in the central area of Shaanxi and local dialects. The latter is sonorous, bright and cheerful, and local intonation (*xiahe yu*) is generally adopted.

The music structure of the traditional singing tune of Shangluo *huagu* features single form and long history, serving as the "living fossil" for the study of the development and evolution of opera music. At present, due to the rich and diverse forms of cultural activities of the masses as well as the lack of inheritors, the opera is in an endangered state and urgently needs rescue and protection.

In 2006, Shangluo *huagu* opera was included in the first batch of China's National Intangible Cultural Heritage List.

合阳提线木偶戏
Heyang Marionette Show

陕西省渭南市合阳县活跃着一个稀有剧种——合阳提线木偶戏。它是我国目前现存木偶戏中历史最悠久的剧种之一。合阳人把提线木偶戏称为"线猴",也叫"线胡""线戏""小戏"。它起于汉,兴于唐,盛于明清,距今已有2,000多年的历史。

合阳提线木偶戏主要有生、旦、净、丑四个行当,其表演方法主要是提线。表演时,根据角色的不同,演员的线分别有五到十根不等。旦角线最多,除了头、耳、手、腰、脚外,还有腹、肘、膝等关节处的加线,有十七八根之多,最长的线有三四米。表演者巧妙地运用提、拔、勾、挑、扭、抢、闪、摇等技巧,控制通常高为80~90厘米的偶

In Heyang county of Weinan city, there is a rare puppet show—Heyang marionette show, also called "string drama" "*xianhu*" "*xianhou*", etc. It is one of the oldest puppet shows in China which has a history of more than 2,000 years. It began in the Han Dynasty, flourished in the Tang Dynasty, and prospered in the Ming and Qing dynasties.

Heyang marionette show has four types of roles: *sheng* (the male role), *dan* (the female role), *jing* (the painted-face role) and *chou* (the comic role). Lifting strings is the major performing technique. On the stage, a puppet's strings vary from five to ten pieces, depending on the role it plays. *Dan* needs the most strings. The head, ears, hands, waist, feet, abdomen, elbows, knees and other joints are attached to the strings, which amount to seventeen to eighteen pieces, and the longest string

人，做出走、跑、跳、坐、骑马、坐轿、舞枪弄棒、腾云驾雾、抢水袖、踢纱帽等难易不等的动作。

木偶的头部以泥土雕塑，风干后彩绘成各类角色，用铁丝将颈部与偶身相连，偶人的躯干四肢以木刻制，偶头和偶身可以灵活搭配，以便组成不同的角色。木偶表演动作丰富，其双手可以细腻地表演人物的各种动作，如开合扇子、撑伞、拿书、写字、斟酒、射箭、舞剑等。

合阳提线木偶戏的唱腔称为线腔，是我国提线木偶戏独具的一种唱腔艺术。线腔带有浓郁的地方音调，悲伤苍凉而不失激情，委婉细腻而不失刚烈，颇具秦人秦地的风韵和特点。表演者根据唱腔和道白，充分表现木偶轻便灵活的特点，在有限的时空里，演出丰富多彩的剧目。合阳提线木偶戏演出的大都是

is three to four meters long. The performers ingeniously use the techniques like lifting, pulling, hooking, picking, twisting, flashing, and shaking to suspend and control the puppets that are usually 80 to 90 centimeters tall to make motions like walking, running, jumping, sitting, riding, sitting in sedan chairs, dancing, shooting, riding on the clouds and mist, throwing sleeves, kicking the gauze cap and so on.

Heads of the puppets are made of clay and painted into various characters after being dried. The neck is connected to the body with a piece of iron wire. The body and limbs of the puppet are made of wood. The heads and bodies can be matched flexibly to form different characters. The puppet is able to perform a variety of movements, especially the hands can vividly perform various motions, such as opening and closing a fan, holding an umbrella, holding a book, writing, pouring wine, shooting arrows, playing sword.

The tune of Heyang marionette show is called *xianqiang*, a unique singing tune very different from those of other types of operas. It features a strong flavor of local accent, sad and gloomy but not losing passion, gentle and smooth but not lacking power, which shows the charm and characteristics of Shaanxi people.

传统剧目，如《李彦贵卖水》《三滴血》《借伞》等。

合阳提线木偶戏自古以来都是以师傅带徒弟的形式传承，现在愿意学习该剧种的年轻人已经很少。合阳提线木偶戏面临着失传的窘境，亟待抢救。

2006年，合阳提线木偶戏被列入第一批国家级非物质文化遗产名录。

According to the singing tune and narration, performers fully make use of puppets' characteristics of being light and flexible to perform rich repertoires in a limited time and space. Most of Heyang marionette shows are traditional works, such as *Li Yangui Sells Water*, *Three Drops of Blood* and *Borrowing an Umbrella*.

Since the ancient times, Heyang marionette show has been inherited in the form of masters-to-apprentices. Unfortunately, now few young people are willing to learn it, thus it faces the dilemma of extinction and needs rescue.

In 2006, Heyang marionette show was included in the first batch of China's National Intangible Cultural Heritage List.

华阴迷胡
Huayin *Mihu* Opera

迷胡是陕西地方戏的第二大剧种。陕西省渭南市华阴市是最早出现迷胡剧种之地和最有影响的迷胡传承地之一。

华阴迷胡，俗称"板凳曲子"，多为弦乐伴奏，因此也叫"清唱曲子"。早期的地摊子是比较单一的小曲演唱，以丝竹弦乐伴奏，以后逐渐形成的系列套曲，由一人或多人合唱一个有情节的故事。华阴迷胡受宋代弹词以及元曲、杂剧的影响，在保持地摊型基本表演形式的前提下，部分开始向高台表演转变，逐渐形成了独立的艺术程式。

华阴迷胡一般分为两类：第一类多为文人雅士茶余饭后的自娱消遣；第二类是江湖曲子，多为艺人卖唱时演唱，

Mihu is the second largest genre of Shaanxi local opera. Huayin City of Weinan City is the region where *mihu* opera originates and it is also one of the most influential regions where *mihu* opera has been inherited.

Huayin *mihu* opera is commonly known as the "Bench Tune". As it is mainly accompanied by string music, it is also called "Accapella Tune". The early stall-type performance featured ditties that were accompanied by stringed and wind instruments. Later, a series of suites gradually formed in which one or more persons sang a story. Huayin *mihu* opera was influenced by *tanci* (storytelling to the accompaniment of stringed instruments) in the Song Dynasty, *yuanqu* (a type of verse popular in the Yuan Dynasty) and *zaju* (an opera popular in the Yuan Dynasty). On the basis of maintaining the basic performing form of the original stall-type performance, some works began to be shown on the stage, and gradually the present *mihu* opera which has independent artistic expression mode took shape.

Huayin *mihu* opera is generally divided into two categories. The first category is the opera sung by literati in their

文词比较通俗,内容贴近社会生活和民众感情。华阴迷胡的音乐曲牌浩繁,有大调七十二、小调三百六十之说。按照情感效能,曲调可分为欢愉性、哀怨性、中性,总体风格柔美细腻,便于抒发内心感情。题材多为男女悲欢离合的爱情故事,代表性剧目有《杜十娘》《孟姜女》《张连卖布》等。

中华人民共和国成立前后,华阴地摊型的"清唱迷胡"班社多达上百个,其中赵坪、南营、康营等村的自乐班社距今已有上百年的历史。随后,华阴迷胡受到有关方面的高度重视,得以发扬光大。

2008年,华阴迷胡被列入第二批国家级非物质文化遗产名录。

leisure time for self-entertainment. The second category is called *jianghu* tunes, which are mostly sung by artists to make a living—the lyrics of the tunes are relatively popular, and the content is related to social life and can easily arouse sympathy from the audience. The opera has numerous tune names. According to the emotional efficacy, the tunes can be divided into joyful tunes, sad tunes and tunes expressing neutral feelings. The tunes are gentle, smooth and delicate, which can easily express people's inner feelings. The themes of the opera are mostly concerned with love stories about the sorrows and joys between men and women, and representative operas include *Du Shiniang*, *Meng Jiangnü*, *Zhang Lian Sells Cloth* and so on.

Around the founding of the People's Republic of China, there were over a hundred stall-type *mihu* opera troupes in Huayin. Among them, the troupes in villages such as Zhaoping, Nanying, and Kangying had a history of over a hundred years. Since then the opera has received great attention from relevant parties and is able to flourish.

In 2008, Huayin *mihu* opera was included in the second batch of China's National Intangible Cultural Heritage List.

眉户曲子戏
Meihu Opera

　　眉户曲子戏是陕西地方剧种之一，也称"陕西曲子"，因眉户发源于陕西的户县和眉县两地而得名；又因其曲调缠绵委婉，使人入迷，故又称"迷糊"。

　　眉户的剧目丰富多彩，以反映劳动群众的日常生活、劳动、爱情、婚姻等内容为主，代表性剧目有《张连卖布》《二姐娃做梦》《文王访贤》《刘秀走南阳》《桃园借水》等。眉户曲子戏音乐的主要素材源于陕西的民歌，如情歌、牧歌、樵歌、渔歌，以及民间小调和童谣。唱词思想内容深刻，易于表现人民群众的生活、习惯、思想、感情、性格以及心理。眉户曲子戏的演唱形式分为两种：一种是一唱到底、很少说白的演唱形式，另一种是有白、有唱、有

　　Meihu opera, also called "Shaanxi Tune", is one of Shaanxi's local operas. It originates from Meixian County and Huxian County of Shaanxi Province, hence the name *meihu*. It is also called *mihu* (which means people feeling enchanted) for its beautiful and melodious tunes can deeply attract people.

　　Meihu opera has rich and colorful repertoires which mainly reflect the daily life, work, love, marriage, etc., of ordinary people. The representative works include *Zhang Lian Sells Cloth*, *The Second Sister Had a Dream*, *The Emperor Visits the Talent*, *Liu Xiu Visits Nanyang*, *Borrowing Water from a Peach Orchard* and so on. The material of *Meihu* opera mainly comes from Shaanxi folk songs (such as love songs, pastoral songs, woodmen' songs, and fishing songs), folk ditties and nursery rhymes. The lyrics of *meihu* opera contain profound theme, and they can well express people's life, habits, thoughts, emotions, character and psychology. The opera includes two types of singing styles: one is singing without narration; the other is singing with narration and performance. The main accompaniment instrument of the opera is *sanxian* (a three-stringed plucked musical instrument) and

表演的舞台演出形式。伴奏乐器以三弦为主，板胡、海笛为辅助乐器。

眉户曲子戏音乐明快，曲调丰富，具有十分迷人的音乐效果，因而大大激发了演唱者和作曲者的创造力。农民可以自由按曲编词，不一定要识字，只要能编出来，唱着顺口，就能表达自己的思想感情。在实际生活中，农民编的曲子切合实际，加上语言生动、形象鲜明，唱起来更有地方味道。眉户曲子戏在农村十分流行。由于它需要的乐器简单，人员可多可少，又不需要搭建舞台，主人家开支较少，所以深受人们的欢迎。

眉户曲子戏优美动听，委婉细腻，有很强的艺术感染力。眉户曲子戏音乐的民歌体、抒情性和它对民间歌谣的天然亲和力、融合力，使得一些散佚的民间小调能及时得以保存并发展，极大地丰富了我国民间音乐。

2008年，眉户曲子戏被列入第二批国家级非物质文化遗产名录。

the auxiliary instruments are *banhu* (a bowed two-stringed instrument with a thin wooden soundboard) and *haidi* trumpet.

The music of *meihu* opera is bright and lively and the tunes are rich, which can create very charming musical effect and greatly stimulate the creativity of singers and composers. Farmers, even illiterate, are able to compose lyrics according to the tune, and they can sing the tune to express their thoughts and feelings. In real life, what the farmers compose are based on their own life, coupled with vivid language and clear images, thus this kind of opera boasts a distinct local flavor. Due to simple musical instruments, flexible number of performers, low performing expenses, the opera is very popular in rural areas.

Meihu opera has strong artist appeal for its melodious, smooth and pleasant tunes. Its folk song style, lyricism, and natural affinity and fusion with folk songs have enabled some scattered folk ditties to be saved and developed in time, which has greatly enriched the Chinese folk music.

In 2008, the opera was included in the second batch of China's National Intangible Cultural Heritage List.

府谷二人台
Fugu Song-and-Dance Duets

府谷二人台流传于陕西省榆林市府谷县和其他各县，属民间小唱艺术。大约在清朝同治年间，府谷二人台已形成艺人班子，但当时尚没有二人台这种称谓，而是叫"打坐腔"。又因二人台的演出与过节闹社火相伴，也叫"唱秧歌"。

府谷二人台可分为民谣体和叙事体两类。作品的内容以农村生活情趣为主，其中反映男欢女爱、反封建的剧目所占比例较大。另外，还有反映旧社会黑暗、苦难生活的剧目，有反映民俗风情的剧目，有反映历史传说的剧目，有描写花名的剧目，有描述货郎、挑夫生活的剧目，有刻画青楼女子、尼姑之苦的剧目。

Fugu song-and-dance duets are a kind of folk singing art, circulated in Fugu County and other counties of Yulin City. During the reign of emperor Tongzhi in the Qing Dynasty, Fugu song-and-dance duet troupes came into being—the performance was called "*Dazuo Tune*" at that time. As the song-and-dance duets are often performed together with the *shehuo* performance which includes a series of entertainment activities like lion dance, dragon dance, walking on stilts and so on, they are also called "Singing *Yangge*"—*yangge* dance is an essential part of *shehuo* performance.

Fugu song-and-dance duets can be divided into two categories: ballads and narratives. The duets are mainly themed on the fun of rural life, among which repertoires that reflect love and anti-feudalism spirit account for a larger proportion. There are repertoires concerning flower names, folk customs and historical legends. Moreover, there are also repertoires depicting people's miserable life in the dark old society, the life of peddlers and porters, the suffering of girls in whorehouses and nuns in nunneries.

The duets roughly involve three

府谷二人台的表演方式大致有三种：一是清唱，一般不化妆；二是跑场，一般由男女对唱并增加念白及表演；三是小戏，多有故事情节，人物超过两人，且分场、分幕。文场伴奏乐器有四弦、三弦、扬琴、海笛、京阳胡五大件，武场的有梆子、板鼓、四页瓦、手锣、小镲、马锣。

府谷二人台的歌词句式丰富，两句段、三句段、四句段、五句段、六句段、多句段均有，词句有五字句、七字句、八字句、九字句、十字句等。说念道白、插科打诨的语言颇具地方性，方言妙语横生，特色显明。演唱采用真假声结合，抑扬顿挫，高亢明亮，自然合韵，悠扬动听。

因府谷与山西、内蒙古毗连，从府谷二人台的音乐和表演中，我们可以看

performing modes: one is singing opera arias without makeup and acting; another is *paochang*, which features a combination of antiphonal singing between a male and a female, narrating and acting; the last is the playlet, which usually has a plot and involves more than two characters and can be divided into several scenes and acts. The orchestral instruments of the duets include *sixian* (a four-stringed plucking instrument), *sanxian* (a three-stringed plucking instrument), dulcimers, *haidi* trumpets, and *jingyanghu* (also called *banhu*, a bowed two-stringed instrument with a thin wooden soundboard); and the percussion instruments include clappers, drums, hand gongs, cymbals, etc.

Fugu song-and-dance duets boast rich lyric patterns. A part of the lyric can be composed of two sentences, or three, four, five, six, or many sentences. A sentence can be made up of five, seven, eight, nine or ten words. The duets are sung in the local dialect which is characteristic and humorous. Actors and actresses combine their real and falsetto voices to sing so that the duets sound natural, rhythmic, sonorous and melodious.

As Fugu County is adjoined to Shanxi Province and Inner Mongolia Autonomous

到其与山西、内蒙古民间艺术相互融合的显著印记。

2008年,府谷二人台被列入第二批国家级非物质文化遗产名录。

Region, Fugu song-and-dance duets feature a distinct flavor of the integration of the three regions' folk arts, both in music and in performing form.

In 2008, the duets were included in the second batch of China's National Intangible Cultural Heritage List.

五

曲艺

Quyi, Folk Vocal Art Forms

陕北说书
Storytelling of Northern Shaanxi

陕北说书流行于陕西省北部的延安、榆林等地。最初是由穷苦盲艺人运用陕北的民歌小调演唱一些传说、故事，后来吸收眉户、秦腔以及道情、信天游的曲调，逐步发展成陕北说书这一民间曲艺形式。

陕北说书的表演形式为一人自弹自唱，说唱相间，伴奏乐器为三弦或琵琶。此外，还有绑在小腿上的以两块木板制成的耍板，以及绑在手腕上的打节奏用的"嘛喳喳"（用竹片做成枣核形状串在一起）。后经民间艺人韩起祥等人改革，一人可同时操作大三弦或琵琶、梆子、耍板、嘛喳喳、小锣或钹五种乐器

The storytelling of northern Shaanxi is popular in Yan'an City and Yulin City. It originated from the performances of poor and blind artists who sang folk songs and ditties themed on legends and stories. Later, it absorbed the tunes of *meihu* opera, *qinqiang* opera, *daoqing* tune and *xintianyou* melody, and gradually developed into the form of storytelling.

The performance form of the storytelling in northern Shaanxi is that one person sings and tells stories in alternation while playing the musical instrument of *sanxian* (a three-stringed plucking instrument) or *pipa* (a plucked string instrument with a fretted fingerboard). In addition, there are also musical instruments like *shuaban* (clappers made of two wooden boards and tied on the player's lower leg), and *mazhazha* (a string of date-pit-shaped wood strips tied on the player's wrist for beating rhythm). After reforms by folk artist Han Qixiang and others, in the storytelling performance one person can simultaneously play five musical instruments

伴奏,从而大大增强了陕北说书的艺术表现力。

陕北说书的唱词通俗易懂,生活气息浓厚,一般采用五字句或七字句,但又不受字数的严格限制,有利于表现生活。陕北说书的曲调丰富,风格粗犷、激越,具有浓郁的陕北地方特色。其中常用的曲调有"单音调""双音调""西凉调""山东腔""哭调""武调"等。20世纪80年代后,陕北说书有了新的发展,由单人说唱发展为多人对说,由坐场改为走场,由地摊搬上舞台,由盲艺人说书发展为健全人、有文化者说书。过去没有女艺人说书,20世纪80年代,韩起祥培养了几位女徒弟。现在说书女艺人已经成为陕北说书的一支活跃的新生力量。

陕北说书种类繁多,曲目丰富,据

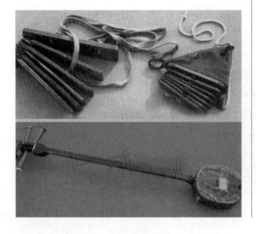

including the big *sanxian* or *pipa*, clappers, *shuaban*, *mazhazha*, small gong or cymbal, which can greatly enhance the artistic expression of the storytelling.

The lyrics of northern Shaanxi storytelling are popular, easy to understand and full of life flavor. They are generally in the form of five-word sentences or seven-word sentences, but not strictly limited by the number of words, which can reflect daily life very well. The storytelling boasts rich tunes and is high-spirited, bold, vigorous and full of strong local characteristics. The commonly used tunes include mono-tune, dual-tune, Xiliang tune, Shandong tune, sobbing tune, martial tune, etc. Since the 1980s, the storytelling of northern Shaanxi has witnessed a new development, from single-person performance to multi-person performance, from sitting-type performance to walking-type performance, from performing on the street to performing on the stage, from blind artists' storytelling to non-disabled and literate people' storytelling. In the past, there were no female storytellers, while in the 1980s, Han Qixiang trained several female apprentices. Now the female storytellers have become active new forces in the storytelling performance.

There are over 20 kinds of storytelling with rich repertoires and various forms of performance. The repertoires fall into two major categories: traditional repertoires and modern

统计，大致有二十几种。其表演形式也是多种多样。陕北说书的书目可分为传统书目和现代书目两大类。传统书目有200多部，主要讲述神话、历史人物传记、英雄豪杰打抱不平、奸臣害忠良等，代表性书目包括《偷鞋记》《金镯记》《万花山》《杨家将》《观灯记》等。现代书目有300多部，主要反映现代人的斗争、生活等，如《王贵与李香香》《李双双》《张玉兰参加选举会》《送金匾》《延安老汉进北京》等。

陕北说书具有很高的历史、艺术与实用价值。2006年，陕北说书被列入第一批国家级非物质文化遗产名录。

repertoires. The traditional repertoires cover more than 200 works focusing on myths, biographies of historical figures, heroes, unscrupulous traitors and so on, and the representative works include *Stealing Shoes, Golden Bracelet, Wanhua Mountain, Generals of the Yang Family, Watching Lantern*, etc. The modern repertoires cover more than 300 works focusing on the struggle and life of modern people, and the representative works include *Wang Gui and Li Xiangxiang, Li Shuangshuang, Zhang Yulan Takes Part in the Election, Present the Plaque, An Elderly Man in Yan'an Visits Beijing* and so on.

The storytelling of northern Shaanxi has great historical, artistic and practical value, and in 2006 it was included in the first batch of China's National Intangible Cultural Heritage List.

榆林小曲
Yulin Ditties

榆林小曲是产生并流传于榆林市井的一种民间说唱艺术形式。相传由明代驻扎在榆林一带的军官蓄养的歌伎从江南带来，后在长期的发展演变过程中，以当地方言演唱并吸收了当地的民歌小调，丰富完善为今天的曲艺品种。

榆林小曲的内容以反映城市生活情趣为主，其中描写离愁别怨、男欢女爱的曲目占较大比例，如《日落西山》《日落黄昏》等。另外还有反映茶肆

Yulin ditties are a type of folk talking-singing art form that comes into being and spreads in Yulin City. According to the legend, they were introduced from the south of the Yangtze River by singing girls who were kept by military officers stationed in Yulin in the Ming Dynasty. In the course of long-term evolution, they were sang in the local dialect and influenced by the local folk songs and ditties, developing into the present artistic form.

The content of Yulin ditties mainly reflects urban life, among which repertoires describing grief of parting as well as love between men and women account for a large proportion, such as *The Sun Sinks Westward* and *Sunset*. There are repertoires reflecting lives of merchants, porters, people in wine houses and tea houses, such as *Opening a Tea House* and *Selling Groceries*. There are repertoires depicting the hatred of prostitutes and the suffering of nuns, such as *A Prostitute Files a Suit* and *The Little Nun*. There are repertoires showcasing folk customs, such as *Flying a Kite*, *Playing on a Swing*, *Stealing Red Shoes*. There are repertoires describing folklore and tales, such as *The Butterfly Lovers*, *Eight Immortals Cross the Sea* and

酒楼、货郎挑夫生活的曲目,如《开茶馆》《卖杂货》;有刻画青楼之恨、尼庵之苦的曲目,如《妓女告状》《小尼姑》;有表现民俗风情的曲目,如《放风筝》《戏秋千》《偷红鞋》等;有关于一些脍炙人口的民间传说故事的曲目,如《梁山伯与祝英台》《八仙过海》等。此外,有些曲目源于当地民歌,如《走西口》《小寡妇上坟》《送大哥》等。

小曲的伴奏乐器为扬琴、古筝、琵琶、三弦、京胡等。小曲既可一人单唱,也可两人对唱;既可坐唱,也可站唱。演唱时采用真假声结合及顿挫抑扬的唱法,合辙押韵,优美动听。

清末民初,民间学唱小曲在榆林蔚然成风。从事演唱、演奏的艺人多是市民阶层中的小手工业者,如银匠、钟表匠、鞋匠、

so on. In addition, there are also repertoires derived from local folk songs, such as *Leave for the West*, *The Young Widow Pays Respect to the Deceased at the Grave*, *See Elder Brother Off* and so on.

The accompaniment instruments of the ditties include the dulcimer, *guzheng* (a 21-stringed or 25-stringed plucked instrument), *pipa* (a plucked string instrument with a fretted fingerboard), *sanxian* (a three-stringed plucked instrument), *jinghu* (a two-stringed bowed instrument with a high register), etc. The ditties can be sung by one person or two persons; the performer can sit or stand while singing. The music rhymes and is pleasant to ears for the singer combines his/her natural voice and falsetto to produce rising and falling tones.

At the end of Qing Dynasty and the beginning of the Republic of China, learning to sing Yulin ditties among the folks became popular in Yulin. Artists engaged in singing and playing the ditties are mostly handicraftsmen in the civic class, such as silversmiths, watchmakers, shoemakers, carpenters. Later, due to frequent wars, Yulin ditties were almost extinct. After the founding of the People's Republic of China, Yulin ditties developed and prospered. Training classes of Yulin ditties were organized and artists went to Xi'an and Beijing to put on performances. After the silence for some time, they entered a new period of development and prosperity after 1985. Yulin City established

木匠等。此后，由于战乱频仍，小曲一度几乎绝响。中华人民共和国成立后，榆林小曲得以重生，小曲演唱培训班诞生，并先后赴省城、进京参加会演。之后榆林小曲经历了一段时间的沉寂，1985年以后进入一个新的发展繁荣时期。榆林市成立了榆林小曲研究会，编印了《榆林小曲专辑》，组建了半专业性的演唱队，使小曲的影响日益扩大。但是，现在榆林小曲仍然面临着后继乏人的困境，急需抢救。

2006年，榆林小曲被列入第一批国家级非物质文化遗产名录。

Yulin Ditty Research Association, compiled and printed *Yulin Ditty Album*, and formed a semiprofessional singing team so that the influence of the ditties has been expanding day by day. However, now Yulin ditties still face the dilemma of lack of successors, so urgent measures are required to save and protect them.

In 2006, Yulin ditties were included in the first batch of China's National Intangible Cultural Heritage List.

陕北道情
Daoqing of Northern Shaanxi

陕北道情是广泛流传于陕北的一种古老的民间曲唱形式，在子长、延川、清涧等县最为集中，并辐射至晋西北、内蒙古河套地区及甘肃、宁夏靠近陕北的地区。它源于唐代道教徒诵经的经韵，后演变为道教徒在民间布道时演唱的道歌。

陕北道情是陕北群众喜闻乐见的艺术形式之一。陕北道情分为东路道情和西路道情两种，二者音乐调式不同，

Daoqing of northern Shaanxi is an ancient folk singing form, which has widely spread in the northern part of Shaanxi. It is mostly concentrated in Zichang County, Yanchuan County, Qingjian County and other counties, and also prevails in northwestern areas of Shanxi Province, Hetao areas in Inner Mongolia Autonomous Region, areas of Gansu Province and Ningxia Hui Autonomous Region which adjoin northern Shaanxi. It originated from Taoist scripture chanting in the Tang Dynasty, and later developed into Taoist songs sung by Taoists in folk sermons.

Daoqing of northern Shaanxi is one of the art forms that are deeply loved by the local people. It is divided into two types: eastern *daoqing* and western *daoqing*, whose music modes are different, but the names of tunes are roughly same, for instance, both have level tune and cross tune. Eastern *daoqing* and western *daoqing* have completely different artistic styles. The former is high-pitched and cheerful, while the latter is delicate and smooth. *Daoqing* of northern Shaanxi was originally sung by one or many-person without makeup and acting. Later, it was combined with performance and gradually developed

但曲牌名称大致相同，如平调、十字调等。二者艺术风格完全不同，东路道情高亢明快，西路道情委婉细腻。陕北道情的演唱形式原为单人或多人清唱，后与表演结合逐渐向戏曲演唱形式发展，同时也转为民间班社演唱。陕北道情的传承模式大体有两种：一种为家庭传承，即父传子，子传孙，代代相传；一种为社会传承，即以村为基本单位传承。

陕北道情的传统曲目保留了许多古老的历史和文化信息，被誉为陕北文化的"活化石"；其音乐与陕北民歌、陕北说书的音乐截然不同，保留了道教音乐风格，有独特的艺术价值。

2008年，陕北道情被列入第二批国家级非物质文化遗产名录。

into the form of opera singing. At the same time, it was also sung by folk troupes. There are basically two inheritance modes for *daoqing* of northern Shaanxi. The first is the family inheritance, that is, it is passed on from generation to generation; and the second is the social inheritance and the village is the basic unit of inheritance.

Traditional repertoires of *daoqing* of northern Shaanxi retain much ancient historical and cultural information and are regarded as the "living fossil" of northern Shaaxi culture. The music of *daoqing* retains the Taoist music style, completely different from the music of folk songs and storytelling of northern Shaanxi, thus it has unique artistic value.

In 2008, *daoqing* of northern Shaanxi was included in the second batch of China's National Intangible Cultural Heritage List.

洛南静板书
Jingbanshu, a Form of Storytelling and Singing in Luonan Dialect

洛南静板书早在清朝道光年间就在雒南（今陕西省商洛市洛南县）盛行。过去演唱洛南静板书多是盲艺人求生糊口的手段和农户办红白喜事时借以助兴的形式。现在洛南静板书已经成为当地群众喜爱的一种民间曲艺形式。

表演洛南静板书时，一人可操六种乐器，融弹、敲、打、说、唱于一身，一人顶七人。田间地头，家庭院落，一张桌椅即可说唱。说唱时在桌子两侧各竖一根竹竿，再用两条绳子牵连，上绳上吊着大

Jingbanshu, a form of storytelling and singing in Luonan dialect, was popular in Luonan (the present Luonan County of Shangluo City) as early as the Daoguang Period of the Qing Dynasty. In the past, it was mostly a means for blind artists to make a living and a way for farmers to provide entertainment for guests at weddings or funerals. Now it has become a popular folk art form among local people.

When performing *jingbanshu*, a performer talks and sings while playing six kinds of musical instruments by himself/herself, which means one person plays seven persons' roles. Whether in the field or at the courtyard, it can be performed as long as a table and a chair are available. Before the performance, one bamboo pole is erected on each side of the table, and then two ropes are used to tie them. A big gong and a small gong are hung on the upper rope, and the lower rope adjoins the gongs to prevent them from swinging during the performance. A small copper cymbal is placed on a hemp rope loop on the table, and a pedal clapper is tied to the leg of the table. The performer has four small pieces of bamboo clappers tied below one of his/her knees and holds *sanxian* (a

锣、小锣，下绳紧靠锣边，防止打击时锣体摇摆。桌上用麻绳圈仰放小铜镲，桌腿上捆着脚踏梆子。说书人的膝盖下绑着四片竹制蚂蚱板，怀抱三弦，自弹自敲，自打自唱。说唱时，唱腔清晰，文文雅雅，脚踏梆子打击节奏，不加杂其他乐器伴奏，过门时才用其他乐器渲染气氛。

根据地域方言的不同，洛南静板书形成了东路、西路、北路三种不同的说唱风格。东路静板书古朴、粗狂，说唱时弦乐运用上、中、下三个韵律，反复演奏三遍，并根据书目情节发展，时带拖腔，时不带拖腔。西路静板书的唱腔注重音韵洪亮，普遍带有拖腔。北路静板书的唱腔力求语言轻巧，吐字清晰，注重抒情，不带拖腔。

洛南静板书的内容有神话故事、历史演义、忠臣孝子、世俗生活、男欢女爱等，篇幅有长有短，深受群众喜爱。

2011年，洛南静板书被列入第三批国家级非物质文化遗产名录。

three-stringed plucked instrument) with his/her hands. During the performance, the performer talks and sings clearly and elegantly to the rhythm of pedal clappers, and other instruments are only played to highlight atmosphere.

According to the dialects in which it is performed, *jingbanshu* has formed three different styles, including the eastern style, western style, and northern style. The eastern style is quaint, bold and unconstrained. Throughout the performance, the string music which consists of three kinds of rhythms is played for three times. Besides, the tune is prolonged when necessary according to the plot development. As for the western style, the singing tune emphasizes the sonorous rhyme, and is often prolonged. The northern style features lyricism and the singing tune is soft and clear without being prolonged.

Luonan *jingbanshu*, in different length and with rich content covering myths, historical romances, stories of loyal ministers and filial sons, secular life, love stories, etc., is deeply loved by the masses.

In 2011, Luonan *jingbanshu* was included in the third batch of China's National Intangible Cultural Heritage List.

陕西快板
Shaanxi Clapper Talk

陕西快板起源于关中一带，由民间顺口溜演变而来，主要分布在关中地区，同时辐射陕北、陕南和整个西北地区。陕西快板作为一种民间艺术形式，以关中方言为标准语言，有单口、对口、群口等形式。其节奏明快，乡音醇厚，高亢激昂，风趣幽默，为群众喜闻乐见。其伴奏乐器主要是七块板和四页瓦。四页瓦的独特打法被视为陕西快板的"绝技"。

陕西快板已有些年头。中华人民共和国成立前后，王老九、谢茂恭等人编演陕西快板，反映劳动人民的疾苦，揭露旧社会的黑暗，歌唱人民翻身解放、当家做主的喜悦。中华人民共和国成立后，随着艺人地位的提高和国家对宣传

Shaanxi clapper talk originated in Guanzhong area (the central part of Shaanxi Province) and evolved from the folk doggerel. It is mainly distributed in Guanzhong area, and meanwhile spreads in northern Shaanxi, southern Shaanxi and the entire northwestern region of China. It is performed in Guanzhong dialect and has different forms such as the single-person talk, cross talk and group talk. As a folk artistic form, it features lively rhythm, strong local accent, high pitch, great passion and humorous language, so it is popular among the masses. Its accompaniment instruments are mainly *qikuaiban* (seven-piece bamboo board clappers) and *siyewa* (four-piece bamboo board clappers). The way of playing the *siyewa* is regarded as a "consummate skill" in the performance of Shaanxi clapper talk.

Shaanxi clapper talk has a long history. Around the founding of the People's Republic of China, Wang Laojiu, Xie Maogong and other artists composed and performed Shaanxi clapper talk, which reflected the suffering of the working people and the darkness of the old society, expressed the joy of the people's liberation and mastery of the country. After the

工作的重视，一批业余快板演员陆续涌现。刘志鹏在陕西快板表演中吸收借鉴山东快书的表演形式，创造了陕西快书，把陕西快板推向新的发展阶段。受其影响，一大批陕西快板演员相继登上舞台，并多次在全国曲艺会演和大赛中获奖，代表人物有刘文龙、董怀义、卢向阳等。

2007年，陕西省曲艺家协会成立了陕西快板（书）艺术委员会，为陕西快板的传承和发展做出了贡献。

2011年，陕西快板被列入陕西省第三批非物质文化遗产名录。

founding of the People's Republic of China, with the improvement of artists' status and the country's emphasis on the propaganda work, a group of amateur clapper talk actors emerged. Liu Zhipeng learned from the performance form of quick patter of Shandong to create Shaanxi quick patter, pushing Shaanxi clapper talk into a new stage of development. Influenced by this, a large number of Shaanxi clapper talk actors, including Liu Wenlong, Dong Huaiyi, Lu Xiangyang, etc., have performed the clapper talk on stage and won a number of awards in national folk art shows and competitions.

In 2007, Shaanxi Folk Vocal Art Association established Shaanxi Clapper Talk Art Committee, which has contributed a lot to the inheritance and development of this art form.

In 2011, Shaanxi clapper talk was included in the third batch of Shaanxi Provincial Intangible Cultural Heritage List.

眉县曲子
Meixian Tunes

眉县曲子最早流传于宝鸡市眉县青化乡风池村，起源于明朝正德年间，距今已有五百多年的历史。

眉县曲子有十多种唱腔，五十一个曲牌，大致分为民歌曲体、说诵性曲体和戏曲化曲体三类。伴奏乐器有三弦、板胡、笛子、碰铃等。眉县曲子的欢音轻快欢畅、优美动听，苦音幽怨深沉、凄楚悲痛，具有很强的感染力。

在民间办红白喜事时，在纳凉广场上，以及冬季的热炕上都可演唱眉县曲子，也可在舞台上表演。演员的化妆、服饰简朴而真实，具有生活气息，颇受群众喜爱。眉县曲子除了表演传统的眉户剧目《张连卖布》《杜十娘》等，也演过《兄妹开荒》《十二把镰刀》《梁

Meixian tunes originally spread in Fengchi Village, Qinghua Township, Meixian County of Baoji City. They originated in the Zhengde Period of the Ming Dynasty and have a history of more than 500 years.

There are more than 10 kinds of singing tunes and 51 tune names. The tunes are roughly divided into three categories: the folk-song-style tunes, chanting-style tunes and opera-style tunes. The accompaniment instruments include *sanxian* (a three-stringed plucked instrument), *banhu* (a bowed two stringed instrument with a thin wooden soundboard), flute, finger cymbal and so on. The happy tune of Meixian tunes is lively, cheerful and dulcet, while the sad tune features hidden bitterness and deep sadness, which arouses much sympathy from the audience.

Meixian tunes are widely sung on various occasions like weddings, funerals, outdoor performances. They can not only be performed on the stage, on the square, in the courtyard, but can also be performed on the *kang* (a heatable brick or earthen bed) in winter. The actors and actresses' makeup and costumes are simple, natural and close to life, deeply favored

秋燕》等新剧目，同时还有表现家庭矛盾等题材的现代新剧目。这些剧目大都是老艺人口授心传，保留了原始的唱腔和技法。眉县曲子的故事浅而寓意深，教育意义极强。特别是那些反映劳动人民生活的曲目，更是鲜明生动、诙谐风趣。

近年来，眉县曲子的抢救保护工作已经引起眉县有识之士和文化主管部门的高度重视。目前，眉县的文化工作者和艺人一起对眉县曲子传统曲目进行了抢救、挖掘、整理，并制订了长期的保护规划。

2011年，眉县曲子被列入陕西省第三批非物质文化遗产名录。

by the masses. In addition to performing traditional works such as *Zhang Lian Sells Cloth*, *Du Shiniang*, some new works have also been staged, such as *The Brother and Sister Reclaim Wasteland*, *Twelve Sickles* and *Liang Qiuyan*. Moreover, there are also modern works which show family conflicts and other themes. Most of the repertoires are taught by old artists by word of mouth so that the original singing tunes and singing techniques are retained. The stories told in Meixian tunes are simple, but imply deep meaning and profound educational significance, and the repertoires that reflect the working people's life are especially vivid and humorous.

In recent years, the saving and protection work for Meixian tunes have attracted attention of people of insight and cultural authorities in Meixian County. At present, the cultural workers and artists of Meixian County are working together to save, collect and file the traditional repertoires, and they have also formulated a long-term protection plan.

In 2011, Meixian tunes were listed in the third batch of Shaanxi Provincial Intangible Cultural Heritage List.

六

传统体育、游艺与杂技

Traditional Sports and Acrobatics

甘水坊高空耍狮子
High-Altitude Lion Dance of Ganshuifang

流行于西安市鄠邑区甘水坊村及其周边村子的高空耍狮子又叫"打狮子",是当地年节时社火表演的一种艺术形式。高空耍狮子主要有以下三种表演形式。

雄狮爬杆:在活动场地中心竖起一根高约15米的高杆,从杆顶拉两条间隔80厘米的粗竹绳固定于地面。竹绳两侧各用一根长约25米的钢绳固定高杆。杆上有平台,平台下面有2个或4个秋千。雄狮爬杆一般由10人表演,其组成是3个耍狮子的武士、3个单人狮子、2个双人

The high-altitude lion dance in Ganshuifang Village and its surrounding villages in Huyi District of Xi'an City is a famous martial art performed during local festivals, which falls into the following three kinds of performances.

The first kind of performance is that lions climb up ropes. A pole about 15 meters high is erected in the center of the performance venue, and two thick ropes with an interval of 80 centimeters are pulled from the top of the pole and fixed to the ground. A steel rope about 25 meters long is used to fix the high pole on either side of the ropes. On the top of the pole is installed a platform with 2 or 4 swings fixed below it. The performance of lions climbing up ropes generally needs 10 persons: 3 warriors who lead lions, 3 single-person lions, and 2 double-person lions. During the performance, the warriors and the lions are fighting, playing and chasing, climbing up and down on the two 25-meter-long steel ropes. After climbing onto the top of the pole, the lions

狮子。表演时，武士和狮子在打斗嬉戏和追逐的过程中，在两条长25米的钢绳上爬上爬下进行表演。狮子爬上杆顶后在平台上进行表演，武士在杆侧的吊棍上进行悬空倒吊等表演。

狮子叼板凳：把25条高低、长短相同的条凳每层放两条摆起来，最上面放一条板凳，共13层，高约8米。此项表演中仅稳凳就需50人，再加上1个武士和1个单人狮子，共52人。表演时，武士和狮子从两边的凳角一直攀登到顶端的一条凳子上，然后进行打斗玩耍表演。打斗五个回合后，武士逐层退下，狮子找不到武士，在暴怒中用嘴叼住板凳将其一条一条往下扔，直到底层。

狮子翻山：把两个高约7米的木梯（或铁梯）的顶端相连，八字形摆在场地

perform various motions on the platform, and the warriors give performances such as hanging upside down on the hanging rod installed on one side of the pole.

The second kind of performance is that the lion throws benches. 25 benches of the same height and length are piled together: 2 benches on each of the first twelve tiers, and 1 bench on the thirteenth tier, a total of 13 tiers, about 8 meters high. This performance needs a total of 52 persons: 50 persons stabilize the benches, 1 person plays as a warrior and 1 person plays as a lion. During the performance, the warrior climbs up from one side of the benches and the lion climbs up from the other side of the benches and finally to the bench at the top, where they fight against and playing with each other. After five rounds of fighting, the warrior retreats from the benches. As the lion can't find the warrior, it holds the bench with its mouth and throws it down one by one.

The last kind is lions' climbing over ladders. The tops of two wooden ladders (or iron ladders) about 7 meters high are connected and the ladders are placed in the middle of the performance venue, the bottom parts tied with ropes. During the performance, 4 persons stabilize the ladders, the

中间，下端用绳绑好。表演时，由4人稳好梯子，武士爬上梯顶。2个双人狮同时爬追武士到梯子顶端，向四方舞动玩耍，找不到武士后，同时爬下梯子。

在以上表演中，均有烟火表演和锣鼓、胡哨伴奏。高空耍狮子属于武狮子，表演惊险，气氛紧张热烈，引人入胜。

2011年，甘水坊高空耍狮子被列入陕西省第三批非物质文化遗产名录。

warrior climbs up to the tops of the ladders. 2 double-person lions chase the warrior to the tops of the ladders at the same time, dancing and playing in all directions. As the lions can not find the warrior, they climb down the ladder.

Accompanied by fireworks, gongs, drums, and whistles, the performance is magnificent and exciting. The high-altitude lion dance of Ganshuifang is fascinating and thrilling with intense and lively atmosphere.

In 2011, it was included in the third batch of Shaanxi Provincial Intangible Cultural Heritage List.

吴东无底鸳鸯秋千
Swing Playing of Wudong

无底鸳鸯秋千是渭南市富平县美原镇吴东村的一项民间游乐竞技活动。据传,清朝嘉庆年间,当地一位刘姓老艺人引进了一种设计巧妙的秋千。后来一对年轻男女在对打秋千的过程中萌生爱意,终结为夫妻。此事在当地传为佳话。于是人们把这种秋千称为"无底鸳鸯秋千"。

无底鸳鸯秋千是美原镇吴东村清明节民俗活动中的一项重要游乐内容。每年清明节前后,村民们便自发地"扶"起秋千,一般有两架秋千,有时村中各

Swing playing is a folk amusement activity in Wudong Village, Meiyuan Town, Fuping County of Weinan City. According to the legend, during the reign of Jiaqing Emperor in the Qing Dynasty, an elderly artist surnamed Liu in the village introduced a thrilling swing of ingenious design. Later, in the process of playing on the swing a young man and a young woman fell in love and finally they got married, which became a popular story in the local area, so people call this kind of swing "mandarin duck swing" (in China, mandarin ducks symbolize enduring love).

Swing playing is an important entertainment of *Qingming* Festival (Tomb-sweeping Day) folk activities in Wudong Village. Every year around the *Qingming* Festival, the villagers spontaneously play on the swings. Generally there are two swings in the village, and sometimes there is one in each commune of the village. All villagers ranging from elderly men and women in their 70s to 80s to children aged 5 to 6 years old all prefer this activity and are able to swing back and forth on the swing.

The mandarin duck swing in Wudong Village is unique in structure and ingenious

in design. Two or three stone rollers are overlapped, on which a drum-shaped stone is placed. A five-meter or six-meter high steel pillar is erected on the drum-shaped stone, and a beam is fixed at the top of the pillar. A swing is hung on each side of the beam, and six ropes are fastened to stabilize the steel pillar and beam. At the junction of the drum-shaped stone and the steel pillar, a supporting wooden stake about 20 centimeters long and 8 centimeters thick is fixed. And an iron ball is installed between the supporting wooden stake and the steel pillar. When the swing sways, the iron ball rolls slowly. The steel pillar also sways with the rolling of the iron ball, which looks dangerous but actually not dangerous at all. For the sake of beauty, a large copper bell and several small copper bells are hung on each side of the swing, and the swings are also decorated with pine and cypress sprays and colorful flags.

组都有。村里的男女老少齐上阵，上至七八十岁的老翁老媪，下到五六岁的孩童，都能在秋千上荡几个来回。

吴东村的无底鸳鸯秋千结构独特，造型巧妙，可谓独一无二。"扶"秋千时，人们要把两个或三个碌碡重叠竖起，再在碌碡上放一鼓石，鼓石上面立一根五六米高的立柱，在立柱顶端固定一根横梁，两边各吊一个秋千，再用六根绳子拉稳。在鼓石和立柱衔接处立一根长约20厘米、粗约8厘米的支木，在支木和立柱间放一铁球。秋千荡起，铁球随秋千的荡悠而缓慢滚动，上边的立柱也随着铁球的滚动而晃动，有惊无险。为

Around the *Qingming* Festival, Fuping County usually suffers from drought. In the old days, in order to pray for rain, local people erected on the swing a more than ten-meter-high wooden pole that pointed to the sky, which means "a pole pierces the sky so that rain can fall to the earth". With the advancement of society and the development of natural science, people play on swings no longer to pray for rain, but to build their bodies and enjoy themselves.

The swing playing in Wudong Village can be divided into various forms

了美观，人们还在秋千两边各挂一个大铜铃和若干小铜铃，并装饰有松柏枝叶和彩旗。

清明时节，渭北干旱少雨，旧时"扶"秋千时，人们为了祈雨，在秋千上端要竖起一根十几米高的木杆，刺向天空，意为"一杆戳破天，甘露降人间"。随着社会的进步和自然科学的发展，人们荡秋千已不再是为了祈雨，而是为了强身健体、愉悦身心。

吴东村的无底鸳鸯秋千可分为单人表演、两人竞打，以及站打、坐打等各种形式。人荡秋千时如同飞燕穿梭，周围彩旗飘扬，观者欢声雷动，场面热闹壮观，令人叹为观止。其间，还会举行丰富多彩的民间文艺活动，吸引十里八乡的人前来观看。

2011年，吴东无底鸳鸯秋千被列入陕西省第三批非物质文化遗产名录。

such as single-person performance, two-person competition, performers standing or sitting on the swing board to play. When performers are swinging, they look like flying swallows, and the audience cheer and applaud thunderously. The scene is lively and spectacular. During the swing performance, various folk art activities are also held, attracting people from surrounding areas to watch.

In 2011, the swing playing of Wudong Village was included in the third batch of Shaanxi Provincial Intangible Cultural Heritage List.

柳池芯子
Xinzi Acrobatic Performance of Liuchi

柳池芯子发端于澄城县庄头乡柳池村。据该村王姓族谱记载，明朝万历年间，王家先祖王宠入选贡生，先后在四川昭化县、甘肃西和县等地任职。王宠为官清正，深受百姓爱戴，告老还乡时当地人赠予他两副芯子。王宠回乡后把一副方形铆套件的芯子分给大儿子，把一副圆形铆套件的芯子分给二儿子。每副芯子有3个大方垛和其他铁件共200余件。大儿子居村东，二儿子居村西，祖

Xinzi acrobatic performance of Liuchi originates in Liuchi Village, Zhuangtou Township, Chengcheng County. According to the family tree of the people surnamed Wang in the village, during the Wanli reign of the Ming Dynasty, Wang Chong, the ancestor of the Wang family, passed the imperial examination to become an official and then served successively in Zhaohua County of Sichuan Province and Xihe County of Gansu Province. Wang Chong was an upright official and loved by the local people. Before he returned to his hometown, the locals gave him two *xinzi* (a prop made of iron used for *xinzi* performance). After returning to his hometown, he gave one *xinzi* to his elder son, and the other one to his younger son. Each *xinzi* had more than 200 pieces of iron parts. His elder son lived in the east of the village, and the younger son lived in the west of the village. The ancestors in the village set unique rules for the *xinzi* performance, and with time going by the current division of the east *xinzi* troupe and the west *xinzi* troupe formed.

Xinzi acrobatic performance of Liuchi Village is a folklore activity focusing on offering sacrifices to the King of Medicine.

辈们定下独特的游戏规则，久而久之便有了现在的东、西两社之分。

柳池芯子是以祭祀药王为主的一项民俗活动，一般在正月十五举行芯子游演。演出前的正月十四下午先要祭风神、祭杆，正月十五芯子活动达到高潮。芯子上由男童女童装扮的传统戏曲、神话传说、民间故事中的人物在行进中表演。

柳池芯子有三奇：一是固定芯童的铁件的端头为锻打而成的各种不同的人头造型或动物形象。动物有龙、凤、虎、豹、羊、马、猴、蛇等，或憨态可掬，或面目狰狞，一个个栩栩如生。二是群众争先恐后地让自己的孩子上杆表

Generally, xinzi performance is held on the fifteenth day of the first lunar month. On the fourteenth afternoon of the first lunar month before the performance, the God of Wind must be worshiped. On the fifteenth day of the first lunar month, boys and girls dressed up as characters from traditional operas, myths, legends, and folk tales are fastened on poles of *xinzi*, performing while the parade team is marching ahead.

Xinzi acrobatic performance of Liuchi Village boasts three unique features. The first one is that the ends of iron pieces of *xinzi* on which the children performers are fixed are forged into various characters or animal images. The animals include dragons, phoenix, tigers, leopards, sheep, horses, monkeys, snakes, etc., which look naive or hideous, and each one is lifelike. The second one is that the local people all

演芯子，芯童一般为四至十二岁。当地群众认为，此项活动可以锻炼孩子的胆量，甚至能祛病强身，使孩子平安成长。三是芯子活动中双方要斗文斗智。东、西两社各自设有文案，由村中有文化、有才华的人担任文官，其中一方根据对方芯子扮演的故事内容编写上联，另一方则对出下联，把芯子活动推向高潮。

2011年，柳池芯子被列入陕西省第三批非物质文化遗产名录。

want their children to perform on the *xinzi* prop. The children are usually four to twelve years old. The local people believe that this activity can increase children's courage, and even cure their illnesses and strengthen their bodies, so that children can grow up safe and sound. The third one is that people get involved in wisdom and literacy competition during the *xinzi* performance. Both the east *xinzi* troupe and the west *xinzi* troupe have their own copywriters, with educated and talented people in the village serving as the head. One copywriter from one troupe writes the first line of a couplet based on the story played by the other troupe, and the copywriters from the other troupe respond with the second line, pushing the *xinzi* performance to a climax.

In 2011, *xinzi* acrobatic performance of Liuchi Village was included in the third batch of Shaanxi Provincial Intangible Cultural Heritage List.

花样跳绳
Fancy Rope Skipping

跳绳运动是民间一项为大众喜闻乐见的体育健身活动，在我国已有数千年的历史。马王堆出土的文物中就有跳绳，称为"长索"。隋唐称跳绳为"透索"，宋称"跳索"，明称"白索"，清称"绳飞"，民国以后才称"跳绳"。

西安市雁塔区刁家村以花样跳绳闻名。中华人民共和国成立后，西安"绳王"胡安民在继承祖传跳绳技艺的基础上有所发展，他所掌握的花样跳绳技艺有十二大类，六十多套绳路，三百多种

Rope skipping, a folk sports and fitness activity quite popular among the public, has a history of thousands of years in China. Skipping ropes were found in the cultural relics unearthed in the Han Tomb of Mawangdui, which were called "long ropes" in the Han Dynasty. In the later dynasties, the skipping rope has different names such as "white rope", "flying rope", and it gets the current name "skipping rope" after the Republic of China.

Diaojia Village in Yanta District of Xi'an City is famous for fancy rope skipping. After the founding of the People's Republic of China, Xi'an "Rope Skipping King" Hu Anmin has developed and innovated rope skipping on the basis of inheriting rope skipping skills handed down from his ancestors. He has mastered 12 categories of fancy rope skipping, over 60 sets of skipping patterns, and more than 300 skipping methods. The 12 categories include rope gymnastics, rope dance, rope boxing, rope athletics, rope arraying, fun rope skipping, long-rope skipping, double-rope skipping, multi-rope cross skipping, rope-skipping relay race, rope-skipping rally and so on. All kinds of rope skipping are divided into various rope

跳法。十二大类为绳操、绳舞、绳拳、绳技、绳阵、趣味跳绳、跳长绳、跳双绳、行进跳绳、多绳交叉跳、跳绳接力赛和跳绳拉力赛等。各类跳绳又分为多种绳路，如绳操有"跳绳八节操""健美跳绳操""中老年人绳舞操"等。各种绳操又有不同的跳法，真可谓变幻莫测，意趣无穷。

花样跳绳不限场地，器械简单，简便易行，可跳可舞，可蹲可跃，可快可慢，适合各个年龄段的人学练。花样跳绳能使人的大脑神经、肌肉细胞、器官同时得到锻炼，有利于促进身体平衡协调发展，是一项深受群众喜爱的健身运动项目。

2013年，花样跳绳被列入陕西省第四批非物质文化遗产名录。

skipping patterns, such as eight-section rope-skipping gymnastics, rope-skipping aerobics, rope-skipping dance, all of which involve a variety of jumping methods and bring great fun to the audience.

Fancy rope skipping is neither confined by place nor special sports facilities. Players can easily do different motions and control the speed according to their physical conditions. Therefore it is suitable for people of all ages to learn and practice. Fancy rope skipping can exercise players' brain nerves, muscle cells and organs at the same time, which can promote the balanced and coordinated development of the body, so it is a fitness exercise preferred by the masses.

In 2013, fancy rope skipping was included in the fourth batch of Shaanxi Provincial Intangible Cultural Heritage List.

少摩拳
Shaomo Boxing

少摩拳是由梅花拳第十二代掌门刘丕显宗师创立的。刘丕显，天津人氏，20世纪早期，他怀着"强身，强种，报效国家"之志向，潜心研究武术，在梅花拳的基础上博采中华传统武术技击之精华，汲取儒家、道家等思想精髓，形成了自己完整的理论体系，创立了少摩拳，并在西安生根发芽，逐渐壮大。少摩拳旨在通过少而精的训练和揣摩，极大地提高人体的灵活性和人的悟性。

少摩拳的训练内容主要包括少摩拳桩功桩法、少摩拳徒手单式训练、少摩拳步法训练、少摩拳特定竞技训练、少摩拳器械训练，其中少摩拳桩功是少

Shaomo boxing was founded by grandmaster Liu Pixian, the twelfth-generation master of plum blossom boxing. Liu Pixian, a native of Tianjin, had the ambition of "strengthening the body and serving the country" and devoted himself to the study of martial arts in the early 20th century. On the basis of the plum blossom boxing, he learned the essence of traditional Chinese martial arts and absorbed the thoughts of Confucianism and Taoism to develop a complete theoretical system of martial arts, and finally founded *shaomo* boxing which took root in Xi'an and gradually became influential. *Shaomo* boxing aims to greatly improve the flexibility of human body and practitioners' power of understanding through less but better training and speculation.

Shaomo boxing mainly involves standing training which is called *zhuanggong* in chinese, bare-handed single movement training, footwork training, athletic training, equipment training, among which the standing training is the foundation and core of *shaomo* boxing. The auxiliary equipment mainly includes *shaomo* sword, *shaomo* stick, *shaomo* spear, *shaomo* broadsword as well as other auxiliary training equipment

摩拳训练的基础和核心。辅助器械主要有少摩剑、少摩棍、少摩枪、少摩刀，还有为提高击打能力的其他辅助训练器械。

少摩拳的理论体系完整、科学。少摩拳把民间击打术运用到极致的技击思想，充分体现了中华传统文化中少而精、揣摩取其变的《周易》思想，强调医武同修、骨骼扣合、气血协调等。训练时少摩拳的桩功和少摩拳的每一个单式，强调人体的整体合一、周身协调，特别是在完成一个动作定式时（如飞腿），定式的一瞬间人体犹如雕塑，展现人体的优美，达到天人合一的境界，具有很强的艺术性和观赏性。

2013年，少摩拳被列入陕西省第四批非物质文化遗产名录。

which can improve the striking capability of the practitioners.

The theoretical system of *shaomo* boxing is complete and scientific. The attack and defense techniques of *shaomo* boxing fully embody the traditional Chinese culture of being less but better and figuring out the changes (thoughts from the book of *Zhouyi*), emphasizing keeping healthy by practicing martial arts, skeletal integration, coordination of *qi* and blood, etc. The standing training and every single posture or movement of *shaomo* boxing stress the overall unity and coordination of the human body. Especially when keeping a movement such as kicking, the practitioner looks like a sculpture, which reaches the realm of the unity between nature and man and embodies the beauty of the human body, creating a strong artistic and ornamental effect.

In 2013, *shaomo* boxing was included in the fourth batch of Shaanxi Provincial Intangible Cultural Heritage List.

周化一魔术
Zhou Huayi's Magic Shows

中华民族的魔术艺术源远流长，深受广大群众喜爱。1957年，家住东北的周化一先生带着自己的魔术团队来陕西表演中国传统魔术，后在陕西扎根，成立了陕西省周化一杂技魔术艺术团，拉开了陕西魔术的发展大幕。

周化一魔术以多种科学手法的综合运用创作多种多样、变化多端的魔术节目，使观众感到神奇与新颖，从而在活跃思维和启发智力中获得美妙的艺术享受。周化一魔术的变化包括生、遁、回、穿、脱、连、断、换、腾、知等。生是无中生有，能凭空变来物品；遁是将物隐去，能把有的变没；回是将毁坏的东西恢复原状；穿是从坚硬的物质中间顺利通过；脱是在坚固的束缚中离

The magic art of the Chinese nation has a long history and is deeply loved by the masses. In 1957, Mr. Zhou Huayi who lived in northeast China led his magic team to Shaanxi to perform traditional Chinese magic, and then took root in Shaanxi and established Shaanxi Zhou Huayi Acrobatic and Magic Art Troupe, which promoted the development of Shaanxi magic shows.

Zhou Huayi uses a variety of scientific techniques to compose various and changeful magic programs, which not only bring audiences magical and novel feelings as well as wonderful artistic enjoyment, but also activate audiences' thinking and enlighten their intelligence. Zhou Huayi's magic shows include a variety of tricks. For example, he can make something out of nothing, make things disappear, restore the destroyed things to their original state, pass through a hard object smoothly, escape from a strong bondage easily, connect unrelated things together, separate the inseparable things, change one object into different objects, make a heavy item hang in the air and perceive something which is difficult to predict.

Zhou Huayi's magic shows are of various forms. According to performing

scenes, they can be divided into large-scale magic shows and small and medium-sized magic shows. His magic shows can also be divided into improvisational magic shows, stage magic shows and other forms of magic shows. He is not only good at performing large-scale magic tricks, but also specializes in using daily necessities for magic performances. Over the years, he has developed some influential magic programs such as "The Cannon Shoots Real Persons" and "Change Torches". In addition, he has also developed many new types of magic machines and written a lot of materials to publicize magic shows.

In 2014, Zhou Huayi's magic shows were included in the fourth batch of China's National Intangible Cultural Heritage List.

开；连是把没有关系的物品连在一起；断是将无法分开的东西分开；换是一个物品的自我变幻；腾是使沉重的物品悬空飘浮；知是能感知不可能知道的事物。

周化一魔术节目形式多样，按照场面来分，有大型魔术，也有中小型魔术。他还将魔术分为即兴魔术、圆场魔术、舞台魔术等。他既擅长表演大型魔术，又善于将日常生活用品拿来进行魔术表演。多年来，周化一研发了"炮台打真人""变更火炬"等在全国有影响力的节目，还研制了不少新型的魔术机器，撰写了大量宣传魔术的资料。

2014年，周化一魔术被列入第四批国家级非物质文化遗产名录。

七

传统美术

Traditional Arts

安塞剪纸
Ansai Paper-Cutting

安塞剪纸是流行于陕西省安塞区的一种民间艺术。大凡喜庆的日子，安塞妇女都要铰剪纸、贴窗花。腊月天，妇女们围在一起，早早就为春节剪纸。临近年关，家家户户的窗户上贴满了各式各样的剪纸。

安塞剪纸的题材多样，内涵丰富，线条粗犷明快，乡土气息浓厚，充满对平安吉祥的祈望之情。安塞剪纸有窗花、窑顶花、衣物配饰花样、婚嫁剪纸、神龛剪纸等，纹饰多为花鸟虫鱼、瓜果菜蔬、家禽走兽以及人物等。剪纸作者运用暗喻、比喻、借喻和象征手法，艺术地表现天人合一、推崇生殖繁衍等思想观念。

安塞剪纸不仅造型美观，剪工精

Ansai paper-cutting is a kind of folk art popular in Ansai District of Shaanxi Province. On happy occasions, women in Ansai cut exquisite paper-cuts and paste them onto windows. In the twelfth lunar month of the year, women gather around and cut paper patterns for the celebration of Spring Festival. Around the Spring Festival, various paper-cuts are pasted onto every household's windows.

Ansai paper-cuts are diverse in themes, rich in connotation, bold in patterns, and full of local flavor, which express people's good wishes for safety and auspiciousness. The paper-cuts can not only serve as decorations on windows and cave roofs, and as embroidery patterns on clothing and accessories, but are also used for marriage and worshiping. The patterns are mostly in shapes of flowers, birds, insects, fishes, fruits, vegetables, poultry, beasts, human figures and so on. The paper-cutting artists employ metaphor, metonymy and symbolism to express ideological concepts of unity between men and nature and the concept of procreation worship.

Ansai paper-cuts are not only beautiful in appearance, exquisite in craftsmanship, but also has profound cultural connotations

致，而且具有深刻的文化内涵，包含美学、历史学、哲学、民俗、考古学、文化、人类学等内容。在安塞剪纸中，花鸟虫鱼绝不是单纯的表现形式，而是蕴含着深刻的古老文化观念。安塞传统剪纸花样是研究我国北方民族文化与民俗的重要史料，有"地上文物"和"活化石"之称。

2006年，安塞剪纸被列入第一批国家级非物质文化遗产名录。

relating to aesthetics, history, philosophy, folklore, archaeology, culture, anthropology and many other fields. In Ansai paper-cuts, the patterns of flowers, birds, insects, fishes, etc., are by no means purely normal expressions of life, but contain profound ancient cultural concepts. Ansai traditional paper-cutting patterns are important historical material for the study of the culture and folk customs in northern China, which are known as the "cultural relics overground" and "living fossils".

In 2006, Ansai paper-cutting was included in the first batch of China's National Intangible Cultural Heritage List.

凤翔泥塑
Fengxiang Clay Sculptures

凤翔区位于陕西省宝鸡市。凤翔泥塑是我国一种独具特色的民间美术品。据《凤翔县志》记载：国内出土的春秋战国、汉唐墓葬中的一些陪葬陶器动物、陶人等近似于当今的泥塑品，故泥塑工艺美术品的历史可追溯至两三千年前。现今凤翔泥塑产地主要集中在距县城东南四千米的城关镇六营村，那里的二百多农户几乎家家从事泥塑生产。

据说，明朝的时候，朱元璋军队的第六营兵士屯扎于此，这个村便被命名为"六营村"。这些来自江西的兵士有制陶手艺，闲暇无事，就和土为泥，捏制各种形态的泥活儿当作玩具，并且

Fengxiang District is located in Baoji City. Fengxiang clay sculptures are a kind of unique folk artwork in China. According to *Fengxiang County Annals*, some of the funeral pottery figurines found in the tombs of the Spring and Autumn Period, the Han Dynasty and the Tang Dynasty in Fengxiang territory are similar to today's clay sculptures, so the history of clay sculptures can date back to 2,000 to 3,000 years ago. At present, the production places of clay sculptures are mainly concentrated in Liuying Village of Chengguan Town, four kilometers southeast of the county seat, where almost all the families, over 200, are engaged in clay sculpture production.

It is said that during the Ming Dynasty, soldiers of the sixth battalion of Zhu Yuanzhang's army settled here, thus the village was named Liuying Village, which means the sixth battalion village. These soldiers from Jiangxi Province mastered pottery craftsmanship and they made various kinds of clay works as toys and then painted them in their spare time. Later when these soldiers became local residents, some

彩绘示人。后军士转为地方居民，其中部分人重拾入伍前的陶瓷制作手艺，利用当地黏性很强的土和泥、制模，捏泥人、泥动物、泥器物，并施以彩绘，然后去各大庙会出售。当地老乡购泥塑置于家中，用以祈子、护生、辟邪、镇宅、纳福。六营村的脱胎彩绘泥偶由此出名，并代代相传，成为我国民间艺术中独具特色的精品，在国内外享有盛誉。

凤翔泥塑的制作方法简单易行，泥塑造型生动，色彩别具一格。其用色不多，以大红、大绿和黄色为主，颜色对比强烈。凤翔泥塑大约有170多个花色品种，基本上分三类：一是泥玩具，以动物造型为主，大多为十二生肖造型；二是挂片，有脸谱、虎头、牛头、

of them resumed their pottery-making skills. They made clay figurines, animals and utensils with the local sticky soil, painted them, and then took them to major temple fairs for sale. Local folks bought clay sculptures and put them in their homes to pray for children, protect creatures, ward off the evil, secure houses, and pray for good luck. From then on, the painted clay sculptures in Liuying Village have become famous and the craftsmanship has been passed down from generation to generation. Now Fengxiang clay sculptures have become a unique artwork in China's folk art and enjoy a high reputation at home and abroad.

The method of making Fengxiang clay sculptures is simple and easy. The sculptures feature vivid shapes and unique colors. Not many colors are employed—red, green and yellow are the major colors, but the color contrast is sharp. The clay

狮子头、麒麟送子、八仙过海等；三是立人，主要为民间传说及历史故事中的人物造像。这些泥塑造型夸张，形神兼备，惟妙惟肖，多用作儿童玩具和镇宅辟邪的吉祥物，近年来也用于装饰居室。

数百年来，泥塑作品不断地继承和发展着，众多优秀的传统泥塑作品都得以传承，尤为典型的是虎的造型。这些虎又可分为挂虎、坐虎等类型。挂虎属挂片类，虎头暴额突睛，虎头的"王"字用牡丹替代，象征富贵。虎面的纹饰多为五谷、花草、蔬果的融合，反映了自然界生生不息、开花结果的永恒规律。虎面上还绘有宝葫芦，象征子孙昌盛。坐虎的前腿立后腿坐，面部紧凑，耳朵夸大，显其威严。躯体饰以莲花、牡丹等纹饰，浓艳大方，富有观赏性。按当地风俗，遇到小孩满月、百天、周岁，亲友们通常以坐虎相赠，置于炕

sculptures have about 170 varieties of patterns, basically divided into three types. The first type is clay toys mainly in shapes of animals, most of which are the twelve Chinese zodiac signs. The second type is hanging sculptures, including sculptures of facial makeup, tiger heads, bull heads, lion heads, kirin sending children, eight immortals crossing the sea, etc. The third type is sculptures of standing persons, mainly characters in folklore and historical stories. These clay sculptures feature exaggerating patterns as well as vivid appearance, and they are mostly used for children's toys and mascots to ward off evil spirits. In recent years, they have also been used to decorate houses.

Over hundreds of years, the clay sculptures have been soundly inherited and developed, and many outstanding traditional clay sculptures have been well inherited, especially sculptures of tigers. These tigers can be classified into hanging tigers and sitting tigers. The hanging tiger belongs to the hanging sculpture category. The tiger's forehead is protruding and the eyes are very big. The usual character of "王" that means "king" on the tiger's head is replaced by peony, which symbolizes wealth. The patterns on the tiger's face are mostly a combination of images of cereals, flowers, vegetables and fruits, reflecting the eternal law of nature's endless growth and reproduction. There is also a gourd painted on the tiger's face, which

头，以表达他们对小孩长命、富贵的祝福。

凤翔泥塑有着丰富的民俗文化内涵和浓郁的乡土气息，因而具有较高的历史文化价值和艺术价值，其中马、猪、羊三种动物的泥塑作品图已被中国邮票采用。

2006年，凤翔泥塑被列入第一批国家级非物质文化遗产名录。

symbolizes prosperity. The sitting tiger's front legs stand and the hind legs crouch. The face is compact and the ears are exaggerating, displaying its majesty. The body is decorated with lotus, peony and other patterns, which are bright-colored and can feast people's eyes. According to local customs, when a child is one month old, a hundred days old, and one year old, the child's relatives and friends usually give him or her a sitting tiger as a gift to express their blessing that the child will live a long and wealthy life.

Fengxiang clay sculptures contain rich folk culture connotation and strong rustic flavor, so they possess high historical, cultural and artistic value. Among them, the images of three kinds of animal sculptures of the horse, pig and sheep have been printed on Chinese stamps.

In 2006, Fengxiang clay sculptures were included in the first batch of China's National Intangible Cultural Heritage List.

凤翔木版年画
Fengxiang Woodblock New Year Pictures

位于关中平原西部的凤翔区是我国八大木版年画产地之一。凤翔木版年画始于唐宋，盛于明清。凤翔木版年画全以手工雕版，土法印刷，局部手绘填染，风格古朴自然，造型夸张饱满，色彩对比强烈，具有鲜明的黄土风情和西部地域的艺术特色。

凤翔木版年画取材十分广泛。不论神、佛、仙、道、达官贵人、庶民百姓的生活画面，还是城、堡、车、船、宫

Located in the west of the Guanzhong plain of Shaanxi Province, Fengxiang District is one of the eight major centers in China producing woodblock New Year pictures. Fengxiang woodblock New Year pictures originated in Tang and Song dynasties, and flourished in Ming and Qing dynasties. They are all hand-carved, traditionally printed, and partially hand-painted. They feature simple and natural style, exaggerating patterns, and strong color contrast, which display distinctive flavor and artistic feature of the Loess Plateau and western region of China.

A great variety of figures and things can be drawn by craftsmen of Fengxiang woodblock New Year pictures, ranging from gods, Buddhas, immortals, taoists, nobles, common people's daily life to cities, forts, carts, boats, palaces, bridges, flowing water, falling flowers, birds, beasts, fishes, insects, etc. According to the theme, the pictures can be classified into five categories: sacrificial pictures, Grain Rain (one of Chinese 24 solar terms) pictures and spring bull pictures, drama pictures, auspicious pictures and genre pictures. Sacrificial pictures are mainly used for worshiping gods during the Chinese New Year, such

as the Door God pictures, the six-household-god pictures, and the Wealth God pictures. Local farmers post Grain Rain pictures and spring bull pictures during the period of Grain Rain. Usually single chicken, double chickens, or Zhang Tianshi (the founder of Daoism) are drawn in Grain Rain pictures, which are considered as mascots to exorcise evil spirits and keep noxious insects away. On the spring bull pictures, there are dates of the 24 solar terms of a particular year, which have the function of guiding farming work. Fengxiang people love to listen to *qinqiang* opera, so a lot of drama pictures are produced. The natural environment in northwest China is tough, so local people's life used to be difficult and hard, therefore they pinned their hopes for a happy life on their children and grandchildren, which resulted in auspicious New Year pictures. Based on local customs, life scenes and people's daily production, artists have created a considerable number of genre pictures.

Fengxiang woodblock New Year pictures occupy an important position in the folk art of Fengxiang County and even Shaanxi Province. As a gem in the world's treasure house of art, the pictures have been deeply favored by domestic and

室、桥梁、流水、落花、鸟兽鱼虫等，都在艺人取材之列。按照题材，凤翔木版年画主要分为祭祀画、谷雨画和春牛图、戏文画、吉祥画、风俗画等五种。祭祀画主要用于过年时祭祀神灵，主要有门神画、家宅六神画、财神画等。到了谷雨时节，农户要张贴谷雨画和春牛图。谷雨画有单鸡、双鸡、张天师等，是降邪镇宅、令毒虫远避的镇物；春牛图上印有当年二十四节气的日期，有指导农事的作用。凤翔人爱听秦腔，因而产生了大量的戏文画。西北的自然环境恶劣，农人生计十分艰难，人们都把对幸福生活的期盼寄望于未来与子孙，因而产生祈福纳祥的吉祥年画。依据当地的风情、习俗和人们的日常生产、生活场景，艺人创作了相当数量的风俗画。

凤翔木版年画在凤翔乃至陕西民间

艺术中占有重要地位,受到国内外艺术家的青睐,为世界艺术宝库中的一朵奇葩。凤翔木版年画大多采用写实手法,真实地记录了某一时期的社会生活片段,充分体现了西北地区的民俗风情、文化教育、宗教信仰、社会变迁以及历史发展,具有重要的历史价值。另外,凤翔木板年画早期的刻板及印刷工艺是研究近代印刷术的宝贵资料,因此凤翔木板年画也具有重要的学术价值。

目前,凤翔能够制作木版年画的人已为数不多,凤翔木版年画的传承和延续面临着危机,亟待抢救和保护。

2006年,凤翔木版年画被列入第一批国家级非物质文化遗产名录。

foreign artists. With the adoption of practical techniques, most of Fengxiang woodblock New Year pictures truly record fragments of social life at a certain time, vividly showcasing customs, education, culture, religious beliefs, social changes, and historical development of the northwest China, hence they have great historical value. In addition, the early block carving and printing techniques applied in making Fengxiang woodblock New Year pictures are valuable materials for the study of modern printing, therefore the woodblock New Year pictures also have important academic value.

At present, there are only a small number of people who can make woodblock New Year pictures in Fengxiang, and the inheritance and continuation of this art faces a crisis, so this craftsmanship urgently needs to be rescued and protected.

In 2006, Fengxiang woodblock New Year pictures were included in the first batch of China's National Intangible Cultural Heritage List.

安塞民间绘画
Ansai Folk Painting

安塞民间绘画多见于陕西省延安市安塞区，是根植于黄土地的民间美术形式，具有鲜明的地方特色，被国外艺术家誉为"东方毕加索"之作。

安塞民间绘画是民间剪纸和民间刺绣的延伸，流行于民间，抒发作者的理想和追求，美化家居生活。其种类有炕围画、锅台画、箱柜画等；内容多有人物、动物、花卉等，以民俗、传说、民歌等为题材。作品讲究装饰性，注重色彩效果，追求强烈的视觉印象。

安塞民间绘画的作者以农村妇女为主体。她们将当地民间艺术独特的构思、造型、色彩、审美情趣和民俗文化融入民间绘画的创作，形成了鲜明而

Ansai folk painting, a form of folk art rooted in the Loess Plateau, is popular in Ansai District of Yan'an City. With distinctive local characteristics, the paintings are hailed as the works of "Oriental Picasso" by foreign artists.

Ansai folk painting, an extension of local paper-cutting and embroidery, is popular among the folks. The paintings express painters' hopes and pursuits and are used to beautify life. The paintings can be classified into different categories including *kangwei* paintings (painted on the exterior wall of the *kang,* a heatable brick bed), cooking stove paintings, cabinet paintings, etc. The subjects of the paintings cover folk customs, legends, folk songs, etc.; the content is mainly figures, animals, flowers and so on. The paintings feature decorative function, color effect, and strong visual impression.

Most of the painters are rural women. They integrate the unique conceptions, images, colors, aesthetic tastes of local folk art and folk culture into the creation of the paintings, hence a bright and unique artistic style is formed. Instead of being confined to the imitation of images of real objects and theoretical rules of painting, they

又独特的艺术风格。她们不拘泥于对客观形象的模拟，不受各种理论法则的约束，而是以大胆的想象和直觉感性的恣意发挥，随意移植手法进行创作。安塞民间绘画作品粗犷而又细腻，古朴沉稳而又活泼灵动，清新浓艳而又不失典雅，带着浓郁的泥土芳香。作品注重表现意境和神态，把现实和理想美妙地结合起来，颜色明快、和谐、鲜活，构图大胆、抽象、夸张、简练、浪漫。

安塞民间绘画在安塞乃至整个延安地区都有重要的地位。它是人民群众主要的文化活动之一，在人民群众的日常生活中占据着重要位置，对安塞乃至全国的精神文明建设、人民群众文化生活的丰富、人民群众素质的提高等都具有重要的作用。

1988年，安塞被文化部命名为"全国民间绘画之乡"。2007年，安塞民间绘画被列入陕西省第一批非物质文化遗产名录。

adopt flexible skills with bold imagination and intuition. Rough yet delicate, primitive yet lively, colorful yet elegant, the paintings carry a strong flavor of the local culture. Stressing the presentation of artistic conception and expression, the folk paintings are a combination of reality and ideals, with the colors bright, harmonious and fresh, and the composition bold, abstract, exaggerating, concise and romantic.

As one of the main cultural practices, Ansai folk painting is important in Ansai County and even the entire Yan'an City, and is of great significance in the daily life of local people. It has played an important role in constructing the spiritual civilization, enriching people's cultural life and cultivating personal qualities of the people in Ansai and even the whole country.

In 1988, Ansai County was acknowledged by China's Ministry of Culture as the "hometown of the Chinese folk paintings". And in 2007 Ansai folk painting was listed in the first batch of Shaanxi Provincial Intangible Cultural Heritage List.

定边剪纸艺术
Dingbian Paper-Cutting

定边剪纸是流行于陕西省榆林市定边县的民间剪纸艺术。定边是古代军事要塞,驻军多是南方人,他们的家眷把南方剪纸带到定边,并与当地的民间剪纸相融合,逐渐形成了独具特色的剪纸。定边剪纸既有陕北剪纸自然、质朴的特点,又有南方剪纸细腻、精巧的风格,因而在陕北剪纸中独树一帜,为人称道。

传统定边剪纸作品的样式主要有四类。第一类用于春节时美化环境,第二类用于嫁娶时装饰洞房,第三类用于制作刺绣、布玩具的底样,第四类用于祭

Dingbian paper-cutting is a folk art popular in Dingbian County of Yulin City. Dingbian was once a military fortress in ancient times and most of the garrison soldiers were southerners. The family of the soldiers brought the southern paper-cutting skills here and integrated them with the local ones, gradually a unique paper-cutting art took shape. Dingbian paper-cuts are special and highly acclaimed in northern Shaanxi in that they have both the characteristics of naturalness and simplicity of northern Shaanxi paper-cuts as well as exquisiteness and delicacy of paper-cuts in southern China.

Traditionally, Dingbian paper-cuts fall into four types. The first one, the most commonly seen in Dingbian, is to beautify environment in the Spring Festival, during which a large number of paper-cuts are used. Patterns of such type include birds, plants, fish, insects, folklore, mythologies, fruits, livestock, lions and tigers, etc. Rich in content, many of them express people's pursuit of auspiciousness. The second type is for wedding room decoration. Festive patterns that symbolize wealth and good luck are very common, such as "the dragon and phoenix bringing prosperity", "a fat

祀礼仪活动。春节是定边剪纸使用得最多的时候，剪纸内容十分丰富，象征吉祥如意的作品很多。作品内容包括天上的飞鸟、地上的花草鱼虫、民间传说、神话故事、劳动果实、保平安的家畜、镇宅避邪的狮子以及老虎等。洞房装饰剪纸多为象征富贵吉祥的喜庆图案，如"龙凤呈祥""连年有余""八狮滚绣球"。刺绣往往先要用剪纸出底样，刺绣品多用于女子出嫁时送给男方家里的老人或者亲朋，准备的绣品以鞋垫、枕头、荷包、烟袋、钱包为主。剪纸底样图案多为花卉、桃、莲、动物等。比较常见的祭祀礼仪活动剪纸有财神爷的门帘、吊帘，多是繁丽的贯钱连续图案；灵堂上的剪纸式样以二龙戏珠、二十四孝为多。

战争时期，定边妇女先后创作了《夫妻识字》《送郎参军》《兄妹开荒》《白毛女》等反映边区人民生活、劳动、战斗的新剪纸；改革开放以后，创作了《家乡》《一路清廉》《养猪》《养兔大户》等以社会发展为主题的作品。

定边剪纸对我国民间美术尤其是剪纸艺术的发展做出了重要贡献。定边剪纸反映了农村妇女对社会发展的认识，

baby carring a carp in the bosom", "eight lions rolling silk ball". The third type is patterns for embroidery and cloth toys. These embroideries are mostly sent by the bride-to-be to the elderly or relatives of the groom-to-be before their wedding, like insoles, pillows, *hebao* (a small bag for carrying money or odds), tobacco pouches and purses, on which there are paper-cut ground patterns of flowers, peaches, lotuses and animals. And the fourth type is used in ritual activities. The most common paper-cuts are door curtains of the God of Wealth with patterns of strings of coins. In addition, paper-cutting patterns like "two dragons playing with a pearl" and "stories of filial piety" are often seen in morning halls.

In the wartime, Dingbian women created new types of paper-cuts to reflect the life, work and fighting of local people, for instance, *A Couple Learn to Read*, *Seeing My Beloved off to the Army*, *Brother and Sister Reclaim Wasteland* and *White-hair Girl*. After China's reform and opening up in 1978, paper-cutting works reflecting social development were created, such as

对研究我国农耕社会的生产发展以及民俗风情、意识形态等具有重要的参考价值。定边剪纸题材丰富，是对青少年进行爱国主义教育、民族传统教育、革命传统教育不可多得的生动材料。

2007年，定边剪纸艺术被列入陕西省第一批非物质文化遗产名录。

Hometown, Honesty and Upright, Raising Pigs, The Rabbit Raising Household.

Dingbian paper-cutting, reflecting the rural women's understanding of social development, has made great contribution to the development of Chinese folk fine arts, especially the development of paper-cutting in China. It also has important reference value for studying the production development as well as folk customs and ideologies of Chinese agricultural society. The paper-cuts cover a variety of themes and are special and vivid teaching materials for the education of patriotism, national tradition, and revolutionary tradition for the young people.

In 2007, Dingbian paper-cutting was included in the first batch of Shaanxi Provincial Intangible Cultural Heritage List.

澄城刺绣
Chengcheng Embroidery

澄城刺绣是一项传统的民间艺术，在澄城县各地很常见。澄城刺绣可追溯到商周时期。明清时期，凡出嫁的姑娘都必须学会刺绣的技艺。

澄城刺绣针工细腻，花形简洁大方，颜色搭配和谐，富有深刻的内涵。其基本特点有以下两个。一是绣品的用途广泛，常见于小到被枕、服饰、衣戴佩物、婚嫁礼品，如裹兜、烟袋、裙子、绣鞋、被面、荷包、腿带、腰带等，大到屏帐、桌单、围裙等。二是图样和题材广泛，大多根据实际需要选择。小孩的肚兜多将花卉、仙桃绣在中

Chengcheng embroidery is a traditional folk art which is common among the folks in Chengcheng County of Weinan City. The embroidery can be traced back to the Shang and Zhou dynasties. During the Ming and Qing dynasties, all married girls have to learn embroidery craftsmanship.

Chengcheng embroidery is famous for its exquisite needlework, simple and elegant patterns, harmonious color matching, and profound connotation. The embroidery has two basic characteristics. First, the embroideries are widely used on quilts, pillows, clothing, clothing accessories, bed-curtains, table cloth, aprons, and wedding gifts like *guodou* (a kind of underwear usually worn on a baby's or girl's belly), tobacco pouches, dresses, shoes, quilt covers, purses, leg straps, waistbands and so on. Second, the embroideries feature a wide range of patterns and themes, most of which are selected according to actual needs. Usually children's *guodou* are embroidered with flowers and peaches, surrounded by patterns of bats, which contain the connotation of health, prosperity, and good luck. The patterns on curtains are mostly based on plots of myths, legends and folk stories. Sometimes, flowers, birds

间，再以蝙蝠"万"字组成边缘图案，表达蒸蒸日上、长命百岁、福禄吉祥之意。门帘上的刺绣多选自神话传说、民间故事等的情节，也有花鸟、蝴蝶，再配以吉祥话语。枕顶上的刺绣既有各种飞禽走兽、花草鱼虫、人物故事等主题的图样，又有各种吉祥文字。

澄城刺绣文化内涵丰富。象征和托物寓意是澄城刺绣的一大特征。人们希望幸福，借同音物，如蝙蝠，以象征"福"。人们希望摆脱贫穷、加官晋爵，常借用美丽的梅花鹿以象征"禄"，含鼓励上进之意。人们希望长寿，凡给老人的衣物都绣有桃、寿星、

and butterflies are also embroidered on curtains with auspicious words. Pillows are often embroidered with various patterns such as birds, animals, flowers, plants, fish, insects, figures and auspicious characters.

Chengcheng embroidery contains rich connotation, which is expressed in the method of symbolization. People hope for *xingfu* which means happiness, so they embroider *bianfu* (referring to bats in English) to symbolize "*fu*" which means happiness and good luck. People want to get rid of poverty and rise to a higher position or status, so they often embroider the beautiful animal *meihualu* (referring to sika deer in English) to symbolize "*lu*" which means get promoted. People want longevity, so whenever clothes for the elderly are made, patterns such as peaches, the God of Longevity and cranes will be embroidered, which symbolize immortality. Magpies, mandarin ducks, dragons and phoenixes are embroidered on quilts and curtains serving as gifts to newlyweds to express the hope that the couple will love each other and have a happy marriage. The pattern "a fat baby holds a lotus flower and embraces a big fish" means abundance year after year. Pomegranates are embroidered on *guodu*

仙鹤，象征长生不老。送给新婚夫妇的被面、门帘多绣着喜鹊、鸳鸯、龙凤等图案，祝愿夫妻恩爱、婚姻幸福美满。胖娃娃手持莲花、怀抱大鱼，寓意连年有余。女儿出嫁，裹肚上绣石榴，寓意多子多福。一些美丽的神话传说和戏曲人物也为刺绣品提供了创作素材。

澄城刺绣体现了当地民众的信仰、人生观、审美观，反映了澄城女性的聪明才智、勤劳淳朴以及她们对艺术的执着追求。

2008年，澄城刺绣被列入第二批国家级非物质文化遗产名录。

for girls who are going to get married to deliver the wish that they will have more children and more blessings. In addition, some figures in touching myths, legends and operas are also commonly seen in Chengcheng embroideries.

Chengcheng embroidery reflects the beliefs, life outlook, and aesthetic idea of the local people, and shows the ingenuity, industriousness, simplicity and persistent pursuit of art of Chengcheng women.

In 2008, Chengcheng embroidery was included in the second batch of China's National Intangible Cultural Heritage List.

西秦刺绣
Xiqin Embroidery

  西秦刺绣是用平面刺绣做成各类工艺用品的通称。西秦刺绣历史悠久，经考古学家证实，宝鸡的西周井姬墓中已有绣品出土。西秦刺绣经过3,000多年的传承和发展，到明清时已经成熟，达到鼎盛时期，平绣、悬绣和拼贴缝制结合的多种技巧形成，并延续至今。

  西秦刺绣具有浓郁的传统风格和鲜明的地方特色。刺绣的内容丰富，包括传统吉祥图案、龙凤狮虎、花鸟鱼

  Xiqin embroidery, also known as Baoji embroidery, is a general name for various art works made by two-dimensional embroidery in Baoji City. *Xiqin* embroidery has a long history. It was confirmed by archaeologists that embroideries had been unearthed in tombs of the West Zhou Dynasty in Baoji City. After more than 3,000 years of inheritance and development, *xiqin* embroidery matured and reached its peak period during the Ming and Qing dynasties. The embroidery employs a combination of various embroidery techniques like

虫、四季蔬果、戏文人物、成语典故、字画楹联等。西秦刺绣的布艺造型简洁夸张,构思奇巧浪漫,色彩强烈鲜明,寓意含蓄积极。它不仅装饰着人们的生活,而且与当地的民情风俗紧密结合。刺绣品被广泛应用于服饰鞋帽、被枕帘帕、儿童玩具、香包挂件、婚嫁礼品、丧葬祭品等,几乎伴随着人的一生。西秦刺绣展现了当地人民的美好祝愿。风调雨顺、五谷丰登、国泰民安、团结和睦、健康长寿、家庭幸福、尊老爱幼、多子多孙等都是各种作品共同的主题。

西秦刺绣布艺表现的思想内涵集中体现在农民对生命、自然、社会生活的热爱和美好祝愿上,对认识和研究农耕社会的民情风俗、意识形态具有参考价值。近年来,由于机绣工艺的发展和普及,西秦刺绣的适用范围大大缩小,这

two-dimensional embroidering, three-dimensional embroidering and patchwork sewing, which have still been used nowadays.

Xiqin embroidery features strong traditional and regional characteristics. It boasts rich patterns, including traditional auspicious patterns and patterns of dragons, phoenixes, lions, tigers, flowers, birds, insects, fishes, fruits, vegetables, drama characters, idioms, allusions, calligraphy, paintings, couplets, etc. The embroidery is simple and exaggerating in composition, imaginative and romantic in design, strong and bright in color, as well as implicit and uplifting in theme. The embroideries are used to embellish people's life and are closely related to local customs. The local ingenious women embroider the above-mentioned patterns on clothes, shoes, hats, quilts, pillows, curtains, handkerchiefs, toys, sachet accessories, wedding decorations, funeral offerings, etc., that almost company people for the whole life. The embroideries carry local people's good wishes for good weather, bumper grain harvests, prosperity and peace, unity and harmony, health and longevity, family happiness, respect for the old and love for the young, etc., which are all common themes of various embroidery works.

The ideological implication contained in *xiqin* embroidery fully reflects local farmers' love and good wishes for life,

一优秀的民间手工技艺迫切需要得到有效的保护和传承。

2008年,西秦刺绣被列入第二批国家级非物质文化遗产名录。

nature and social life. Thus it has reference value for understanding and studying the folk customs and ideologies of the farming society. In recent years, due to the development and popularity of machine embroidery technology, *xiqin* embroidery has been in crisis, which urgently needs effective protection and inheritance.

In 2008, *xiqin* embroidery was added to the second batch of China's National Intangible Cultural Heritage List.

黄陵面花
Huangling Dough Figurines

黄陵县位于陕西省延安市。黄陵面花是当地一种独特的民间手工艺品，自古以来就和黄帝陵的祭典活动紧密联系。起初，人们用猪、牛、羊三牲祭祀黄帝。随着社会文明水平的日益提高，人们开始用面粉做成各色动物和花卉的造型来代替三牲，因而面花产生。在民间，人们也普遍用面花祭祀祖先和神灵。

用面花祭品祭祀祖先这一形式经过漫长的发展演变，逐渐由官方向民间转

Huangling County belongs to Yan'an City of Shaanxi Province. The dough figurines made by people in Huangling are a kind of characteristic local folk art, which have been closely integrated with the sacrificial activities at the Yellow Emperor's Mausoleum since ancient times. At first, people offered sacrifices like pigs, cattle, and sheep to the Yellow Emperor. With the progress of social civilization, people began to use flour to make colored animals and flowers to replace real animals, thus dough figurines came into being. Among the folks, the dough figurines are also commonly used to worship ancestors and deities.

The tradition of worshiping ancestors with dough figurines has undergone a long process of development and evolution, and has gradually been transformed from the official activity to the folk activity. At the same time, dough figurines have also been closely combined with local people's life, for example they are widely used on birthdays, at weddings, funerals or other ritual activities. Nowadays, the dough figurines can be seen everywhere in the daily life of the local people and they have become indispensable things in the sacrificial activities as well as in people's

化，同时也紧紧地与当地的生产生活、婚丧嫁娶、生儿育女等结合起来。到今天，面花在当地群众的日常生活中也随处可见，成为祭祀活动中和日常生活中不可或缺的重要组成部分。

制作黄陵面花的主要原料是面粉、食用色素、高粱皮、麦穗、彩色纸等。心灵手巧的妇女们把经过发酵的面粉捏成惟妙惟肖的"十二生肖"、家畜家禽、吉祥动物、花卉等小件作品，上锅蒸熟，再用颜色涂染，进行美化装饰，制成面花。也可将这些小件进行组合，组成具有各种寓意的面花作品。

长期以来，黄陵人民积累了丰富的制作面花的经验和技巧。面花不仅可作为一种庄重、严肃的礼仪祭品，而且因其做工精细、造型美观、色彩艳丽，也成为颇具审美价值的民间工艺品。

2008年，黄陵面花被列入第二批国家级非物质文化遗产名录。

daily life.

The main materials for making Huangling dough figurines are flour, food colourant, sorghum husk, ears of wheat, colored paper, etc. The ingenious women knead and shape the fermented dough into small and lifelike images like Chinese zodiac signs, livestock, poultry, auspicious animals, flowers, etc., which are steamed in the pot, then painted with color, beautified and combined to make vivid figurines that have various symbolic meanings.

In the long practice, Huangling people have accumulated rich experience and techniques in making dough figurines. The figurines have become not only solemn ceremonial sacrifices, but also valuable folk crafts boasting exquisite craftsmanship, beautiful appearance and bright color.

In 2008, Huangling dough figurines were included in the second batch of China's National Intangible Cultural Heritage List.

陕北匠艺丹青
Danqing Painting of Northern Shaanxi

陕北匠艺丹青是陕北民间画匠以建筑、木工、石工等各种工艺手段为依托,将之与各类实用器物相结合,以多种技术完成的一种民间绘画艺术,在陕西省榆林、延安两市各个区县的城镇及乡村很常见,多见于民众窑居、城镇公共景观建筑和乡村的大小庙宇。

Danqing painting of Northern Shaanxi is a folk art created by the folk painters who apply various arts and crafts like architecture, carpentry, masonry, etc., to all kinds of instruments and objects. The painting is very common in the towns and villages in Yulin City and Yan'an City, commonly used to decorate kiln dwellings, public landscape architectures and temples in the countryside.

Danqing paintings of Northern Shaanxi mainly include temple murals, architectural color paintings, *kangwei* paintings (painted on the exterior wall of the *kang,* a heatable brick bed), cooking stove paintings, cabinet paintings, household wooden furniture paintings, mirror plaque paintings, etc., which boast rich humanistic connotation and distinctive local characteristics. Most of the craftsmen are farmers, many of whom are from famous folk painting families. *Danqing* painting integrates various techniques like painting, sculpture, woodwork,

陕北匠艺丹青主要包括庙宇壁画、建筑彩画、炕围画、灶台画、箱柜画、家用木器装饰画、玻璃镜匾画等，其人文内涵丰富、地方特色鲜明。绘画者多为农民，其中不少人出身于著名的民间绘画世家。陕北匠艺丹青兼具画、塑、木作、石刻、建筑设计等多项技能。它借助土、石、木、布、纸、陶、桐油、石色等材料，在公共建筑、宗教神器及民居环境和家具上施行工艺，将当地居民的现实物质生活与精神生活联系在一起，是人们追求美好幸福生活的精神寄托。经过数百年的发展，陕北匠艺丹青形成了独特而完备的艺术创造与生态体系，其传承谱系和图像图案谱系完整而清晰。

陕北匠艺丹青在当地比较常见，与群众生活的各个方面都有关联，表现形式多样，已成为当地民众生活中的有机组成部分。它以民间工匠为创作和传承

stone carving, architectural design and so on. Craftsmen make use of materials such as soil, stone, wood, cloth, paper, pottery, tung oil, to paint on public architectures, religious artifacts, houses and furniture. The paintings link the material life with the spiritual life of local residents, serving as the spiritual sustenance of local people's pursuit of a good and happy life. After hundreds of years of development, *danqing* painting has developed into a kind of unique art with complete and clear inheritance patterns.

Danqing painting of Northern Shaanxi which features various forms of expression has been widely spread among the folks and has become an integral part of local people's life. With folk craftsmen as the main body of its creation and inheritance, the painting is characterized by diverse cultures related to farming, animal husbandry, industry and commerce. Due to the mixture of various cultural elements, the painting possesses unique artistic characteristics and high research value concerning art, folklore, religion, and fine art, etc.

主体,是扎根于山沟草原的农耕文化,同时纵向连接农牧工商的市井文化。多种文化元素的杂糅形成了独特的艺术特点,显示了艺术学、民俗生态学、宗教学、美学等方面的研究价值。

2008年,陕北匠艺丹青被列入第二批国家级非物质文化遗产名录。

In 2008, *danqing* painting of Northern Shaanxi was included in the second batch of China's National Intangible Cultural Heritage List.

澄城手绘门帘
Chengcheng Hand-Painted Door Curtains

流行于陕西省渭南市澄城县的手绘门帘俗称"门帘画",是用传统水墨画的手法,直接画在特制的粗布上的一种民间艺术表现形式。手绘门帘的绘画内容多以神话传说、历史典故、民俗风情等为体裁,其作品细腻传神,风格朴素清新、简洁明快,有强烈的乡土生活气息。

The hand-painted door curtains, commonly known as "door curtain paintings", are popular in Chengcheng County of Weinan City. The painters directly paint on specially-made homespun cloth by using traditional ink-wash painting techniques. The paintings are mostly themed on myths, legends, historical stories, folk customs, etc. With simple and fresh style, the paintings are delicate and expressive, concise and bright, featuring a strong flavor of local life.

The layout of the painting is divided into three parts. The upper and bottom parts are symmetrical human patterns, and a group of flower and bird patterns are painted in the middle to separate the two groups of human patterns. The upper part is painted with round patterns, meaning that the sky is round, and the bottom part is painted with square patterns, meaning that the earth is square. The four corners surrounding the round patterns are painted with various flowers and butterflies. The two

画面分为三大部分，上、下两部分均为对称的人物图案，中间用一组花鸟图案把两组人物画面隔开。上部以圆形画面表现，意为天圆；下部则用方形画面表现，意为地方。上部圆形四角配以各类花卉、蝴蝶等角隅纹样，两边常用对称的二方连续或四方连续的花卉图案装饰镶边。整体画面方圆有致，构图饱满，典雅大方。在画法上，先用浓墨勾勒轮廓，再填上轻重不同的墨色加以烘托，增加艺术表现效果。图案多以"连生贵子""五子夺魁""二十四孝"等为主，借以传达民俗生活理念，表现劳动人民对美好生活的向往。

澄城手绘门帘吸收借鉴了传统壁画和民间庙画的表现手法，并将实用与装饰的功能融为一体而走进澄城每一个村舍、每一个家庭，把古老的图案和先祖的教诲以及长辈的祝福送到每个人的面前，把真、善、美送到每个人的心中。

手绘门帘用代表着人生价值和生活理念的吉祥图案表现人们对美好生活的期盼。"连生贵子"代表多子多福，"鸳鸯戏水"代表白头到老、相伴一生，"五子夺魁"表达了人们对富贵和仕途的美好憧憬。总之，手绘门帘倾注

sides are often decorated with symmetrical rectangular floral patterns. The overall composition is full and elegant. As for the painting method, the paintings are outlined with thick ink, and then filled with different colors to enhance the artistic effect. Most of the paintings have auspicious patterns like "a baby playing the musical instrument *sheng* beside lotus flowers" (which means giving birth to more babies), "five boys competing to get a helmet" (which means they are competing to be number one), "stories of filial piety" and so on, such patterns well convey the concept of folk life and express people's wish for a better life.

Chengcheng door curtain painting draws on the expression techniques of traditional wall painting and folk temple painting. The paintings are widely used in the rural houses in Chengcheng County for their practical and decorative functions, presenting the local people with quaint patterns, ancestors' teachings and elders' blessings, and bring the true, the good and the beautiful to everyone's heart.

With auspicious patterns representing the value and concept of life, the curtain paintings express local people's expectation for a better life. The pattern "a baby playing *sheng* beside lotus flowers" stands for "the more children, the more blessings"; "two mandarin ducks playing merrily in the water" stands for a happy and long-last marriage; "five boys competing to get a helmet" shows people's longing for riches

着人们对生活的热爱，散发着清香的泥土气息，不但给人以美的享受，还给人以生活的启迪，在当地百姓的精神生活中发挥着重要的作用。

2009年，澄城手绘门帘被列入陕西省第二批非物质文化遗产名录。

and successful career. In short, the curtain paintings feature distinct local flavors and reflect people's love for life. They bring people the enjoyment of beauty, give people enlightenment and play an important role in local people's spiritual life.

In 2009, Chengcheng hand-painted door curtains were listed in the second batch of Shaanxi Provincial Intangible Cultural Heritage List.

洛川刺绣
Luochuan Embroidery

洛川刺绣流行于陕西省延安市洛川县，是当地颇具特色的民间工艺。洛川刺绣种类繁多，题材广泛，内容丰富，常见于枕头、玩具、肚兜、香包、帽围帘、马甲、鞋、云肩等。其表现主题有动物、人物、花鸟、草虫、瓜果以及戏剧故事、神话故事等。

在施针用线和配色上，洛川刺绣不拘一格。洛川刺绣表面上看似千变万化，事实上大多数来自生活与自然，是依据各种自然原型创造的一种基础纹形，并逐渐演变、扩展而形成。各基本纹形的原型依据大致分为：生殖崇拜类，代表作品有《麒麟送子》《观音送子》等；图腾崇拜类，如将蝎子、蛇、

Luochuan embroidery which spreads in Luochuan County of Yan'an City is a characteristic local folk art. With a wide range of categories, subjects and rich content, Luochuan embroideries include pillows, toys, *dudou* (a kind of underwear wore on the belly), sachets, hat brims, vests, shoes, *yunjian* (a piece of embroidery similar to a cape wore over the shoulder as decoration), etc. Themes of the embroideries cover animals, people, plants and birds, grass and insects, fruits, stories from dramas and myths, and so on.

Luochuan embroidery is eclectic in the use of needles, thread and color matching. The patterns seem to be ever-changing, while in fact most of them come from daily life and the nature. The patterns are based on and evolved from various natural prototypes and can be roughly divided into three major categories. The first category is related to reproductive worship, such as the pattern of "the Unicorn delivering a son", "the Goddess of Mercy bringing a child for the family". The second category is about totem worship. Exaggerating patterns of scorpions, snakes, spiders, centipedes, and toads are embroidered on clothes and utensils to ward off evil spirits. The third

蜘蛛、蜈蚣、蟾蜍等五毒绣在衣物及用具上，用以辟邪，其纹样夸张大胆。此外，还有民间神话故事类和一些无法解释的抽象纹样。

过去结婚时，女方要绣花枕头顶、鞋垫、门帘送给男方，同时还要准备一些香包、针扎送给男方的亲戚朋友，以展示女方的心灵手巧。外婆给孙儿做布老虎、布娃娃、布马、布狗等玩具，洋溢着浓郁温馨的生活情趣。小孩满月时，姑姑、姨姨要给娃娃送虎头鞋、虎头帽、虎头枕、肚兜、布老虎，为孩子消灾避难，保佑孩子长命百岁。姑娘给心上人绣"马上封侯""二龙戏珠"等，象征大富大贵。这些绣品精细入微，寓意深刻。

随着社会经济迅速发展，城市化的步伐加快，遗存于民间的古老绣品已日渐稀少，因而洛川刺绣显得弥足珍贵。

2009年，洛川刺绣被列入陕西省第二批非物质文化遗产名录。

category is patterns concerning folk myths, and abstract patterns which are beyond explanation.

In the past, the bride-to-be needed to prepare embroideries of pillow cases, insoles, and curtains to the groom-to-be, and sachets and needlework for his relatives and friends to show that she was clever in mind and skillful in hand. The grandmother embroidered toys like dolls, cloth tigers, cloth horses, cloth dogs for her grandchildren to express her love and best wishes. When babies were one month old, their aunts would embroider for them tiger-head shoes, tiger-head hats, tiger-head pillows, *dudou*, and cloth tigers, wishing that the babies would avoid accidents and live a long and healthy life. Girls embroidered for their sweethearts handicrafts with auspicious patterns like "a monkey riding on a horse" which means to be successful or promoted and "two dragons playing with a pearl" which denotes great fortune and success. Such embroideries are exquisite in patterns and profound in meaning, so they are deeply preferred by people.

With the rapid development of the social economy and the fast pace of urbanization, the ancient embroideries left among the folks are becoming scarcer, hence Luochuan embroidery is more valuable.

In 2009, Luochuan embroidery was listed in the second batch of Shaanxi Provincial Intangible Cultural Heritage List.

延川布堆画
Yanchuan Cloth-Paste Pictures

延川布堆画多见于陕西省延安市延川县的各个乡镇，尤以延川镇、土岗乡、延水关镇、文安驿镇的最具代表性。延川布堆画起源于劳动人民的日常生活，由妇女给孩子的衣服打补丁演变而来，具有广泛的群众性和鲜明的地域性，是广大劳动人民喜闻乐见的一种艺术形式。

黄土高原自然条件艰苦，但心灵手巧的婆姨们在物质贫乏的生活中依旧怀着对生活最美的希望，在打补丁时有意剪成一定的图案。如小孩的鞋尖破了，心灵手巧的母亲特制一块虎头形状的布缀在鞋尖，就成了"虎头鞋"；枕头破

Yanchuan cloth-paste pictures are very common in various towns in Yanchuan County of Yan'an City. Originated from the daily life of the working people, they evolved from patches that women sewed on children's clothes. With distinctive regional characteristics, the cloth-paste pictures are an art form popular among the working people.

Although the physical conditions of the Loess Plateau were tough, the ingenious women had good wishes for life, and they scissor patches into lovely patterns deliberately. For example, if the tip of a child's shoe was broken, a piece of cloth in the shape of a tiger head was adorned on it, hence a "tiger-head shoe" was produced. If a pillow was broken, plants or animals stitched by colored cloth would be sewn on it. If the quilt or sheet was broken, a cloth-made flower or character of *xi* (meaning happiness) with different colors would be sewn on it. The local ingenious women made the originally damaged clothes become both good-looking and durable. Later, with the development of society, the cloth-paste pictures were used not only for practical function. People employed them on daily necessities such as bellybands,

shoe uppers, shoulder pads, wallets, tobacco pouches, thus exquisite artworks were made.

The raw materials for Yanchuan cloth-paste pictures are mainly homespun. The colors and shapes vary depending on the patterns. Colors of red, yellow, blue, black and white are mainly used. A characteristic cloth-paste picture is made through the following steps. Firstly, conceive an artistic conception. Secondly, draw a pattern or scissor out a sketch. Thirdly, match the color according to the pattern. Finally, paste, splice, inlay, and stack the cloth pieces on the base cloth, most of which need to be stitched. The content of the pictures mainly includes folklore, drama characters, folk customs, plants and animals. With vivid images and bold imagination, most of the pictures are exaggerating and bright. The small-sized works can be produced by one person alone, while large ones require cooperation of several persons.

Yanchuan cloth-paste pictures boast conciseness, simplicity and roughness. The patterns are based on folk paper-cuts but more general and concise; the colors are based on folk embroideries but more vivid and brighter. The pictures have been exhibited in Beijing, Shanghai, Xi'an, Hefei and other places in China for many times. Especially after the National Art Museum of China introduced Yanchuan cloth-paste pictures to the whole country in 1995, the pictures have drawn widespread attention

了洞，找几片上了色的布头拼剪成花草鸟兽等样式缝缀好，称"堆花枕头"；铺盖烂了，选用不同颜色的布块做个团花、喜字，就成了"堆花被褥"。巧婆姨们细针纳缀，别出心裁，层层堆摞，厚厚缝衲，让那些原本破损的衣物变得好看耐穿。后来，随着社会的发展，布堆画渐渐脱离了纯粹的实用性，人们特意将它装饰在裹肚、鞋面、垫肩、钱包、烟袋等生活日用品上，成了精美的艺术品和收藏品。

延川布堆画的制作原料主要是农妇纺织的土布，主要颜色有红、黄、蓝、黑、白五种。也可用一般下脚料，色彩和形状因造型不同而有所变化。其基本的制作工序是构思意境、绘出图样或剪出样品，然后依样配料填色，在底布上逐次进行贴块、拼接、镶花、堆叠，多数还要缝合，最终制作出极具民俗特色的图案。延川布堆画以民间传说、戏剧人物、民俗生活、花鸟禽兽为主题，画面大多夸张绚丽、意象生动、想象奇特。小型作品可一人单独制作，大型图景则需众人分工合作。

延川布堆画的造型基础是民间剪纸，但它比剪纸更加概括简练；其色彩基础是民间刺绣，但它比民间刺绣更加强烈鲜明，具有简练、概括、粗犷、纯朴的艺术风格。延川布堆画作品多次在北京、上海、西安、合肥等地展出，特别是1995年中国美术馆向全国推出延川布堆画后，布堆画引起了国内外艺术界的广泛关注，获得了高度评价，成为国内外专家和美术馆收藏的珍品。《黄河》《烈日》《辉煌的岁月》《手拉手》等多幅作品被中国美术馆、毛主席纪念堂等有关单位以及美术界人士收藏。

2009年，延川布堆画被列入陕西省第二批非物质文化遗产名录。

and received praise from domestic and foreign artists, and have become treasures collected by experts and art galleries at home and abroad. Many works such as *The Yellow River*, *The Scorching Sun*, *Glorious Days* and *Hand in Hand* have been collected by artists and organizations like the National Art Museum of China, Chairman Mao Memorial Hall, etc.

In 2009, Yanchuan cloth-paste pictures were listed in the second batch of Shaanxi Provincial Intangible Cultural Heritage List.

吴起油漆画
Wuqi Oil Painting

吴起油漆画多见于陕西省吴起县各个乡镇，由北方民族早期岩画演变而来，不仅用于家庭装饰，也用于寺庙修整。其在传承中不断完善，在完善中广泛流传，并形成了自己的风格，是优秀的传统民间文化之一。

吴起油漆画不同于一般绘画，它在颜色搭配上有冷有暖，在表现手法上有写实和素描，但在应用中主要以写实为主。其内容朴实，色彩鲜艳，线条流畅，美观大方，形象逼真；构图极为巧

Wuqi oil painting is popular in various townships of Wuqi County of Yan'an City. The painting evolves from the rock painting of the northern ethnic groups. It has been continuously perfected by generations of artisans and finally formed its own style, becoming one of the excellent traditional folk cultures of China. The painting is not only used for home decoration, but also for temple repair.

Wuqi oil painting is different from other oil paintings. As for the color matching, cool colors are combined with warm colors in the paintings; as for the techniques of expression, both realism and line drawing techniques are employed by the painter, with realism as the main expression technique. With simple content, bright colors, smooth lines, the paintings are beautiful and vivid, boasting ingenious composition, unique artistic conception and elegant style. The materials and tools for the paintings include paint of different colors as well as paint brushes and writing brushes of different types.

The paintings, often used in the decoration of furniture, walls, doors, windows, and household appliances, can protect surfaces of those things from the

妙，表现意境独特，风格高雅，是一种民俗性绘画形式。其原料和绘画工具主要有各色油漆和各种型号的油漆刷、毛笔等。

吴起油漆画常用于家具、墙壁、门窗以及生活用具的装饰，可以保护其表面不受破坏，既可防晒，又可防潮，集美观、实用于一体，备受青睐，被广泛应用。在民间，吴起油漆画比较常见的作品有《福寿图》《吉祥如意图》《五谷丰登图》以及动物和山水图，表现的内容离不开劳动人民的生活与信仰，是陕北劳动人民精神生活的写照。

吴起油漆画带有浓厚的北方气息，反映了北方人民淳朴善良、热情豪放、勇敢强悍的性格特征。

2009年，吴起油漆画被列入陕西省第二批非物质文化遗产名录。

damage of sunshine and moisture, hence they are favored and widely used for their beauty and practical function. The painting works that are popular among the folks include *Fu Shou Tu* (an old man with long gray beard holding a peach in his hands, symbolizing good health and longevity), *Jixiang-Ruyi Tu* (the Chinese characters "*Jixiang-Ruyi*" mean good luck and happiness), *A Bumper Grain Harvest*, as well as animal paintings and landscape paintings. Such paintings are inseparable from the working people's life and beliefs and well reflect the spiritual life of people in northern Shaanxi.

Wuqi oil painting features a strong flavor of northern China, reflecting the character of people in northern China, such as honesty, kindness, enthusiasm, and bravery.

In 2009, the painting was listed in the second batch of Shaanxi Provincial Intangible Cultural Heritage List.

旬邑彩贴剪纸
Xunyi Colorful Paper-Cuts

根据《旬邑县志》记载,陕西省咸阳市旬邑县的旬邑彩贴剪纸,是清末民初以来由旬邑民间单色剪纸发展演变而成的一种剪纸形式。当地农村结婚、逢年过节时妇女都要剪彩贴剪纸贴于门窗、炕头、墙围、窑顶和箱柜之上,以增添节日的喜庆气氛。

According to the *Annals of Xunyi County*, the colorful paper-cuts of Xunyi in Xianyang City have evolved from Xunyi monochrome paper-cuts since the late Qing Dynasty and the early period of the Republic of China. In rural areas, on wedding days and during festivals like the Spring Festival women scissor colorful paper-cuts and paste them on doors, windows, walls, cave-house roofs, and cabinets to intensify festive atmosphere.

Xunyi colorful paper-cuts are mainly seen in the towns and villages of the central highland regions of Xunyi County. The content of the paper cuts mainly includes people, animals, flowers, folk-customs, and religious beliefs. First a basic pattern is cut out in the traditional method, then pieces of paper of different colors are cut into many small dots and large patterns, which are pasted on the

旬邑彩贴剪纸多见于旬邑县中部塬区的乡镇，其主要内容有人物、动物、花卉、民俗、宗教信仰等。旬邑彩贴剪纸以民间剪纸为基础图像元素，用彩色纸剪出许多小圆点和大片形体图案，用剪、贴、衬工艺粘拼、点缀，从而形成一幅完整的作品。

旬邑彩贴剪纸风格独特，讲究对称，阴阳和谐，天人合一。剪纸作品多层次，多色彩，抽象，夸张，繁而不乱，艳而不俗。剪纸者注重作品表现意念和内涵，不重神态，不讲人物比例，也不讲视角三维效果，重在表现富丽华贵。剪纸人物形象饱满，眼目夸张，形态诡谲，基调浪漫。从整体上看，旬邑彩贴剪纸给人以鼓舞与想象，有健康、朴实、喜庆之感。剪纸尺寸可大可小，大的有4米长、1米宽的巨幅作品，小的可在16开的纸上创作。

旬邑彩贴剪纸表达了作者的生活情

basic pattern through techniques of cutting, pasting, lining and interspersing to form a piece of complete paper-cutting work.

With a unique style, Xunyi colorful paper-cuts stress symmetry, harmony of *yin* and *yang* as well as man and nature. The paper-cuts feature multi-layer, rich and bright colors as well as abstract and exaggerated patterns. Instead of emphasizing the figures' facial expression, body proportion, or the three-dimensional effect, attention is paid to the concepts, connotation and gorgeousness expressed by the paper-cuts. The paper-cut figures are vivid with exaggerating eyes and unique shapes. Viewed as a whole, they are plain and festive, giving people a sense of encouragement and imagination. The size of the paper-cuts can be as large as four meters long and one meter wide, while the small ones can be created on a small piece of paper.

Xunyi colorful paper-cuts, which are mainly used to beautify the environment, can well express the makers' views of life, dreams and pursuits. With personalized means of artistic expression, this kind of

感和理想追求，可美化家居生活。它以全新的个性化的艺术手法，开辟了一个既传统又现代、既原生态又超前的剪纸艺术新领域，具有教化、表意、抒情、娱乐、社交等多种价值。

2011年，旬邑彩贴剪纸被列入第三批国家级非物质文化遗产名录。

paper-cutting is both traditional and modern, primitive and advanced, opening up a new field of paper-cutting art. The paper-cuts have great significance in educating and entertaining people, expressing people's emotions and promoting social contact.

In 2011, Xunyi colorful paper-cuts were included in the third batch of China's National Intangible Cultural Heritage List.

汉中民间木版图画
Hanzhong Folk Woodblock Pictures

汉中民间木版图画是在陕南文化生态环境中生长的一种传统美术类文化遗产，主要有以下几类。第一类为木版年画，包括天官、状元、武将和寓意祥瑞的年画以及门神、灶王、龙王、财神等，在春节时张贴，表达美好愿望，烘托节日气氛。第二类为春帖，是一种将年历、节气表以及预报来年气象与农作物收成形势的《春牛图》集于一体的印刷品，具备提示生产生活的功用。其制作过程中的历法推算、《春牛图》描绘、版式设计、雕版工艺等需运用相关的天文学知识和绘画、雕刻技能。第三类为纸马、龙票，是一种刻印有图像和纹饰的神像、符印或纸币，供祀神、祭奠时焚烧。汉中民间木版年画始

Hanzhong folk woodblock pictures, a kind of traditional cultural heritage, originates in the cultural and ecological environment of southern Shaanxi. The pictures can be divided into three major types. The first type is woodblock New Year pictures, posted during the Spring Festival to express good wishes and to add festivity. The patterns on the New Year pictures include heavenly officials, generals, *zhuangyuan* (the number one scholar; a title in ancient times conferred on the most brilliant candidate who gets the highest score in the imperial examination), the God of Door, the God of Kitchen, the God of Wealth, the Dragon King and other patterns that imply auspiciousness. The second type is *chuntie*, a piece of printed paper as a reminder of work and life that combines calendar, solar terms and the *Picture of the Spring Bull* which can forecast the weather and grain harvest of the coming year. The calendar calculation, the depiction of *Picture*

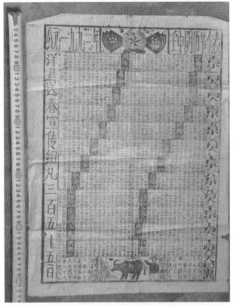 

于清代中叶，盛于民国初年，已有200多年的历史。据传春帖始于隋唐，已有千余年历史。

汉中民间木版图画有很大的社会影响。1942年，中法汉学研究所在北京举办的民间新年神像图画展览会上展出的汉中门神画引起各界关注；1979年以来，汉中门神画先后参加"陕西省民间美术展览""中国陕西乡俗手工艺

of the Spring Bull, the layout design, and the engraving technique all involve astronomy knowledge as well as painting and carving techniques. The third type of folk woodblock pictures serve as sacrificial things which are burned for worshiping gods or ancestors, including pictures of gods, pictures of incantation symbols and joss paper, all of which are printed with patterns or images. Among the three types of folk woodblock pictures, the New Year pictures (the first type), originated in the middle of the Qing

Dynasty and prevailed in the early years of the Republic of China, having a history of over 200 years. It is said that *chuntie* (the second type) dated back to the Sui and Tang dynasties and has a history of more than a thousand years.

The woodblock pictures have a great social influence. In 1942, Hanzhong woodblock door god pictures were exhibited in the New Year God Pictures Exhibition held by Franco-Chinese Sinology Institute in Beijing, and they attracted the attention of people from all walks of life. Since 1979, Hanzhong door god pictures have been displayed in Shaanxi Folk Fine Arts Exhibition and Shaanxi Folkloric Handcraft Exhibition. They have also been displayed and won wide acclaim in different exhibitions in Chinese cities like Beijing, provinces like Jiangsu, Sichuan, Zhejiang, Taiwan, regions like Hong Kong, Macao, as well as in foreign countries like the US, France and Britain. Wang Shucun, an expert of folk fine arts, wrote "there are many places where door gods are painted and printed in China, among which Hanzhong door god pictures are vivid with simple and beautiful colors and striking postures", "reflecting the local artist characteristics and the fine traditions of ancient Chinese folk painting".

In 2011, Hanzhong folk woodblock pictures were included in the third batch of Shaanxi Provincial Intangible Cultural Heritage List.

展"，在我国北京、江苏、四川、浙江和港澳台地区，以及美国、法国、英国等地展出，获得广泛赞誉。民间美术专家王树村先生撰文说："中国印绘门神的地方很多……其中神态生动、姿势威猛而色彩仍能保持古朴典丽的门神，要首推汉中门神了。"汉中门神"能保持地方的艺术特色……尤能体现我国古代民间绘画艺术之优良传统"。

2011年，汉中民间木版图画被列入陕西省第三批非物质文化遗产名录。

黄陵木雕
Huangling Woodcarving

黄陵木雕是一种具有民族特色的传统手工技艺，与人们的生产生活密不可分。黄陵木雕大多以柏木为原料，因为柏木木质红润，纹路清晰，材质坚硬，气味芳香，耐腐蚀，易保存。除此之外还可用枣木、梨木、核桃木等材质较为坚硬的木料做原料。黄陵木雕主要用于古建庙宇的建筑装饰和飞檐、门窗隔扇、联匾等的制作，也用于台、几、案、架、座以及床、橱、箱、桌、椅等家具的装饰雕刻。现在最常见的主要是寿木雕刻，棺椁雕刻的图案取材于民间传说中的二十四孝故事、龙、凤、福禄寿喜等，其构图严谨，刀工细腻，雕刻极其讲究，人物细致，花鸟逼真，装

Huangling woodcarving is a kind of traditional handicraft with national features, which is inseparable from people's work and life. Cypress is most often used as the raw material because the wood is smooth, hard, aromatic, corrosion-resistant, easy to store and with clear grain. In addition, hard wood from jujube tree, pear tree, and walnut tree can also be used. Huangling woodcarving is mainly applied to architectural decoration of overhanging eaves, doors, windows, gatepost couplets, plaques of ancient buildings and temples, and it is also used for decoration of desks, tables, shelves, pedestals, beds, cabinets, boxes, chairs and other domestic furniture. Now what is the most commonly seen is coffin carvings. The patterns of coffin carvings are based on folklore like the stories of filial piety, dragons, phoenixes and auspicious characters. The composition of the woodcarvings is rigorous; the carving technique is exquisite; the patterns of characters, plants, birds, clothes, etc., are vivid and lifelike.

Huangling woodcarvings are peculiar in shape, lifelike in expression, flowing in line, smooth in surface, and gorgeous in color. Finely carved with different carving

饰、服饰都栩栩如生。

黄陵木雕的主要特点是造型特异、神态逼真、线条优美、表面光滑、色泽艳丽，经过圆雕、深雕、透雕、浮雕的工艺流程，精雕细刻而成，具有石雕和其他雕刻不能媲美的优点。大多数木雕工艺品以民间神话传说、人物为题材，匠人巧妙地刻画出生动的故事情节，将传说中的人物形象、神态栩栩如生地呈现在观赏者面前。

数百年来，黄陵木雕工匠在继承传统木雕艺术的基础上，打造了独具黄陵特色的艺术风格。黄陵木雕具有较高的观赏性、艺术性和收藏价值。

2011年，黄陵木雕被列入陕西省第三批非物质文化遗产名录。

skills, they have the advantages that stone carvings and other carvings don't have. Most woodcarvings are based on the plot or characters of myths and legends. The craftsmen vividly portray and present the plot and characters for the viewers.

Over hundreds of years, craftsmen have endowed the woodcarvings with a unique artistic style based on traditional woodcarving craftsmanship, so that the woodcarvings have high ornamental, artistic and collectible value.

In 2011, Huangling woodcarving was included in the third batch of Shaanxi Provincial Intangible Cultural Heritage List.

东龙山狗娃咪泥哨
Donglongshan Animal-Shaped Clay Whistles

狗娃咪，也称狗娃哨，是用胶泥烧制而成的一种儿童玩具与民间工艺品。东龙山狗娃咪具体出现年代无从考证。据传，早在清朝就有狗娃咪在当地庙会上出售。狗娃咪的捏制手艺在龙山村代代相传，几乎家家都精于此技。20世纪80年代之前，狗娃咪是当地儿童的重要玩具。此后，随着社会经济的发展，狗娃咪已逐渐被现代玩具所取代，但仍有一部分远销外地，甚至走出国门。

东龙山狗娃咪的制作共分为制泥坯、捏制、烧制上釉色三个工序。制泥坯：取东龙山特有的黏土（俗称红胶泥土），碾碎过筛，置于青石上日晒，待

Donglongshan animal-shaped clay whistles are a kind of toys and folk craftwork in Shangzhou District of Shangluo City. The exact time when the clay whistles appeared in Donglongshan Village is unclear. It is said that as early as in the Qing Dynasty, there were clay whistles for sale at local temple fairs. The craftsmanship of making the clay whistles has been passed down from generation to generation in Donglongshan Village, and almost every family were proficient in the craftsmanship. Before the 1980s, the whistles were important toys for local children. However, with the development of society and economy, the whistles have been gradually replaced by modern toys, but still some were sold to other places and even abroad.

The process of making the whistles is divided into three steps. The first step is making the clay dough. The craftsmen collect the unique local reddish clay, crush, sieve, and then place it on a flagstone to dry, then sprinkle water over it, leave it for a few hours to let the clay fully moisten, then shape it into

干后再用水洒湿，置几个时辰，待黏土充分濡湿后和成泥团，用锤捶打，直至泥团柔韧光滑，装于瓦罐中待用（可储存数月，甚至数年）。捏制：取出瓦罐中的泥坯，揪成小团，开始捏制。捏制人全凭自己的手艺，先捏住一截泥条，捏出狗娃咪的头部，再捏出狗娃咪的4条腿。然后，捏制人一手拿着捏好的狗娃咪，一手用一根细枣木棍一端按出狗娃咪的两只眼睛，再用枣木棍从狗娃咪嘴部到脖子捅一个小孔，最后用枣木棍从脖子一端的出口往狗娃咪肚子上再捅一个小孔。就这样，一个憨厚、充满稚趣的狗娃咪便做成了。烧制上釉色：捏制好的成坯待干后置于农家的柴草灶膛中，用烧饭时的火候烧制半个多小时后取出，待温度适中时，以松香涂其身，此时狗娃咪通体乌黑锃亮，再以黄胆红点缀，便制作完成。

东龙山狗娃咪的造型多为小狗、小猫、小鸟、小狮、小猴、人骑狮、人骑狗、猴骑狮、狗骑狮，以及十二生肖

a clay dough, hammer the clay dough until it is malleable and smooth, then put it into an earthen jar for later use—the clay can be stored for months or even years. The second step is kneading. Take out the clay dough from the earthen jar, split it into small pieces, and then start to shape the whistle. The craftsman fully relies on his experience and craftsmanship to make the work done. He holds a piece of clay dough with one hand, shapes the head of the animal with the other hand, and then shapes the legs of the animal. Next, he holds the animal with one hand, and presses one end of a thin jujube stick against the upper part of the animal's head with the other hand to make the eyes. After that he pierces through the mouth and neck of the animal with the jujube stick to make a hole, and pierces another small hole on the animal's stomach. Through the above procedures, a cute animal-shaped whistle is completed. The last step is firing and glazing. After the animal-shaped whistle is molded and dried, it is baked in a stove full of burning firewood for more than half an hour and then taken out to cool down. Then, the animal is coated with rosin to make it black and shiny, and finally it is embellished with

等。狗娃咪形制小巧，最小的仅有半寸（约1.6厘米），憨态十足，稚趣可爱，地方特点鲜明。

2011年，东龙山狗娃咪泥哨被列入陕西省第三批非物质文化遗产名录。

red color.

Most of Donglongshan animal-shaped clay whistles are in the shapes of dog, cat, bird, lion, monkey, a man riding a lion, a man riding a dog, a monkey riding a lion, a dog riding a lion, and twelve zodiac signs. They are small in size, the smallest only about 1.6 cm long, and the largest no more than 6.6 cm long. They look charmingly naive and interesting, full of local flavor.

In 2011, Donglongshan animal-shaped clay whistles were included in the third batch of Shaanxi Provincial Intangible Cultural Heritage List.

商州花灯
Shangzhou Lanterns

花灯又称灯彩。商州花灯历史悠久，多在传统节日、婚寿喜庆时悬挂，以烘托热烈气氛，增添喜庆色彩。在商州，每年腊月三十至次年正月十五，庄户农家、城市居民、机关单位等的门前都要悬挂红灯。尤其是在元宵节的晚上，人们赏花灯、猜灯谜、放鞭炮，在灯的海洋里尽情享受节日的欢乐。

商州花灯内容丰富，形式多样，常见的有十二生肖灯、胖娃娃灯、狮子灯、白菜灯、西瓜灯、飞机灯、坦克灯、汽车灯、船灯，还有妙趣横生的转灯、盒子灯等。这些花灯大小各异，有挂、提、拉之别，也有人物、动物之分。花灯中融入了深厚的民俗文化内涵和奇特的创意。每年正月十五前，外公

Shangzhou lanterns, lanterns made and popular in Shangzhou District of Shangluo City, have a long history. They are usually hung during traditional festivals, on weddings and birthdays to enhance the festive atmosphere. Red lanterns are hung in front of doors of farmers' houses, urban residences, and workplaces every year from the New Year's Eve to the Lantern Festival (the fifteenth day of the first lunar month). Especially on the night of Lantern Festival, people watch lanterns, guess riddles written on lanterns, set off firecrackers, and enjoy the festive joy in the sea of lanterns.

Shangzhou lanterns are of different sizes and forms. The lanterns are in shapes of zodiac animals, fat dolls, lions, cabbages, watermelons, airplanes, tanks, cars, boats, etc., and there are also interesting rotating lanterns and box lanterns. The lanterns convey profound folk cultural connotations and fantastic creativity. Every year when the Lantern Festival comes, grandparents send lanterns to their little grandchildren. According to the local custom, it is necessary to send lanterns for three years consecutively after the grandchildren's birth, one pair of lanterns in the first year, two pairs in the second year, and three pairs

外婆要给小外孙送灯。按照习俗，要连续送灯三年，第一年一对，第二年两对，第三年三对。送灯颇有讲究，花灯要系在柏树枝上，还要配上鱼形的面馍，祝愿外孙长命富贵，祝福女儿家年年有余。送莲花灯，寓意连年来财；送龙灯、狮子灯，象征吉祥如意、四季平安；送小红宫灯，象征日子红火、人丁兴旺。

商州花灯大多采用传统工艺手工制作而成，做工精细，形象逼真，色彩艳丽，造型夸张，特色鲜明。

2013年，商州花灯被列入陕西省第四批非物质文化遗产名录。

in the third year. The lanterns should be tied to a cypress branch. Besides lanterns, grandparents should also prepare fish-shaped steamed buns to convey their wishes that the grandchildren will live a long and rich life and their daughter's family will be prosperous. A lotus lantern means continuous wealth; dragon lanterns and lion lanterns suggest peace and good luck; small red lanterns indicate a rich life and a prosperous family.

Shangzhou lanterns are mostly hand-made. They feature fine traditional craftsmanship, lifelike images, gorgeous colors, exaggerating shapes, and distinctive characteristics.

In 2013, the lanterns were listed in the fourth batch of Shaanxi Provincial Intangible Cultural Heritage List.

八

传统技艺

Traditional Craftsmanship

耀州窑陶瓷烧制技艺
Firing Technology of Yaozhou Kiln Porcelain

耀州窑位于陕西省铜川市黄堡镇。此地在宋代辖于耀州，耀州窑由此得名，其产品被称为耀州瓷。耀州瓷创烧于唐代，成熟于五代，鼎盛于宋代，是宋代"六大窑系"中最大的一个窑系，耀州瓷是北方青瓷的代表。

耀州瓷以铜川黄堡镇为中心，沿漆河两边密集布陈，史称"十里陶坊"。同时还有陈炉镇、上店村、玉华村等的窑场依次排列，绵延百里。金元兵灾之后，各窑场已日趋衰落，至明代中期终烧，唯有陈炉镇制瓷延续至今，成为西

Yaozhou kiln is located in Huangbao Town of Tongchuan City. In the Song Dynasty, Huangbao was under the jurisdiction of Yaozhou, thus the name of Yaozhou kiln and Yaozhou porcelain. Yaozhou porcelain started in the Tang Dynasty, matured in the Five Dynasties, and flourished in the Song Dynasty. It was the largest kiln of the "Six Kilns" in the Song Dynasty. And its products are the representatives of the celadon in northern China.

Yaozhou porcelain is mainly produced from kilns in Huangbao Town and other kilns densely distributed along both sides of the Qi River, which are known as "Ten-mile Kilns". At the same time, there are kilns in Chenlu Town, Shangdian Village, Yuhua Village, etc., which are scattered in order and stretch for hundreds of miles. Since the Jin Dynasty and Yuan Dynasty, all kilns declined due to wars and finally closed down in the middle of the Ming Dynasty except the kilns in Chenlu Town, which have survived and continued their business till now. Now Chenlu Town has become a major porcelain-making town in the northwest of China. In the 1970s, with the help of experts, the traditional

北地区的制瓷重镇。20世纪70年代，在有关专家的帮助下，耀州窑的传统工艺得以恢复，生产耀州青瓷、黑釉及剔花瓷、白釉及剔花瓷、蓝花瓷、铁锈花瓷、花釉六大系列陶瓷。

耀州窑陶瓷烧制技艺主要体现在原料的采配及加工、泥料的储备及揉炼、手工拉坯、手工雕花、釉药的配制及敷施、装窑及烧成等方面，掌握相关技艺的人被称为"匠人"。一件成品要经过采料、精选、风化、配比、耙泥、揉泥、手拉坯、修坯、施釉、装饰、装窑、烧窑等17道工序，主要产品有碗、盘、瓶、罐、壶、盆、炉、枕等，凡生活需要的产品应有尽有。

装饰手法以刻花和印花为主，刀法犀利流畅，刚劲有力，立体感较强。纹饰丰富多彩，有动物、人物、花卉和几何图案。纹样中的动物有龙、凤、狮、

firing technology of Yaozhou porcelain was restored and people began to produce six varieties of porcelain, including Yaozhou celadon, black glaze porcelain engraved with patterns, white glaze porcelain engraved with patterns, blue flower porcelain, porcelain with rust-colored patterns and colorful glaze porcelain.

The firing technology of Yaozhou porcelain is mainly embodied in the aspects of collecting, preparing and processing raw material, storing and rubbing the ceramic mud, hand-molding, hand-carving, preparing and applying glaze, stacking the earthenware in the kiln, firing, etc. Those who master the professional skills are called *jiangren* which means craftsmen. One product is finished through 17 procedures including collecting, selecting, weathering, proportioning, rubbing, molding, fettling, glazing, decorating, firing, etc. The porcelain products feature rich varieties, including bowls, plates, bottles, pots, basins, censers, pillows and so on.

Craftsmen mainly adopt decoration techniques of carving and printing to create smooth, exquisite and stereoscopic patterns. The ornamental patterns mainly fall into four categories: animals, figures, flowers and geometric patterns. The animal patterns include dragons, phoenix, lions, rhinos, horses, sheep, dogs, cranes, geese, ducks, fish, mandarin ducks and so on. Figure patterns include playing kids, etc. Flower patterns are represented by lotus,

犀牛、马、羊、狗、鹤、鹅、鸭、鱼、鸳鸯等，人物有婴戏等，花卉有莲花、牡丹、菊花、梅花等。几何图案纹有三角纹、回纹等。

近年来，在现代化工业的冲击下，耀州陶瓷业一度举步维艰。特别是年纪大的匠人相继去世，年轻人大多不愿意从事陶瓷制作，流传了一千多年的传统技艺面临着后继乏人的困境，亟待抢救。

耀州窑作为中国古代六大名窑之一，在中国陶瓷史上甚至世界陶瓷史上都占有重要的历史地位。

2006年，耀州窑陶瓷烧制技艺被列入第一批国家级非物质文化遗产名录。

peony, chrysanthemum, plum blossom, etc. Geometric patterns include triangle, Chinese character "回" and other auspicious patterns.

In recent years, under the impact of modern industry, the porcelain industry of Yaozhou kiln is under a difficult circumstance. Especially as elderly craftsmen passed away and most young people are reluctant to engage in porcelain production, this traditional workmanship is endangered, which is badly in need of rescue.

Yaozhou kiln, as one of the six famous kilns in ancient China, has an important position in the history of Chinese ceramics, even the world's ceramics.

In 2006, firing technology of Yaozhou kiln porcelain was included in the first batch of China's National Intangible Cultural Heritage List.

澄城尧头陶瓷烧制技艺
Yaotou Ceramic Firing Technology in Chengcheng

陕西关中东部的澄城县尧头镇生产粗瓷。此地煤炭资源丰富,又有坩土矿分布于沟涧的石崖,夹生白、紫两色的原料,便于烧制陶瓷、砂器。

澄城县历史悠久,考古发现的仰韶文化遗址有十多处。从遗址发掘出土的陶器和陶片中可以看出,在新石器时期这里已经有了相当成熟的彩陶烧造技艺。又据明代县志记载,尧头瓷砂始于唐。经过长期的发展,尧头陶瓷烧制至明清时达于兴盛。两千多年来,尧头镇的陶瓷业久盛不衰,延续至今。

尧头陶瓷主要产于尧头镇尧头村。"收秋不收秋,等到五月二十六,二十六日滴一点,快到尧头买大碗,买来大碗喋(吃)米饭。"这首古老的民谣反映了

Yaotou Town of Chengcheng County, located in the east of central Shaanxi, is famous for coarse porcelain production as it boasts abundant coal resources and soil which is suitable for firing ceramics.

Chengcheng County has a long history, and there are more than ten sites of Yangshao cultural ruins discovered here by archaeologists. From the potteries excavated from the ruins, it can be seen that the skills for firing pottery were quite mature during the Neolithic Period. According to the county records in the Ming Dynasty, Yaotou ceramic firing began in the Tang Dynasty. After a long period of development, it flourished during the Ming and Qing dynasties. For more than 2,000 years, the ceramic industry in Yaotou Town has continued to this day.

Yaotou ceramics are mainly produced in Yaotou Village of Yaotou Town. "If you want to know whether there will be a good harvest, please wait until the 26th of the fifth lunar month. If it rains on the 26th, go to Yaotou Town to buy a big bowl to eat rice." This old ballad not only reflects people's expectation for harvest, but confirms that Yaotou ceramic products are indispensable implements in people's

人们对丰收的期盼，也印证了尧头陶瓷是人们生活中不可缺少的必备用品。尧头陶瓷以当地出产的坩土为原料，全部用土法手工生产，加工过程包括浆泥、制坯、施釉、煅烧四道工序，有碗窑、黑窑、瓮窑、砂窑四个传统窑系，主要烧制人们日常生活中使用的盆、瓮等大件器皿和碗、碟、瓶、枕、罐等较为精细的瓷器。

尧头粗瓷以它特有的黑瓷、黑釉剔花瓷、青花瓷和铁锈色瓷器闻名一方。粗瓷釉色多用白、黄、黑三种，还有蓝色及棕红色。各种器物上装饰的花

life. *Gantu*, a special soil produced locally, is used to make Yaotou ceramics. All the ceramics are manually produced in indigenous methods. The production process includes four steps, namely mud-refining, modeling, glazing and calcining. There are four kinds of traditional kilns, namely the bowl kiln, black ceramic kiln, jar kiln, and sandy-soil ware kiln. Such kilns mainly produce big implements such as pots and jars used in daily life, and more elaborate porcelain wares such as bowls, plates, bottles, pillows, pots and so on.

Yaotou coarse porcelain is well-known for its unique black porcelain, black glazed porcelain carved with flowers, blue and white porcelain and rust-colored porcelain. The glazes are mostly in colors of white, yellow and black as well as blue and brownish red. The patterns of flowers and animals decorated on all kinds of ceramic implements are similar to the patterns of local paper-cuts and dough figurines. The patterns mainly include lotus, peony, chrysanthemum or the Chinese characters like *Fu, Lu, Shou, Xi* (meaning fortune, promotion, longevity, and happiness respectively) and so on. Yaotou ceramics are closely connected with the production and life of the masses. The modelling and patterns of the ceramics combine roughness with exquisiteness,

卉、动物与当地的剪纸、面花造型同出一源，内容多为莲花、牡丹、菊花或福、禄、寿、禧等字样。尧头陶瓷与群众的生产、生活紧密相连，其造型粗中见细、拙中寓巧，给人以朴实自然的美感，与南方陶瓷细腻精巧的风格迥异。

近年来，人们的生活方式和消费观念发生了很大变化，对尧头瓷器的需求日益减少。尧头镇仅存的一个陶瓷小作坊只能视市场需求断断续续地生产少量应时产品，加之后继乏人，尧头陶瓷烧制技艺已处于濒危境地，亟待抢救。

2006年，澄城尧头陶瓷烧制技艺被列入第一批国家级非物质文化遗产名录。

which embody the simple and natural beauty, very different from the delicate and exquisite style of ceramics in the south of China.

In recent years, people's lifestyles and consumption concepts have changed greatly, and the need for Yaotou porcelain has been decreasing. Therefore a small ceramic workshop, the only one which has survived in Yaotou Town, can only produce a small number of timely products according to the market demand. Due to the lack of successors, the ceramic firing technology of Yaotou Town is in an endangered situation and urgently needs to be rescued.

In 2006, Yaotou ceramic firing technology was included in the first batch of China's National Intangible Cultural Heritage List.

华县皮影制作技艺
Craftsmanship of Making Huaxian Shadow Puppets

皮影是陕西省渭南市华州区县的一个独特的民间艺术品种。华县皮影制作技艺一般有以下几个步骤：

1. 选皮。一般选用6岁左右的秦川黄牛的牛皮。

2. 制皮。将浸泡后的牛皮刮铲成半透明的皮子，经打磨后方可刻制皮影。

3. 画稿。制作皮影时所用的画稿称为"样谱"，是历代艺人相传的设计图稿。

4. 过稿。用钢针笔把各部件的轮廓

Shadow puppet is a unique folk art in Huazhou District of Weinan City. The making process of Huaxian shadow puppets generally includes the following steps:

Step one, selecting the cow hide. Generally cow hides of *Qinchuan* yellow cattle that are about six years old are used.

Step two, processing the cow hide. The cow hide is soaked in the water first, then is scraped and polished into translucent leather.

Step three, drawing patterns. The patterns for carving the shadow puppets are called *yangpu*, which are handed down by artists of the past generations.

Step four, copying the patterns. Copy the outline and patterns of each part of the puppet on the leather with a steel needle.

Step five, carving. Artists are very particular about carving knives, and generally they have 11 to 12 knives of different shapes and usage.

Step six, coloring. After the parts of the shadow puppets are carved, they will be colored. The experienced artists are very particular about coloring. They are good at color matching as well as speck dyeing, which can give the puppets gorgeous colors.

和设计图案纹样分别拷贝在皮面上。

5. 雕镂。雕刻艺人十分讲究雕刻刀具，一般都有十一二把刀具，其中有宽窄不同的斜口刀、平刀等。

6. 敷彩。皮影雕完后开始敷彩。老艺人十分讲究用色，善于配色，再加上点染的浓淡变化，使色彩异常绚丽。

7. 发汗熨平。将皮影放在两块特制的土坯中间，高温加热土坯，将皮影中的水分烘烤出来。

8. 缀结完成。一个完整的皮影人物

Step seven, drying and flattening. The parts of the shadow puppets are placed between two specially made adobes, then the adobes are heated at a high temperature to evaporate the moisture in the shadow puppets.

Step eight, connecting the parts together. A complete shadow puppet usually has 11 parts from head to toe, including the head, chest, abdomen, legs, arms, elbows and hands. Each joint of the shadow puppet must be pierced a hole called "bone eye", and combined with nails carved from cow hide or thread made of fine cow hide strips to form a complete shadow puppet.

The producers of Huaxian shadow puppets are all folk artisans and most of them are hobbyists. Nowadays, due to the diversification of mass cultural entertainment, shadow plays are no longer favored by young people as before, so the audiences keep dwindling. As a result, shadow puppet production also declines.

的形体从头到脚通常有头颅、胸、腹、双腿、双臂、双肘、双手等十一个部件。皮影人物的各个关节部位都要刻出"骨眼",并用牛皮刻成的枢钉或用细牛皮条搓成的线缀结合成一个完整的皮影人。

华县皮影的制作者均为民间艺人。学习皮影制作技艺的人大多是爱好者。现在由于大众文化娱乐形式的多样化,皮影戏已不再受到年轻人的青睐,观众日益减少,皮影制作也直接受到影响,日渐萎缩。目前,这一技艺面临着可能r失传的危险,亟待抢救。

2007年,华县皮影制作技艺被列入陕西省第一批非物质文化遗产名录。

At present, this craftsmanship is facing the danger of extinction and urgently needs rescue.

In 2007, the craftsmanship of making Huaxian shadow puppets was included in the first batch of Shaanxi Provincial Intangible Cultural Heritage List.

中华老字号西凤酒酿造技艺
Brewing Technology of China's Time-Honored Brand *Xifeng* Liquor

西凤酒产于陕西省宝鸡市凤翔区柳林镇。这里土地肥沃，水质甘美，有着得天独厚的酿酒优势，是我国著名的酒乡。西凤酒以优质高粱为原料，大麦、小麦、豌豆制曲，配以甘美的柳林井水，采用土窖发酵法，老五甑续渣混烧而得新酒。新酒贮存三年以上，经自然老熟后精心勾兑而成。一瓶西凤酒的诞生要经过多名专业人士层层把控，以确保品质。

西凤酒是中国四大老牌著名白酒之一，始于殷商，盛于唐宋，发展于明清，至今已有三千多年的历史。西凤酒是中国凤香型白酒开宗之祖和典型代表，在中华名优白酒中独树一帜。西凤酒清亮透明，醇香芬芳，融清香、浓香

Xifeng liquor is produced in Liulin Town, Fengxiang District of Baoji City. The land in Liulin Town is fertile and the water here is sweet, so it is a good place to make liquor and it is renown for its liquor production. *Xifeng* liquor is made from high-quality sorghum, the local Liulin water and distiller's yeast made from barley, wheat and pea. The raw materials are fermented in the cellar and brewed in a unique way to produce the liquor. The liquor is stored for more than three years, and is meticulously blended after natural maturation. A bottle of *xifeng* liquor has to be checked and controlled by many professionals to ensure the quality.

As one of the four well-known liquors in China, *xifeng* liquor is renowned as the ancestor and representative of the Chinese *feng*-style liquor. Its production has a history of over 3,000 years, which started in the Shang Dynasty, flourished in the Tang and Song dynasties, and developed in the Ming and Qing dynasties. The liquor is crystal clear, mellow and fragrant, combing mild aroma and strong aroma, characterized by the mixed and coordinated flavors as "sour, sweet, bitter, spicy and fragrant" as well as lingering aftertaste. Moderate

之优点于一体，具有醇香典雅、甘润清爽、诸味协调、回味悠长的独特风格，"酸、甜、苦、辣、香五味俱全而各不出头"，适时适量饮用，有活血驱寒、提神祛劳之益。

西凤酒在中华美酒之林中占有重要位置，博大精深的西凤酒文化为中华民族的酒文化宝库增添了光辉灿烂的篇章。西凤酒的大曲及酿造发酵过程也对研究微生物发酵具有重要的参考价值。

2007年，中华老字号西凤酒酿造技艺被列入陕西省第一批非物质文化遗产名录。

drinking at proper time can help drinkers invigorate blood circulation, expel cold, reduce fatigue and get refreshed.

Xifeng liquor involves profound liquor culture and occupies an important position in Chinese spirits family. Its distiller's yeast and brewing process also have important reference value for studying microbial fermentation.

In 2007, the brewing technology of *xifeng* liquor was included in the first batch of Shaanxi Provincial Intangible Cultural Heritage List.

甘泉豆腐和豆腐干制作技艺
Skill of Making Ganquan Fresh Tofu and Dried Tofu

甘泉豆腐和豆腐干闻名古今，距今已有1,400多年历史。甘泉俗称"美水之乡"，甘泉豆腐和豆腐干的品质优良与当地泉水有很大关系。从20世纪80年代起，甘泉豆腐采用延安市出产的一种双青豆制作。双青豆墨绿如翡翠，香气四溢，含人体必需的18种氨基酸及多种维生素，特别是维生素B含量丰富，营养价值高，是理想的高蛋白、低脂肪的"绿色食品"。

Ganquan fresh tofu and dried tofu are well-known in ancient and modern times, which have a history of more than 1,400 years. Ganquan is known as the "hometown of sweet water". The high quality of Ganquan fresh tofu and dried tofu owes a lot to the local spring water. Ganquan tofu has been made from a kind of green soy beans produced in Yan'an City since the 1980s. The beans are dark green, like the emerald, and have lingering fragrance. They contain 18 essential amino acids and multiple vitamins, especially vitamin B, thus they have high nutritional value. They are ideal high-protein and low-fat "green food".

The making process of fresh tofu and dried tofu can be divided into several procedures.

Soaking beans. Sift the beans to remove the small stones and withered beans; wash them; then soak them in water until they swell.

Grinding. In the old days, a stone mill was used to grind beans. After being ground, the bean slurry would be filtered through a piece of gauze for four to five times until the thick liquid and bean dregs are separated. Nowadays, professional

豆腐和豆腐干的制作过程可分为以下几个步骤：

泡豆。首先将大豆过筛洗净，把小石粒和不饱满的豆粒筛出去，洗净后泡入水中，直至泡胀。

磨浆。旧时采用石磨磨浆，豆腐包过浆，需4~5遍过完。现在均采用磨浆机作业，3遍即可保证浆渣分离。

烧浆。小作坊在大锅内把浆烧熟。现代化作业多使用自动烧浆机。

点卤。浆烧熟后盛入容器（小作坊直接在锅内点卤），温度保持在90℃以上，用3%的卤水将浆点成块状。

压榨。小作坊用木板做成大小不等的框架容器，将纱布衬入其中，倒入块状浆汤，用布包好，放上砖（石）压榨。现代化作业采用的是豆腐压榨机，每块用纱布包成50厘米×50厘米大小，每次可压45层，30分钟即可完成。

豆腐只用以上五个步骤即可做好。

machines have replaced the stone mill. The liquid and bean dregs can be separated easily.

Boiling. In the small workshop, the bean slurry is thoroughly cooked in a large pot, while the modernized production is realized by using an automatic machine.

Adding the brine. After the slurry is cooked thoroughly, put it into a container (the small workshop directly adds the brine in the pot). Under the condition that the temperature is kept above 90°C, add the brine (the concentration is 3%) to make the slurry become lumps.

Pressing. The small workshop uses wooden boards to make containers of different sizes. Line the container with gauze, pour the lumps into the container, wrap the lumps with gauze, and place bricks or stones above the lumps to press out the water. The modernized production is realized by using a tofu presser. The lumps are wrapped with gauze into blocks of 50 cm×50 cm, and 45 layers of blocks can be pressed each time. The pressing can be done in 30 minutes.

Through the above five procedures, tofu is made.

Drying. In the old days, tofu was cut into one-inch square pieces, boiled in the water with seasonings like anise, cumin, clove, pepper, salt and so on. The small pieces of tofu need to be simmered with mild heat for better flavor. After that, they are placed on the hot *kang* (a heatable

晾晒。旧时制作豆腐干，把豆腐切成一寸见方的小块，入锅煮味。用的调料主要有大茴、小茴、丁香、花椒、盐等。用文火煮，以便更好入味。入味后，先在热炕上烤去大部分水分，再把一个个豆腐干用线穿起来，一串串地挂到屋檐下晾干。现代化作业是将豆腐切成面积约为10厘米×5厘米的块状，放在盐水中浸泡30分钟，然后在90℃的烤箱中烤干。

切丝。块状豆腐干整齐地按块包装，无需切丝。其他要用切丝机切成长短不等的丝状。

包装。把豆腐丝按不同的口味装入袋中，经过"抽空机"抽出空气，包装成袋。

杀菌。为确保产品质量，把包装好的豆腐干放入高温杀菌箱中消毒30分钟。

装箱。每30袋（60克装）装一箱，

brick or earthen bed) to remove most of the water, and then threaded into strings and hung under the eaves to be dried. The modernized production involves 3 steps. First fresh tofu is cut into pieces of about 10 cm × 5 cm, then soaked in the salt water for 30 minutes, and lastly baked in an oven at a temperature of 90°C.

Shredding. Blocks of tofu in regular shape are packed in blocks, and others need to be cut into long or short strips with a cutter.

Packaging. Put dried tofu strips into different bags according to the flavors, and then vacuumize the bags.

Sterilizing. To ensure the quality, put the packaged dried tofu into a high-temperature sterilization box for 30 minutes to sterilize.

Cartoning. 30 bags, 60 grams per bag, are packed in a box, and all manufacturers in Ganquan County adopt the unified cartoning standard. After acceptance check, the dried tofu can leave the factory for sale.

In the past, Ganquan fresh tofu sold well, while the dried tofu was only used as

全县各厂家统一标准。验收合格后方可出厂。

旧时甘泉豆腐销售较快，而豆腐干被人们当作一种零食，或者是饮酒时的小菜，销售量并不大。20世纪40年代以后，甘泉镇上销售豆腐和豆腐干的店家和摊点大幅增多，产量大幅增加，形成了一个颇具规模的产业。20世纪80年代以后，甘泉豆腐干声名鹊起，已成为陕西省地方传统名牌食品之一。

2007年，甘泉豆腐与豆腐干制作技艺被列入陕西省第一批非物质文化遗产名录。

a snack or a side dish for drinking alcohol. Thus, the sales of dried toufu were not large. Since the 1940s, the number of shops and stalls selling fresh tofu and dried tofu in Ganquan has increased significantly, so has the output of fresh tofu and dried tofu, which have gradually developed into a large-scale industry. Since the 1980s, Ganquan dried tofu has become famous and been regarded as one of the local traditional brand-name foods in Shaanxi Province.

In 2007, the skill of making Ganquan fresh tofu and dried tofu was listed in the first batch of Shaanxi Provincial Intangible Cultural Heritage List.

岐山臊子面制作技艺
Skill of Making Qishan *Saozi* Noodles

陕西省宝鸡市岐山县的臊子面起源于3,000多年前西周时的祭祀制度。岐山人吃面前所进行的祭祀活动与《周礼》中敬天敬地敬祖先的礼仪大体吻合：臊子面做好后，第一碗用来祭祀天地神灵和祖先，然后宾客方能按长幼次序入席食用。岐山臊子面历经数千年代代相传而长盛不衰。

岐山臊子面的制作原料有面粉、大肉、豆腐、胡萝卜、青菜、香菜以及辣椒、食盐、醋等调料。岐山臊子面的吃法相当别致，只吃面，不喝汤。这种面是当地百姓四时八节、婚丧嫁娶、接待贵客的上等美食。

岐山臊子面的制作工艺如下：

1. 燣臊子。岐山臊子肉是岐山地方传统风味食品，是制作名吃岐山臊子

The *saozi* noodles in Qishan County of Baoji City originated from the sacrificial system of the Western Zhou Dynasty more than 3,000 years ago. The sacrificial activities practiced by Qishan people before they eat noodles are largely in line with the etiquette of worshiping the heaven, the earth and ancestors described in the *Rites of Zhou*—when the *saozi* noodles are prepared, the first bowl of noodles is sacrificed to the heaven, the earth, the gods and ancestors, and then guests can take their seats at tables and eat noodles according to the order that the elder is prior to the younger. The skill of making Qishan *saozi* noodles has been passed down from generation to generation through thousands of years and the noodles have always been preferred by the people.

The raw materials of Qishan *saozi* noodles are flour, pork, tofu, carrots, greens, coriander and seasonings including chili, salt and vinegar. As for the eating method, it's very unique as people are only supposed to eat the noodles but not to drink the soup. Qishan *saozi* noodles are the superior food served on such occasions as festivals, wedding ceremonies, funerals and important guest receptions.

Qishan *saozi* noodles are made

面的主要辅料之一。该产品制作工艺考究，口味酸辣爽口，油而不腻，香酥味美，经济实惠，易于长期贮存。燥制臊子时要选用最好的猪肉，也就是猪后腰部位的大肉，把肉切成1厘米大小的方片，切法很讲究刀功。肉片要薄，肥瘦搭配，大小均匀。燥臊子的火不宜大，把猪油先化开，加入适量的菜油，猪肉和菜油的比例是10∶3，烧热后放入切好的肥肉，用文火加热20分钟左右；再倒入瘦肉，加热搅动至能掐动肉皮；油变清后，依次放入适量的姜皮、调料粉，加入酿造的食醋（量以醋味出头为宜），文火烧沸5分钟后，加入适量的食用盐；待肥肉片达到透明状后，将秦椒面加入，暂不宜搅动，煮沸3分钟左右，炼掉辣面的烈辣味，搅匀出锅即成。

2. 擀面。岐山人对面要求严格，

through the following steps:

The first step is making *saozi*. Qishan *saozi*, a traditional food in Qishan County, is one of the main ingredients used to make Qishan *saozi* noodles. It is sour, hot, tasty, oily but not greasy. Besides, it is characterized by its low cost, good quality and easy storage for a long time. Its making skill is very demanding. The best pork from the back of the pig's waist is used for making *saozi*. The pork is cut into one-centimeter-square slices. In this step, a high slicing skill is required because the slices should be thin, with both fat and lean meat, and of the similar size. The heat stir-frying the *saozi* should not be too high. After the lard in the pan is melted, add an appropriate amount of rapeseed oil— the ratio of lard to rapeseed oil is 10 to 3. When the oil becomes hot, put the fat meat into the pan and heat it for 20 minutes with slow fire, and then add the lean meat and stir until the pork skin can be pierced with a chopstick. When the oil becomes clear, add an appropriate amount of ginger peel, seasoning power and vinegar—the vinegar is added until the meat tastes a little sour. After the meat sauce is boiling for 5 minutes with slow fire, add an appropriate amount of salt into it. When the fat meat looks transparent, add chili powder, but don't stir the meat for the time being. Boil the sauce for about 3 minutes to remove the hot taste of the pepper. Lastly, mix *saozi* well and ladle it out of the pan.

一丝不苟。选优良白小麦三种，混合细磨，每百斤出面七十斤。每十斤面掺碱三钱（15克），加水搅拌。十斤面粉加三斤水，水应分次加入。先拌后搓，以硬为宜；反复揉搓，形成面块，盘起回醒，以软为宜。口诀是拌硬揉软，擀薄切细（厚不超过1毫米，宽不超过2毫米），面条互不粘连，粗细均匀滚水下面，煮熟为止。

3. 配菜。岐山臊子面的配菜叫底菜和漂花。把它们和臊子一并放入锅中，随汤入碗。底菜和漂花取料于可食用植物的根、茎、叶、花、藻五端，取色于细萝卜之红、金针菜之黄、豆角蒜苗之绿、黑木耳之黑、鲜豆腐之白，配菜丰富，五色俱全。在人民生活富裕的今天，岐山臊子面的漂花菜还加上鸡蛋饼，即把鸡蛋打破，装在碗里，搅成糊状，用平底锅在火上把鸡蛋糊摊成薄

The second step is making noodles. Qishan people have strict requirements on making noodles. Three kinds of high-quality wheat are mixed and finely ground, and every 50 kilograms of mixed wheat produces 35 kilograms of flour. Firstly, add 15 grams of alkali into every 5 kilograms of flour, and then sprinkle water into the flour and stir—1.5 kilograms of water should be slowly added into 5 kilograms of flour. Secondly, stir and knead the flour until a relatively hard dough is formed. Then wait for some time until the dough becomes soft and smooth. Thirdly, roll the dough into a flat and thin sheet (not thicker than 1 mm) and cut it into even noodles (not wider than 2 mm). Lastly, boil noodles in water until they are cooked.

The third step is preparing side dishes. The side dishes and *saozi* are put into the pot together. After being cooked, they will be poured into the bowl with boiling soup. The ingredients of the side dishes mainly come from roots, stems, leaves, flowers and algae of different edible plants like carrots, dried lily, green beans, garlic sprouts, ect., which have different colors and can increase people's appetite greatly. Today eggs are often included in the side dishes. Beat eggs in a bowl, stir them into batter, fry the batter in a pan so that it becomes a thin pancake, cut the egg pancake into diamond-shaped square pieces, and add them into the soup.

The last step is cooking soup. Cooking

饼,切成不大于1厘米的菱形方片,加入臊子面汤锅。这样臊子面的汤锅之中,表面的漂花真是五颜六色,使人食欲大增。

4. 炝汤。臊子面的调汤也很重要。烹汤要专设一口锅,锅内先放少许菜油,烧热后倒入鲜姜末、盐、醋、调料粉、味精等,再加入适量开水,浇沸二三分钟,然后放入臊子、底菜、漂花、鸡蛋饼。岐山臊子面的汤内忌用酱油。若有人不吃大肉,就不加臊子,放入油泼辣子;若有人既不吃臊子,又不吃辣子,则放入熟菜油;若有人想吃鸡蛋,则炒点鸡蛋放入汤中。

改革开放以来,岐山臊子面得到了当地政府的重视和推广,保持了原汁原味的传统制作工艺,已经形成独特的产业,成为当地群众日常生活中和餐饮业的一种特色食品,广受群众喜爱。

2007年,岐山臊子面制作技艺被列入陕西省第一批非物质文化遗产名录。

soup is also very important. A special pot is needed for cooking the soup. Sprinkle a little rapeseed oil in the pot, heat it, and add some fresh ginger powder, salt, vinegar, seasoning powder, monosodium glutamate, etc., then add an appropriate amount of boiling water, boil the water for two to three minutes, then put the *saozi*, side dishes and egg pancake pieces into the soup. Do not add soy sauce into the soup. If someone doesn't eat pork, add chili powder into the soup instead of *saozi*; if someone eats neither the *saozi* nor chili, add cooked rapeseed oil into the soup; if someone likes to eat eggs, scramble eggs can be put into the soup.

Since the Reform and Opening-up, Qishan *saozi* noodles have been valued and promoted by the local government. The noodles which maintain the original taste and traditional making skill have gained popularity and become a special food of the local people.

In 2007, the skill of making Qishan *saozi* noodles was included in the first batch of Shaanxi Provincial Intangible Cultural Heritage List.

岐山空心挂面制作技艺
Skill of Making Qishan Hollow Dried Noodles

陕西省宝鸡市岐山县的空心挂面是传统手工面食中独特的上品。千百年来，岐山空心挂面是当地群众最喜爱的面食之一，也是馈赠亲朋好友的佳品。

岐山空心挂面以优质小麦为原料，把小麦簸、筛、淘、晾后磨成精细的面粉，然后经过十余道工序制作而成。

把面粉用盐水和成团块状，用手使劲反复揉压，以能拉成圆条状为宜；把和好的面块放在案板上，用力揉搓成大条，粗如水杯，长约尺许；把搓成的大条盘入盆内，用湿毛巾苫住约40分钟；给大条上撒上糜面，搓成小拇指那么粗的小条，再盘入盆中捂30分钟左右；将捂好的小条绕在手指那么粗的竹柱棍

The hollow dried noodles in Qishan County of Baoji City are top-grade among the traditional handmade noodles. For thousands of years, Qishan hollow dried noodles have been regarded as one of the most favorite noodles of the local people, and they are also a kind of good gift for relatives and friends.

Qishan hollow dried noodles are made of high-quality wheat. The wheat is winnowed, sieved, washed and dried, and then ground into fine flour with which hollow dried noodles are made through more than ten procedures.

Mix the flour with salt water to form a dough, repeatedly knead the dough until it can be pulled into a round strip. Put the dough on a chopping board and knead it into thick strips that are as thick as a cup and about one foot long. Put the thick strips in circles into a basin, and cover them with a wet towel for about 40 minutes. Sprinkle some proso millet flour on the thick strips, then knead them into thin strips that are as thin as little fingers. Put the thin strips in circles into the basin and cover them for about 30 minutes. The thin strips are winded around two bamboo sticks and placed in a special noodle trough (in the

上，放在特制的挂面槽内（温度保持在36℃）约1小时；将槽内的柱棍架放在特制的开床之上，从上至下拉动，直至底端，又依次放入槽内捂30分钟；待槽内面条醒动下坠后取出，开始上架；用柱棍把上架的面条划拨均匀，直到挂面摆动挂吊成一排排雪白的细面，晾至七成干，放置屋内；再上架，剪去下部面头；完全晾干后，将做好的挂面放在案板上切截包装。

trough, the temperature is about 36°C) for about one hour. Fix one stick in a relatively high position and pull the other stick from the top downward, and then put the two sticks winded with noodles into the warm trough again for 30 minutes. When the noodles begin to drop, take them out of the trough and hang them on a shelf. Evenly spread the noodles on the shelf with a pole until the noodles swing and become thin ones. When the thin noodles are almost dry, place them in the room; then hang them on a higher shelf and cut off the noodle ends. When the noodles are completely dried, place them on the chopping board and cut them into short ones, then pack them up.

The noodles are completely handmade throughout the whole making process. The making skill is passed down from masters to apprentices, and can only be mastered after long-term practice.

Qishan hollow dried noodles feature unique recipe and special making techniques, and they do not contain any additive. They are well-known in China for

岐山空心挂面从原料加工到成品，全由手工完成。岐山空心挂面制作工艺全靠师徒传承，长期实践后才能掌握。

岐山空心挂面工艺独特，配方考究，不含任何添加剂，以条细心空、耐煮不糊、营养高、易消化等特点闻名三秦内外。然而，近年来机械加工的面条对手工制作的挂面产生了很大的冲击，岐山空心挂面制作技艺急需得到保护和传承。

2007年，岐山空心挂面制作技艺被列入陕西省第一批非物质文化遗产名录。

their fineness, hollowness, pliability, high nutrition, easy digestion and other features. However, in recent years, machine-made noodles have had a great impact on hand-made noodles, and the skill of making Qishan hollow dried noodles is in urgent need of protection and inheritance.

In 2007, the skill of making Qishan hollow dried noodles was listed in the first batch of Shaanxi Provincial Intangible Cultural Heritage List.

秦镇米皮制作技艺
Skill of Making Qinzhen Rice Noodles

秦镇是陕西省西安市鄠邑区最东边的一个镇,距今已有3,000多年历史。秦镇的水土、气候条件适宜种植水稻,秦镇大米面皮正是这一丰腴之地特有的传统名牌饮食品种。秦镇大米面皮用料考究,制作精细,其制作过程如下:

选择上等大米,用清水浸泡30分钟,捞出后放置10小时左右,在石碾上碾成大米面粉,用细箩子箩面。用一定量的温水把大米面粉和成稀粥状,水

Qinzhen Town, with a history of more than 3,000 years, is the easternmost town in Huyi District of Xi'an City. The water, soil and climatic conditions of Qinzhen Town are suitable for planting rice, thus a traditional brand-name food, Qinzhen rice noodles, is widely made and gains popularity here. The making process of the rice noodles is as follows:

Soak rice of high quality in clean water for 30 minutes, then remove it from the water, and put it aside for about 10 hours. Grind it into rice flour on a stone mill, and sift the rice flour with a sieve. Add a certain amount of warm water into the rice flour, stir it until it becomes gruel-like liquid. The amount of warm water must be appropriate. If there is too much water, the steamed noodles will be too soft without elasticity; if the water is not enough, the steamed noodles will be thick without toughness. The water temperature should be properly controlled. If the temperature is too low, the noodles will be too hard and taste bad; if the temperature is too high, the noodles will not be chewy. The next step is to put a piece of clean wet cloth in a steamer, spread the gruel-like rice liquid of about 0.6 cm thick and smooth it on

不能多。水一多，蒸出来的面皮就会软塌塌的，没有弹性；水一少，面皮就厚而没有韧性。水温要合适，低了面皮太硬，口感不好；高了面皮不筋道，吃着无味。把干净的湿布铺在笼上，摊上米浆，约0.6厘米厚，抹平，上笼，用旺火蒸约10分钟即熟，取出晾凉。食用时，用约1米长、20厘米宽、5千克重的专用大铡刀，一手抵住面皮，一手端起铡刀，刀头按住不动，将面皮一刀一刀切成条状。

秦镇大米面皮色白如雪，光润如脂，页薄如纸，吃时调上红辣椒油、香醋、食盐、味精、蒜泥、酱油，并佐以焯熟的绿色菠菜叶和黄豆芽，具有筋、薄、细、软等特点，吃在口中，香在心里，回味无穷，男女老少都爱吃，一年四季皆宜。米皮有凉、热两种吃法，但不论凉吃或热吃，辣椒是其最上味的调

the wet cloth, then steam it on a hot fire. After about 10 minutes, take the sheets of rice out to cool when they are well-done. Finally cut the sheets of rice into strips with a special chopping knife that is nearly 1 meter in length, 20 centimeters in width, and 5 kilograms in weight. When cutting, one hand presses against the steamed rice sheets and one hand holds the knife to cut the rice sheets into strips.

Qinzhen rice noodles are as white as snow, as smooth as jelly, and as thin as paper. Before being served on the table, the rice noodles can be added with red chili oil, vinegar, salt, monosodium glutamate, mashed garlic, soy sauce, boiled green spinach leaves and soybean sprouts according to eaters' preference. The rice noodles boast characteristics of toughness, thinness, softness and so on, and are loved by people in different ages. The rice noodles usually serve as a cold dish, but can also be a hot dish. But no matter as a cold dish or a hot one, chili oil is the most flavorful and essential seasoning. If there is no red chili oil, the rice noodles will be less delicious. Therefore, the making of chili oil is particularly demanding, which includes the following procedures: Choosing the best red chilies, drying them under the sun, grinding them into powder, adding some sesame into the powder, then heating the oil until it's boiling, cooling the oil for about one minute and then pouring it into the chili powder. The temperature of the oil should

料，倘缺少了红油辣椒，便少了灵魂。因此，辣椒油的制作特别讲究。选用上等的红尖椒，晒干后磨成细面粉状，加一些芝麻，然后将油烧至沸腾，稍晾1分钟后泼在辣椒面上，以辣椒不变成黑色为最佳。

秦镇大米面皮是我国北方民间传统饮食中的典型代表品种之一，是一种深受群众喜爱的特色食品。

2007年，秦镇米皮制作技艺被列入陕西省第一批非物质文化遗产名录。

be well controlled so that the color of chili powder will not turn dark.

Qinzhen rice noodles, a kind of special food popular among the masses, are one of the typical representatives of traditional folk foods in northern China.

In 2007, the skill of making Qinzhen rice noodles was included in the first batch of Shaanxi Provincial Intangible Cultural Heritage List.

狄寨徐文岳泥哨制作技艺
Xu Wenyue's Craftsmanship of Making Clay Whistles

西安地区的泥哨制作起源于鱼化寨，已有数百年的历史。西安市灞桥区狄寨街道的徐文岳继承了鱼化寨泥哨制作的传统工艺，几十年来坚持不懈，使这一濒临灭绝的技艺获得新生。

徐文岳制作的泥哨是一种民间手工艺玩具。泥哨制作分为选土、和泥、做胎、通哨、烧制、彩绘六道工序，需要三四天才能完成。制作泥哨所需土质应细腻柔软，不易开裂。制作泥哨前，需制作模具。用模子做的泥人原型，经过几天的晾晒、烘烤后，再给它们画上眉毛、胡子和花花绿绿的衣服，这些泥人就变成了"赵子龙""姜子牙"或"二郎神"等。头上有窟窿的泥人，一吹就

The making of clay whistles in Xi'an City originates from Yuhuazhai and has a history of hundreds of years. Xu Wenyue, an artisan who lives in Dizhai Community, Baqiao District of Xi'an, has inherited the traditional craftsmanship of making clay whistles and has been striving for decades to bring this endangered skill to life.

The clay whistles made by Xu Wenyue are a kind of folk handicraft toy. Making clay whistles includes six procedures, namely selecting clay, making clay dough, modeling, making whistles soundable, firing, and painting, which take three to four days to be completed. The clay required for making clay whistles should be fine, soft and not easy to crack. Before making clay whistles, molds need to be made which are used to make clay figurines. The clay figurines made from molds are dried and baked for a few days and then eyebrows, beards and colorful clothes are painted to make them look like historical or legendary figures like Zhao Zilong, Jiang Ziya or Erlang God and so on. The clay figurine with a hole on its head can make a sound when it is blown—it is called "baby whistle". The clay figurine with a hole on one of its feet can't produce a sound—it is

可以发出声音,叫"娃娃哨"。窟窿在脚底下的泥人吹不响,只能插在祭祀盒子上面,叫"祭祀泥人",用于丧事送礼。

泥哨的种类有50～60种,多是传说中的神仙形象和戏剧人物形象,也有体形小巧的胖娃、小动物。泥哨的主要用途是娃娃当作玩具吹,同时可作为民间的祭祀品。由于其造型小巧,色彩绚丽,声音清脆响亮,颇受群众喜爱,特别是受到孩子们的喜爱。

徐文岳老人是目前唯一健在的泥哨制作艺人。现在徐文岳老人年事已高,泥哨制作技艺亟待保护、传承。

2007年,狄寨徐文岳泥哨制作技艺被列入陕西省第一批非物质文化遗产名录。

called "sacrificial clay figurine", which can only be inserted on the sacrificial box and be used as a funeral gift.

There are 50 to 60 types of clay whistles, which mostly range from legendary fairy images and drama characters to small fat babies and small animals. Clay whistles are mainly used as kids' toys and folk sacrifices. Because of their compact body, brilliant colors as well as clear and loud sound, they are quite popular among the masses, especially among children.

Xu Wenyue, a man of advanced age, is the only living artist who can make clay whistles. This craftsmanship needs to be protected and inherited with urgency.

In 2007, Xu Wenyue's craftsmanship of making clay whistles was included in the first batch of Shaanxi Provincial Intangible Cultural Heritage List.

狄寨竹篾子灯笼编织技艺
Craftsmanship of Making Dizhai Bamboo Strip Lanterns

西安市灞桥区狄寨竹篾子灯笼是具有鲜明地方特色的民间工艺品,已有300多年的历史。

狄寨地处西安东郊的白鹿原。这里的竹子是制作竹器的理想材质。民间艺人就地取材,利用这种优质竹子编织灯笼。编织前需先用篾刀把竹子划成细而匀的竹篾子,再编织成各种大小不同的灯笼造型,上面糊上红色彩纸,再装上可插蜡烛的圆木片,便可拿到集市上出售。

竹篾子灯笼有寡灯(即大灯)、中型灯、星星灯三种,所有灯笼都是用大红色皱纹纸贴面,而且只贴中间一部分,上下两边露出细致的竹篾子。每年春节时,寡灯或中型灯由娘家送给新婚出嫁的女儿;星星灯由舅舅送给外甥,以祈求平安吉祥、幸福美满。狄寨竹篾子灯笼在这种民俗活动中得以发展保存下来。狄寨街道办塘村的

Dizhai bamboo strip lanterns in Baqiao District of Xi'an City are a kind of folk crafts with distinctive local characteristics, having a history of more than 300 years.

Dizhai is located on Bailuyuan (the White Deer Plain) in the eastern suburb of Xi'an. The bamboo here is a good material for making bamboo utensils, and folk artists use the high-quality bamboo to make lanterns. Making bamboo strip lanterns involves the following procedures: First cut the bamboo into thin and even strips with a knife, weave the strips into lanterns of different shapes and sizes, then paste red paper on the lantern frame, and install a round wood chip inside the lantern for inserting a candle. Through such procedures, the hand-made lanterns can be sold in the market.

There are three types of bamboo strip lanterns, namely, the big lanterns, medium-sized lanterns, and star lanterns. All lanterns are veneered with red crepe paper—only the middle part is pasted, the upper and

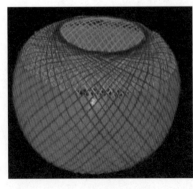

王学坤老人是当地一位手艺精湛的编织竹篾子灯笼的民间艺人。

现在从事竹篾子灯笼编织的人已寥寥无几，这一技艺急需抢救、保护，使之得以传承。

2007年，狄寨竹篾子灯笼编织技艺被列入陕西省第一批非物质文化遗产名录。

lower sides are uncovered so that delicate bamboo strips can be exposed. During the Spring Festival every year, big or medium-sized lanterns are given by the natal family to the newly married daughters, and the star lanterns are given by the uncle to the nephew to pray for peace, good fortune and happiness. Via such folk practices, craftsmanship of making Dizhai bamboo strip lanterns has been passed down from generation to generation. Wang Xuekun, an elderly man in Bantang Village of Dizhai Community, is a local folk artist who is skilled in making bamboo strip lanterns.

Nowadays, there are very few people engaged in making the bamboo strip lanterns, and the craftsmanship urgently needs to be rescued and protected so that it can survive.

In 2007, the craftsmanship of making Dizhai bamboo strip lanterns was included in the first batch of Shaanxi Provincial Intangible Cultural Heritage List.

凤翔草编技艺
Craftsmanship of Fengxiang Straw Plaiting

凤翔草编起源于北宋,迄今已有1,000多年历史。凤翔农村妇女利用农闲时间以当地盛产的麦秆、马莲为原料,做成草帽、提篮、坐垫、门帘等生活用品和屏风、吊篮、挂花等装饰用品。凤翔草编作品色泽明亮自然,质地结实,柔韧轻便,式样新颖独特,富于想象,深受国内外消费者的喜爱。

改革开放以来,凤翔草编又有了不少新品种,有山水风景、壁挂(配有山水、人物、花草、风景等)、风铃、立体小动物、节日礼品等10多个门类,共120多个品种。

凤翔草编在产生、发展、成熟的漫长历程中,已进入了当地民俗用品行

Fengxiang straw plaiting originated in the Northern Song Dynasty and has a history of more than 1,000 years. Rural women in Fengxiang County of Baoji City use straws which are abundant in the local area to make daily necessities such as straw hats, baskets, cushions, curtains and ornaments like screens, hanging baskets and hanging flowers. Fengxiang straw-plaited handicrafts are bright and natural in color, durable and pliable in texture, portable, novel, unique and imaginative in style, and are deeply loved by consumers at home and abroad.

Since the reform and opening-up, Fengxiang straw-plaited handicrafts have developed into more than 10 categories which amount to more than 120 varieties, such as ornaments of landscapes, wall hangings (with patterns of landscapes, figures, flowers and plants, scenery, etc.), wind bells, three-dimensional animals, festival gifts.

In the long process of birth, development and maturity, Fengxiang straw-plaited handicrafts, with strong regional characteristics, have been included in the local folk products and have become an indispensable part of local folk customs.

列，成为当地民俗中不可或缺的有机组成部分，具有极强的地域性特征。其从业者全部为当地农民，最初的消费者主要是西北地区的农民，具有纯粹的农村文化特征。草编制作者几乎全是农村妇女，成品具有极强的女性化倾向，具有女性文化特征。

近年来，由于几位老艺人相继去世，学习该项手艺的年轻人又大幅减少，凤翔草编处于濒危状态，亟待保护。

2007年，凤翔草编技艺被列入陕西省第一批非物质文化遗产名录。

All craftspeople are local peasants, and the original consumers of the straw-plaited handicrafts are mainly peasants in the northwestern region of China, therefore the handicrafts possess rural cultural characteristics. In addition, almost all craftspeople are rural women, thus the handicrafts also boast strong feminine cultural characteristics.

In recent years, the straw plaiting craftsmanship of Fengxiang is in an endangered state and needs protecting urgently as the few old artists have passed away successively and the number of young people who want to learn this skill has greatly decreased.

In 2007, this craftsmanship was included in the first batch of Shaanxi Provincial Intangible Cultural Heritage List.

阎良核雕技艺
Craftsmanship of Yanliang Peach Pit Carving

核雕，亦称果核雕刻，在我国有着悠久的历史。据名噪文坛的魏学伊的《核舟记》记载，核雕艺术在明代就已达到了博大与精细相结合的至高水平。传说桃木能驱邪灭灾，早在几千年前我们的祖先就用桃木刻制各种制品，以供人们佩戴。桃核亦是桃木，人们佩戴用桃核雕成的饰品，祈求吉祥、幸福和平安。贴身佩戴的时间越长，桃核就越光润漂亮，令人爱不释手。

我国的核雕技艺分南、北两大流派，两派又分出很多支脉。西安市的阎良核雕技艺属北派西安脉。此脉源于清朝同治年间的山东地区。该技艺流传至西安后，由我国著名核雕老艺人孙光明先生传授给阎良的赵秉科，遂形成此脉

Pit carving, also known as fruit pit carving, has a long history in China. According to Wei Xueyi's essay *A Boat Carved from a Peach Pit* which is well-known in the literary circles, the art of pit carving reached its highest level of combining profoundness and fineness in the Ming Dynasty. It is said that the peach wood can exorcise evil and calamity, so as early as thousands of years ago, Chinese people used the peach wood to make various things for people to wear. The peach pit also belongs to peach wood, so people wear ornaments carved from peach pits to pray for good luck, happiness and peace. The longer the peach pit is worn on the body, the smoother and more beautiful it will be.

Chinese pit carving craftsmanship can be divided into two major schools, namely, the northern school and southern school, and the two schools have many branches respectively. The pit carving craftsmanship in Yanliang District of Xi'an City belongs to Xi'an branch of the northern school. This branch originated in Shandong Province during the Tongzhi period of the Qing Dynasty. When the craftsmanship spread to Xi'an, it was taught to Zhao Bingke who lived in Yanliang by Sun Guangming, a well-known

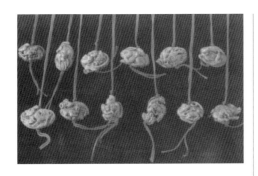

系，以桃核雕刻为主。桃核质地坚硬，不易破碎。雕刻刀具皆由创作者根据多年经验需要特制而成，有剜刀、刻刀、削刀、刮刀等。主要刀法有剜、刻、拨、挑、刮等十多种技法。

阎良核雕的工艺十分复杂。首先要备料，而备料则先要选择纹路清晰、质地良好的桃核，选好后要对桃核表面进行初步的清洗、消毒。为防止刻好的作品变形还要将其放入锅中蒸，然后对桃核表面再次进行仔细的清洗，除掉残余的果实杂质后，将其放置阴凉处晾干。然后根据桃核的纹路、大小进行构思雕刻，技艺熟练的可以直接下刀，不熟练的可以用铅笔勾画图形后再行下刀。雕刻时需要雕刻者眼、手、心合一，稍有差错都可能会前功尽弃。在雕刻的过程中，为了使桃核纹路清晰便于观察，需不断用核桃油刷洗。为了防止作品生虫，作品大致成型后还须用细针

pit carving veteran artist in China, and thus Xi'an branch formed, which mainly deals in peach pit carving. The peach pit is hard in texture and not easily broken. The carving knives are specially made in accordance with the carvers' experience and needs, including gouging knives, carving knives, paring knives, scraping knives, etc. There are more than 10 techniques of using knives, such as gouging, carving, plucking, scraping, and cutting.

The peach pit carving craftsmanship of Yanliang is very complicated. The first step is to process peach pits. The craftsmen need to choose peach pits with clear lines and good texture. After the selection, the surface of peach pits must be cleaned and disinfected. In order to avoid being deformed, peach pits should be steamed in a pot first, and then their surface should be carefully cleaned again to remove the remaining pulp impurities, and then the peach pits should be put in the shade to dry. Next, the carver conceives carving patterns according to the lines and size of the peach pit. If the carver is proficient, he can carve directly; and if the carver is a green hand, he can draw the patterns with a pencil and then starts to carve. While carving, the carver's eyes, hands, and heart should coordinate as even a slight mistake may lead to failure. In the course of carving, in order to make the lines of the peach pit clear and easy to be observed, it is necessary to brush the pit with walnut

将桃仁掏净。然后要用砂纸对成型作品进行细致的打磨，俗话称"三分刻，七分工"。这一环节对作品的面世尤为重要。打磨完后再用核桃油浸润擦拭，一件作品才算圆满完成。

阎良核雕技艺精湛。所雕人物只有米粒大小，五官清晰，造型生动；所刻的舟，船舱有门，船后有锚，锚链环环相扣，令人拍手叫绝。代表性作品有《陕西八大怪》《长安八景》《八仙过海》《渔家乐》《龙舟》等。

阎良核雕是立体微雕中美冠群芳的一绝，显示了我国传统工艺的悠久、博大、精深，是我国民族艺术宝库中的稀有瑰宝。

2007年，阎良核雕技艺被列入陕西省第一批非物质文化遗产名录。

oil from time to time. The peach pit must be cleaned with a needle after the work is roughly done so as to keep insects away from the carved work. Then, sandpaper should be used to polish the work carefully. This part is vital for the success of the work, just as the saying goes "a piece of exquisite carved work is done by 30 percent carving skill and 70 percent labor". After being polished, the carved peach pit should be soaked into and wiped with walnut oil again. Through such procedures, an art work is successfully completed.

The peach pit carving craftsmanship is superb and impresses people deeply. The carved figures with clear facial features and vivid shapes are only in the size of a rice grain; the carved boats are lifelike and amazing—even their doors and anchor chains are vividly and exquisitely carved. The representative carved works include *Eight Wonders in Shaanxi*, *Eight Sceneries in Chang'an*, *Eight Immortals Cross the Sea*, *Happiness of Fishermen*, *Dragon Boat* and so on.

The craftsmanship of Yanliang peach pit carving, which fully shows the richness and exquisiteness of traditional craftsmanship of China, represents the best three-dimensional micro-carving craftsmanship and the carved works are regarded as rare treasures in the national art treasure house of China.

In 2007, the craftsmanship was included in the first batch of Shaanxi Provincial Intangible Cultural Heritage List.

中华老字号德发长饺子制作技艺
Dumpling-Making Skill of China's Time-Honored Defachang Restaurant

德发长手工饺子是西安的特色饮食之一。德发长饺子馆由赵辑五先生创建于1936年。改革开放后，魏玉芳、马运生等几任总经理抓住机遇，大胆创新，将原来单一的饺子发展为融南北风味于一体的饺子宴、二十四节气饺子，并添加菜点以满足不同顾客的消费需求。经过几代人的不懈努力，德发长饺子馆现已发展成为全国餐饮业的品牌企业。

德发长饺子在选料上坚持"好"字，制作流程上坚持"精"字，口味上坚持"特"字。饺子宴博采众长，将选料与多味、烹饪与营养、形态与艺术、饮食与文化等巧妙地融合，具有"一饺一形一态，百饺百馅百味"的特点。饺

The handmade dumplings of Defachang Restaurant are one of the special diets in Xi'an City. Defachang Dumpling House was founded in 1936 by Mr. Zhao Jiwu. After China's reform and opening-up, several general managers such as Wei Yufang and Ma Yunsheng seized opportunities and boldly innovated to develop the original single-type dumplings into dumpling feasts with a combination of flavors in northern and southern China and dumplings themed on China's twenty-four solar terms. In addition, they also added dishes and desserts to meet needs of different customers. With the unremitting efforts of several generations, Defachang Dumpling House now develops into a brand enterprise in China's catering industry.

Defachang dumplings stick to the word "good" in the selection of materials, the word "fine" in the making process, and the word "special" in the taste. The dumplings feasts integrate strengths of other cuisines, blending ingredients with flavors, cooking with nutrition, form with art, food with culture, etc., which boast the characteristics of "one dumpling having one form, and 100 dumplings having 100 kinds of fillings and 100 flavors". The

子造型千姿百态，花鸟虫鱼栩栩如生，制作上综合了捏塑、雕塑、组合、点缀等技艺，每一款饺子的造型都与现代艺术巧妙地结合在一起。二十四节气饺子，是依照我国古代创立的"四季二十四节气"学说，选用每一个节气里最先长成、最为鲜嫩、最具有营养价值的动植物性食物作为原料制作而成的时令饺子。

德发长饺子充分体现了中华民族的勤劳智慧和非凡的创造力，寄托着老百姓期盼团圆、追求祥和的美好心愿。作为广受海内外人们喜爱的中华传统美食，德发长饺子不仅沟通着人们的情感，而且有助于世界人民了解中华传统文化的精髓——"和合"文化。

2007年，中华老字号德发长饺子制作技艺被列入陕西省第一批非物质文化遗产名录。

dumplings are in various shapes, such as lifelike flowers, birds, insects and fish. The making skills integrate kneading, sculpturing, matching, embellishing and other techniques. The shape of each kind of dumplings is cleverly combined with modern art. The dumplings of twenty-four solar terms are seasonal dumplings made according to China's twenty-four solar terms, the fillings being the freshest and most nutritious meat and vegetables available in each solar term.

Defachang dumplings fully embody the industriousness, wisdom and extraordinary creativity of the Chinese nation, and convey people's good wish for reunion and harmony. As a traditional Chinese food deeply loved by people at home and abroad, the food not only promotes people's relations, but also helps people around the world understand the essence of traditional Chinese culture — harmony and unity.

In 2008, the dumpling-making skill of Defachang Restaurant was included in the first batch of Shaanxi Provincial Intangible Cultural Heritage List.

中华老字号张记馄饨制作技艺
Skill of Making China's Time-Honored Zhang's Wontons

陕西省咸阳市的中华老字号张记馄饨已有近百年历史,其传统手工制作技艺也一直流传至今。

张记馄饨皮由手工擀制而成,皮薄透亮,筋斗耐煮;肉馅刀剁棒捶,细腻黏润;包捏的馄饨,形状美观;鸡骨汤经数小时大火煮、小火炖,汤鲜味美不油腻。馄饨盛入碗中,浇上鲜美的鸡骨汤,还要放上虾皮、紫菜、香菜、榨菜、韭黄、蒜苗等十多种佐餐的菜蔬,

Zhang's wontons in Xianyang City, a kind of time-honored Chinese brand, have a history of nearly one hundred years, and the traditional hand-making skill of this food has been passed up to now.

The wrappers of Zhang's wontons, which are thin, translucent, chewy and good-looking, are hand-made with a rolling pin; the meat filling is made by knife chopping and stick beating—it is smooth and sticky; the chicken bone soup is boiled on high heat for several hours and then stewed on low heat—it is delicious and not greasy. When the wontons are cooked and ladled into bowls, they are added with some delicious chicken bone soup, topped with dried little shrimps as well as over ten kinds of vegetables like nori, coriander, pickled mustard tuber, hotbed chives, garlic sprouts, etc. Lastly, thin chicken shreds are added. The hot wontons in the bowl are beautiful in color and shape, like goldfish, butterflies, gold ingots, ancient official hats .... The food is rich in nutrients, good for health, and has a good aftertaste. Traditionally, Zhang's wontons are soup wontons. Besides, according to the needs and tastes of different customers, the cooks also use a variety of cooking methods to serve boiled,

最后放入细细的鸡肉丝。一碗热腾腾的馄饨似金鱼戏水,又似蝴蝶飞舞,似水中元宝,又似古时官帽……真可谓色香味形俱佳,营养丰富,强身健骨,食后回味无穷。张记馄饨以传统带汤馄饨为主,同时根据不同顾客的需要,还采用多种加工制作方法,制作出水煮、生煎和蒸笼馄饨等品种。

张记馄饨是咸阳的著名特色小吃,当地有"汤鲜味美馄饨张"的说法。张记馄饨不但深受当地民众的喜爱,而且在西北地区乃至全国也颇有名气。

2007年,中华老字号张记馄饨制作技艺被列入陕西省第一批非物质文化遗产名录。

fried and steamed wontons.

Zhang's wontons are a kind of famous special snack in Xianyang City, and there goes a popular saying that "Zhang's wontons make your mouth water ". They are not only loved by the local people, but are also quite famous in the northwestern China, and even the whole country.

In 2007, Zhang's wonton-making skill was included in the first batch of Shaanxi Provincial Intangible Cultural Heritage List.

同盛祥牛羊肉泡馍制作技艺
Skill of Cooking Pita Bread Soaked in Beef or Mutton Soup of Tongshengxiang Restaurant

同盛祥牛羊肉泡馍是西安最具特色的清真美食。牛羊肉泡馍有着悠久的历史。《诗经》中就有记载，西周时周人祭祀祖先时"献羔祭韭"，年终举行宴会是"朋酒斯飨，日杀羔羊"的礼仪风俗。明崇祯年间，西安就已有了第一家专营牛羊肉泡馍的"天锡楼"。1920年，回民张文祥兄弟三人在竹笆市南头开设泡馍馆，定名"同盛祥"。

同盛祥牛羊肉泡馍的制作工艺十分考究，从选料、煮肉、熬汤、加料、调味到泡馍，始终坚持做到精细、标准、规范。其制作方法是：将泡洗净的牛羊

The time-honored food—pita bread soaked in beef or mutton soup cooked by Tongshengxiang Restaurant is the most distinctive Muslim cuisine in Xi'an. In *The Book of Songs*, it is recorded that during the Western Zhou Dynasty, Zhou people sacrificed mutton and leek to worship their ancestors; and in the end of the year, mutton is a must in the banquet for people to treat their friends. In the Ming Dynasty, Xi'an had the first restaurant named Tianxi Restaurant that specialized in cooking pita bread soaked in beef or mutton soup. In 1920, the Hui people Zhang Wenxiang brothers ran a restaurant named Tongshengxiang in Zhuba Street of Xi'an, which specialized in cooking this kind of food.

Cooks of Tongshengxiang Restaurant cook pita bread soaked in beef or mutton soup in a very sophisticated way. All the cooking procedures, from selecting materials, cooking meat, braising soup, adding ingredients, seasoning to shredding pita bread, are elaborate and standardized. The cooking methods are as follows. First, put clean mutton or beef into bone soup, add a variety of seasonings; boil the soup with high heat, then slowly simmer it with

low heat until the meat is well done and the soup is thick; shred the pita bread into small pieces like peas and put them into the soup with precooked mutton or beef as well as vermicelli; then sprinkle some coriander. When the food is done and served to customers, sugared garlic and chilli sauce can be added to make the food more tasteful.

肉放入骨头汤中，加入装有多种调料的料包，先用大火煮开，再用文火慢炖，至肉烂汤浓。泡馍时需把烙成的饦饦馍掰成豌豆粒大小，与牛肉或羊肉、粉丝一同放入肉汤中煮，再撒上香菜，吃时佐以糖蒜和辣椒酱。

同盛祥牛羊肉泡馍以其"料重味醇，肉烂汤浓，馍筋光滑，香气四溢，口味纯正"的独特风味闻名古城，长期以来深受陕西乃至西北人民的喜爱。

The shredded pita bread in beef or mutton soup cooked by Tongshengxiang Restaurant is very famous in Xi'an and is deeply loved by people in Shaanxi even in northwestern China for its unique flavor of "well-cooked meat, thick soup, chewy pita bread, lingering aroma and good taste".

牛羊肉泡馍具有鲜明的民族饮食特色和独特的地域风味，在全国久负盛名。近百年来，同盛祥饭庄在继承传统的基础上继续创新发展，使牛羊肉泡馍在色、香、

Pita bread soaked in beef or mutton soup in Tongshengxiang boasts distinctive national dietary characteristics and unique regional flavor, and has been very popular throughout the country. In the recent one

味、形等各方面都有了很大的提高，成为陕西最具清真风味的代表性饮食。

2008年，同盛祥牛羊肉泡馍制作技艺被列入第二批国家级非物质文化遗产名录。

hundred years, Tongshengxiang Restaurant has continued to innovate and develop this food on the basis of inheriting traditions so that the color, aroma, taste and shape of the food have been greatly improved and it has become one of the most representative Muslim diets in Shaanxi.

In 2008, the cooking skill of pita bread soaked in beef or mutton soup of Tongshengxiang was included in the second batch of China's National Intangible Cultural Heritage List.

蒲城杆火技艺
Technology of Making Pucheng Pole Fireworks

蒲城杆火多见于陕西省渭南市蒲城县荆姚镇雷坊村，是目前唯一存世的宫廷低空焰火的母体形态，为该村李氏家族传人掌握。据专家研究，蒲城县的火药生产源于唐宋，杆火则兴于金元，盛于明清，距今已有近千年历史。

蒲城杆火主要用铁棍、竹条等材料做成架子（火斗），支撑火斗的底架为木杆，火斗上安装爆竹、花筒等，外表用彩纸装潢。蒲城杆火全部为手工制作，工艺繁复。杆火以蒲城盛产的硫磺、芒硝、柳木炭为主原料，白糖、蓝墨水、酱油也是必备原料，按比例配制，配好火药后将其装入按需要卷好的大小不同的花筒内，封口，待用；然后以精湛的纸扎造型、秘不示人的火线布

Pucheng pole fireworks are very common in Leifang Village, Jingyao Town, Pucheng County of Weinan City. The fireworks are the only surviving prototype of the royal low-altitude fireworks and the firework-making technology is mastered by the descendants of the Li's family in the village. According to experts' study, the production of gunpowder in Pucheng County originated in the Tang and Song dynasties, and pole fireworks came into existence in the Jin and Yuan dynasties, flourished in the Ming and Qing dynasties, having a history of about 1,000 years.

The supporting frame (called *huodou*) of the pole firework is mainly made of iron rods, bamboo strips and other materials. *Huodou* is supported by a wooden pole and installed with firecrackers, fireworks, etc., and its surface is decorated with colored paper. The pole fireworks are completely handmade, featuring quite complicated craftsmanship. Sulfur, thenardite, and willow charcoal that are abundant in Pucheng are used as the main raw materials of the pole fireworks. In addition, sugar, blue ink, and soy sauce are also essential materials. The materials are prepared in proportion, then are filled into firework

tubes of different sizes and sealed. Then the fireworks are decorated exquisitely with paper, installed with blasting fuse, and fastened on the frame. The pole fireworks are mainly divided into two categories: the *wen* fireworks and the *wu* fireworks. Most of the *wen* and *wu* fireworks are 4 to 12 meters high and each one takes 3 to 5 days to make. The production of some fireworks are very complicated which takes several months to complete. When being set off, the *wen* fireworks display various shapes and patterns without producing any sound, while the *wu* fireworks not only show different shapes and patterns, but also make thundering sounds.

Pucheng pole fireworks create magnificent scenes, which combine splendor of sound, light and color, and can artistically present rich and different patterns like beautiful mountains and rivers, images in folk tales, myths and legends, places of interest, historical figures, architectures and so on. The firework images in the night sky are vivid, brilliant, colorful, changeable, dazzling and dreamlike, which have won the name "a wonder of China". When set off, the pole fireworks are automatically ignited by the rocket-shaped fuse, which is lit by the most distinguished guest or host present.

局和骨架扎结，制成文、武杆火。一般的文、武杆火高4～12米，一杆火需要3～5天制作，有些杆火制作繁杂，需要数月方可完成。文杆没有声音只燃放造型礼花，武杆在燃放造型礼花的同时还有雷鸣般的响声。

蒲城杆火场面宏大，气势恢宏，燃放时具有声、光、色俱全的特点，可以展现秀美山川、民间故事、神话传说、名胜古迹、时代人物、建筑造型等相关内容的艺术造型。在夜空中燃放的杆火形象逼真，璀璨夺目，五光十色，变化无穷，令人眼花缭乱，如梦如幻，堪称"中华一绝"。燃放杆火时，用"码子"（火箭式导火索）自动点火燃放，而"码子"由在场的最尊贵的嘉宾或主人点燃。燃放杆火时首先以火船、火马等为开场花火，火船、火马一般有人驾驶，在全场跑动，渲染气氛，然后依次燃放文火、武火。

蒲城杆火历史悠久，形式独特，具有很高的历史文化研究价值。杆火有着很大的市场前景，作为一种焰火艺术，可为大型活动、旅游项目表演服务，具有经济效益。杆火展示了中华民族古老的文明，可以让世界了解中华焰火文化的神奇，让世界了解中国深厚的文化。

2008年，这一民间技艺被列入第二批国家级非物质文化遗产名录。

The firework show begins with fireworks in shapes of boats and horses, which are usually driven by people and move around the whole venue to render the atmosphere; then the *wen* and *wu* pole fireworks are set off in turn.

Pucheng pole fireworks feature a long history, unique form, high historical and cultural research value, and significant market prospects. The fireworks can be displayed for large-scale activities and tourism projects to create economic benefit. Moreover, the pole-firework making technology shows the ancient civilization of the Chinese nation, which enable people across the world to understand the magic of Chinese fireworks and the profoundness of Chinese culture.

In 2008, Pucheng pole-firework making technology was included in the second batch of China's Intangible Cultural Heritage List.

太白酒酿造技艺
Brewing Technology of Taibai Liquor

陕西省宝鸡市眉县酿酒历史悠久。根据历史记载，东汉灵帝时扶风郡眉人孟陀以眉地产酒为礼送于当朝权贵张让，后就任凉州刺史，亦将酿酒技艺带到凉州，带动了当地酒业的兴起。

太白酒酿造的基本技艺流程有制曲、发酵、蒸馏、贮存四个步骤。太白酒不同于其他酒的特殊生产环节有以下三个：

1. 特殊大曲。其他白酒一般用一种大曲作为糖化发酵剂，而太白酒在制作过程中用了三种大曲，各种大曲原料相同，但在制曲过程中由于控制条件不同而有了差异。

Liquor brewing in Meixian County of Baoji City has a long history. According to historical records, during the reign of Emperor Ling in the Eastern Han Dynasty, Yu Tuo, a native of Fufeng County, gifted the local liquor to Zhang Rang, an influential official in the imperial court, and then he got the post of the governor of Liangzhou. He brought liquor brewing skill to Liangzhou, which led to the rise of the local liquor industry.

The basic brewing process of Taibai liquor includes four steps: yeast making, fermentation, distillation and storage. Taibai liquor production differs from other liquor production in the following three ways.

The first one is the special yeasts. Usually one kind of yeast is used as the saccharification ferment in liquor making, while three types of yeasts are used in Taibai liquor production. Although the raw materials of the three kinds of yeasts are the same, the yeasts have different functions due to different control conditions in the yeast making process.

The second one is fermentation in the earthen pits. Generally, stone pits and pottery vats are often used as places or containers for fermentation, while

2. 土暗窖发酵。一般白酒发酵多用石窖、地缸等作为发酵池，而太白酒则采用土暗窖进行发酵。建窖土坯很有特色，工序多，周期长，经过上百次的人力拍打，形成了独特的韧性，不仅保证了窖池的正常发酵，而且为微生物提供了一个良好的栖息之地。再加上每年换一次窖泥，为微生物的新陈代谢提供了必要的条件。

3. 特制酒海。太白酒使用的酒海不同于一般的储酒容器。酒海是用秦岭生长的藤条编织而成，里边用猪血、石灰、麻纸裱糊上百层，再打上蜂蜡、清油、鸡蛋清，真可谓一个纸糊的容器。正是酒海贮存赋予了太白酒独特的味道。酒海营造了一个弱碱性环境，用它贮存基酒，酒质老熟快，并把酒海味浸入酒中。这是祖辈相传的容器，一个酒海的使用寿命可长达上百年。

earthen pits are used for Taibai liquor fermentation. The adobe used to build the cellar is made through many procedures within a long period. After hundreds of times of manual beating, the adobe has a unique toughness, which not only ensures fermentation, but provides a good habitat for microorganisms. Besides, changing the mud in the cellar once a year provides the necessary conditions for the metabolism of microorganisms.

The third one is special container for liquor storage. The storage container used for Taibai liquor is different from others. They are woven from the rattan grew in Qinling Mountains. The inside of the container is pasted with over a hundred layers of pig blood, lime, and hemp paper, and then topped with beeswax, vegetable oil, and egg white. It is the special container that endows Taibai liquor with its unique taste. With a weak alkaline environment, the container is used to store the base liquor so that the liquor matures quickly, and the flavour of the container can be infused into the liquor. The liquor containers are passed down from generation to generation, and their life span can be as long as more than a hundred years.

Before 1956, Taibai liquor was produced in traditional methods and by experience, staying at the workshop-style stage. Since 1956, the production model has changed gradually and machines have been employed to enhance productivity, but at

自产生至1956年以前,太白酒完全沿用传统方法,凭经验进行生产,停留在作坊式阶段。1956年之后才逐步改变生产模式,加入机械元素,但仍坚持在关键环节运用传统手工艺进行操作,在提高生产效率的同时又保证了太白酒的独特性。

2009年,太白酒酿造技艺被列入陕西省第二批非物质文化遗产名录。

crucial stages the traditional methods have still been used to ensure the uniqueness of the liquor.

In 2009, the brewing technology of Taibai liquor was included in the second batch of Shaanxi Intangible Cultural Heritage List.

陈仓传统银器制作技艺
Traditional Craftsmanship of Making Chencang Silverware

陈仓传统银器制作技艺是陕西省的传统手工技艺，多见于宝鸡市陈仓区慕仪镇东城村。大约在明末清初，这里就有了银器制作加工技术和银匠，距今已有400多年的历史。这里的银器名扬西北，销售到西安、银川、兰州等地。

陈仓传统银器的制作工序有十道。

第一步熔化银水：将银块、碎银放入坩埚，用木炭烧到一定温度后，银子化成银水。第二步浇铸毛坯：将银水倒入铸铁的油槽（即模具）中，制成银毛坯。第三步打叶出条拉丝：根据需要把银毛坯加热，用铁锤在铁砧上将其打制成薄片，叫"出叶"；把银毛坯搓成圆柱，叫"出条"；把银条用专用工具拉

The craftsmanship of making silverware mastered by the folks in Chencang is one of the traditional manual skills in Shaanxi Province. The craftsmanship mainly prevails in Dongcheng Village, Muyi Town, Chencang District of Baoji City. Silversmiths and silverware-making craftsmanship appeared here around the end of Ming Dynasty and early Qing Dynasty, which has a history of over 400 years. The silverware is famous in the northwest of China and has been sold to Xi'an City, Yinchuan City, Lanzhou City and other surrounding places.

The traditional silverware-making process of Chencang includes the following ten steps.

The first step is to melt the silver lump. Put silver bars and lumps into a crucible, heat the crucible with charcoal until the silver bars and lumps turn into silver water. The second step is to cast blank. Pour the silver water into the mold (an oil groove made of cast iron) to make a silver blank. The third step is to heat the silver blanks according to the need, then put them on an anvil and beat them into thin flakes with an iron hammer—this procedure is called making silver flakes; roll the silver blanks into cylinders—

成丝，叫"拉丝"。第四步冲压出形：把银片放在用锡制成的模具中，用锤敲打，冲压出银器的基本轮廓，此道工序也叫"括形"。第五步上胶版：把松香、清油等制成胶泥，把胶泥涂在木板上约1厘米厚，用木炭烤胶泥，待胶泥松软，将银器大形压在胶版上即可。第六步錾花：用专用小钢钎及相关工具在银器大形上砸出山水花鸟、福禄寿禧等各类花纹。这一道工序是银器制作工艺中最复杂、技术含量最高的。花形图案在匠人的心里，心到手到，心手合一，一幅幅精美的图画便雕在银器的大形上。第七步焊接：按照银器的形状需要，把相关部件焊接起来，装饰上花纹。第八步打磨抛光：把成形的容器放在响铜制成的小砧子上，用小榔头轻轻敲打，用钢锉打去毛边，使银器表面光滑发亮。第九步美化去污：把制好的银器放在稀

such a procedure is called making silver cylinder; pull the silver blanks into silver wires with a special tool—it is called making silver wire. The fourth step is to stamp out the general pattern. Put the silver flakes in a mold made of tin, beat it with a hammer to stamp out the basic shape of the silverware, which is also called "shaping". The fifth step is to apply the glue plate. Make a special glue with rosin, vegetable oil, etc., spread the glue on the wooden board about one-centimeter thick, heat the glue with burning charcoal until it is softened, and press the silverware model on the glue plate. The sixth step is to carve patterns. Use special tools to carve various patterns such as landscape, flowers, birds, and Chinese characters like "*Fu, Lu, Shou, Xi*" (represent blessing, promotion, longevity, and happiness respectively) on the silverware, which is the most complex step with the highest technical content in the silverware making process. The silversmith's ingenious design and exquisite techniques breed exquisite patterns on the silverware. The seventh step is to weld. According to the design and shape of the silverware, relevant parts are welded together, then patterns are decorated. The eighth step is to polish. Put the silverware on a small anvil made of copper, gently beat it with a small hammer, remove the burrs with a steel file to make the surface of the silverware smooth and shiny. The ninth step is decontamination. Put the silverware in

硫酸或白矾水中清除霉斑和污垢。第十步上翠点蓝：把银器专用颜料研成面，用小汤匙点在银器上，点燃煤油灯，把银器靠近火焰，用吹筒吹火焰，使银与颜料互相粘连在一起。

通过以上主要工序，一件精美的银器就完成了。

陈仓传统银器以其质地纯正、做工精细、图案优美、色泽明亮而闻名。陈仓银器制品蕴含着丰富的民间文化和民间习俗，寄托着人们热爱生命、追求美好生活的理想和愿望，具有很高的金属工艺美术价值和审美价值。

2009年，陈仓传统银器制作技艺被列入陕西省第二批非物质文化遗产名录。

dilute sulfuric acid or alum water to remove mildew and dirt. The tenth step is coloring. Grind the special pigment for silverware into powder, sprinkle it on the silverware with a small spoon, ignite the kerosene lamp, put the silverware close to the flame of the lamp, blow the flame with a blowing tube to make the silver and the pigment stick to each other.

Through the above main procedures, a piece of exquisite silverware is done.

Chencang traditional silverware, which contains rich folk culture and folk customs and reflects people's love of life and longing for a better life, is famous for its pure texture, fine workmanship, beautiful patterns, bright color, as well as high aesthetic value.

In 2009, the traditional craftsmanship of making Chencang silverware was included in the second batch of Shaanxi Provincial Intangible Cultural Heritage List.

张氏风筝制作技艺
Zhang's Craftsmanship of Making Kites

张氏风筝制作是西安张天伟的独特技艺。张天伟从小受家庭影响酷爱风筝。张氏风筝的骨架以传统竹材为主，对竹材的选用有严格要求，必须有三至五年生长期，要密度好、弹性好、竹节长。绑扎线以细线或麻为主。蒙面材料为洋纺绸、丝绢、薄尼龙绸，但事先必须经上浆处理。绘画颜料根据风筝主题以及大小不同可选用丙烯、品色（碱性染料）、荧光色等。因张氏风筝增加了机械传动装置，所以在材料选用上又增加了

Zhang's craftsmanship of making kites is a unique skill mastered by Zhang Tianwei who lives in Xi'an City. Zhang Tianwei, influenced by his family, has deeply loved kites since his childhood. The framework of Zhang's kites is mainly made of bamboo pieces, and the bamboos are meticulously selected, which must have a growth period of three to five years, with good density, nice elasticity and long bamboo joints. The binding thread is mainly thin thread or linen thread. The covering materials are silk fabric, tiffany and thin nylon silk, which must be starched in advance. According to the theme and size of the kite, the paints used to color the kite include acrylic, magenta (a kind of basic dye), etc. As some mechanical transmission devices are used in Zhang's kites, materials like aluminum alloy, copper or stainless steel sheets, various metal wires, bakelite plates, etc., are also used. The binders used to stick the kite framework mainly include high-quality white latex, 502 glue, AB glue, all-purpose adhesive, etc.

The making process of Zhang's kites are as follows. First, draw the sketch of a kite according to a conceived theme, design the dynamic parts, and draw the components

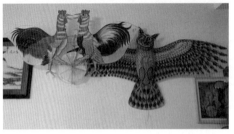

一些铝合金、铜或不锈钢薄板、各种金属丝、胶木板等。风筝骨架的黏结剂主要采用优质白乳胶、502胶、AB胶、万能胶等。

张氏风筝的基本制作过程是：首先根据设想的主题按比例画出图纸，设计动态部位，并画出零部件图。再根据风筝骨架各部分特点劈成不同粗细薄厚的竹条，依照图纸将各部位竹条在酒精灯上烤弯，做成所需形状，然后绑扎成形。与此同时，要进行机械传动零部件的精细加工，之后将二者合一，方完成风筝骨架的制作。其次将丝绸面料逐块平整地裱糊到风筝骨架上。接着根据风

and parts of the kite. Then, according to the characteristics of each part of the kite framework, cut bamboo into strips in different width and thickness, bake and bend the bamboo strips into the required shapes on the alcohol lamp according to the drawings, then tie the strips into a frame. At the same time, the mechanical transmission parts should be meticulously processed and fixed. Next, combine the bamboo frame and the mechanical transmission parts to complete the kite framework. The following step is to evenly paste the silk fabric or other covering materials onto the kite framework, then beautify the kite with the above mentioned paints according to the type of the kite (some kites are painted first and then pasted). Finally tie the leading

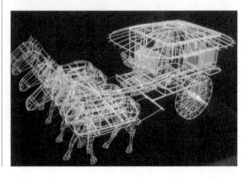

筝类别用颜料加以美化（有些风筝是先画后糊）。最后拴好风筝的引线，等待放飞。

"张氏风筝"享誉国内外，不仅具有很高的艺术欣赏价值，有一定科技含量，而且具有极高的收藏价值与经济价值。

2009年，张氏风筝制作技艺被列入陕西省第二批非物质文化遗产名录。

string to the kite, then a marvelous work of art is done.

Zhang's kites, with certain technological content, are well-known at home and abroad. They not only possess high artistic value, but also have high collection and economic value.

In 2009, Zhang's craftsmanship of making kites was included in the second batch of Shaanxi Provincial Intangible Cultural Heritage List.

武功手织布技艺
Hand-Weaving Craftsmanship of Wugong Cloth

陕西省咸阳市武功县的手织布起源于后稷"教民稼穑"之后。早在东晋时期，武功才女苏蕙因织出的《璇玑图》名扬天下。数千年来，手织布技艺遍及武功各乡村，祖祖辈辈传承至今。

武功手织布技艺全凭手工操作，靠经验、悟性和长期实践才能掌握。其技艺复杂，约有72道工序，主要包括四方面。一是纺线，即先用棉花搓捻子，再在纺车上纺出细细的白线。二是把纺锭上卸下的线穗子上的线上拐、成束、

The hand-woven cloth in Wugong County of Xianyang City came into being after Hou Ji who is regarded as the God of Agriculture in China taught people to plant and harvest crops. As early as the Eastern Jin Dynasty, the talented woman Su Hui who lived in Wugong County woven *Xuanji Tu* (841 Chinese characters on a piece of brocade, which can constitute different poems by reading in different ways). Due to this piece of hand-woven work, she gained great reputation. For thousands of years, the hand-weaving craftsmanship of cloth has been circulated throughout the villages in Wugong County, and has been passed down from generation to generation.

The hand-woven cloth of Wugong County is completely done by hands, therefore in a large part weavers have to rely on experience, understanding and long time practice to master the cloth-weaving craftsmanship. The craftsmanship is complicated, including about 72 procedures that can be categorized into four major steps. The first step is to spin cotton into thread. The cotton is twisted into thick strips first and then the cotton strips are spun into threads with the spinning wheel. The second step is to twine the threads

浆洗、晾干，缠成线筒子。三是进行"经线"工艺组合，设计配色型，俗称"经布"，然后再梳理经线，俗称"刷布"。四是把经线滚子架上织机织布。

武功手织布的质感润柔，图案别致，细密平整，纹理清晰，有吸汗保暖、环保健康的特点。千百年来，武功手织布对农耕文化的发展和中华文明的延续具有重要作用。

2009年，武功手织布技艺被列入陕西省第二批非物质文化遗产名录。

removed from the spindle into bundles, then wash and dry the thread bundles, and finally wind the threads in each bundle onto thread bobbins. The third step is to design the color matching pattern by matching warps of different colors, and then comb the warp threads. The fourth step is to put the warp thread bobbins on the loom to weave cloth.

The hand-woven cloth of Wugong County boasts unique and clear patterns as well as fine and smooth texture. It can absorb sweat, keep warm, and is environmental-friendly and good for health. For thousands of years, the hand-woven cloth has played an important role in the development of Chinese farming culture and the continuation of Chinese civilization.

In 2009, the hand-weaving craftsmanship of Wugong cloth was included in the second batch of Shaanxi Provincial Intangible Cultural Heritage List.

普集烧鸡制作技艺
Skill of Cooking Puji Braised Chicken

陕西省咸阳市武功县普集烧鸡制作技艺的创始人是河南人郭志平。1940年，为避战乱，郭志平携带家眷来到武功县普集镇投友定居，以祖传清宫烧鸡技艺谋生。因普集镇火车站人流量大，烧鸡被旅客带到四面八方，因而定名为普集烧鸡。

普集烧鸡香酥鲜嫩，色味俱佳，名声远扬，其制作工艺极为讲究。首先要严格选鸡，一般选用一年生的嫩鸡，严禁使用病鸡、死鸡。宰杀时要让鸡血流净，脱毛时要水温适中。宰好的白条鸡用清水冲洗，并在凉水中浸泡六个小时后再用大火油炸。油炸时火候逐渐由大到小，要保持皮黄色亮。调料要用优质的干姜、花椒、桂皮、丁香等。配好

The cooking skill of Puji braised chicken in Wugong County of Xianyang City was originated by Guo Zhiping who came from Henan Province. In 1940, in order to avoid war, he brought his family to Puji Town of Wugong County to settle down because his friend lived there, where he made a living by braising chicken with the skill which his ancestors used to braise chicken for the imperial family. Due to the large flow of people at the train station in Puji Town, the braised chickens were taken by passengers to different places, so this food was named Puji braised chicken.

Puji braised chicken, characterized by crispiness, tenderness, good color and delicious taste, enjoys a widespread reputation. The cooking process is very demanding. First of all, it is important for the cook to strictly select chickens. Generally, the one-year-old chickens are preferable. Sick and dead chickens are contraindicated. After being slaughtered, the chickens' blood must be drained, and the water temperature should be moderate when depilating the chickens. Rinse the depilated chickens with clean water, soak them in cold water for six hours, and then deep-fry them with high heat. During

调料后再将少许冰糖放入加水的原汁汤中，再把炸过的鸡入锅，先大火烧开，再以小火慢卤，使料味渐入肉内。烧鸡煮熟后捞出，再涂上香油，以保持鸡肉原色。做烧鸡的原汁汤，俗称陈年老汤。据说郭志平当年来武功时，担子里就有一个密封的陶瓷罐，内盛陈年鸡汤，汤内有党参、人参、天麻、丁香等多种原料。

普集烧鸡制作技艺主要流传于武功县普集镇。现在武功县已采取措施保护普集烧鸡制作技艺，使之得以传承。

2009年，普集烧鸡制作技艺被列入陕西省第二批非物质文化遗产名录。

frying, the heat needs to be gradually turned down and the skins of chickens should keep yellow and bright. The seasonings include high-quality dried ginger, Chinese red pepper, cinnamon, clove and so on. After adding seasonings, put a little rock sugar, some water and the fried chicken into the stock. Boil the chicken on high heat, and then slowly stew it on low heat to make the flesh gradually have the flavors of the seasonings. After the chicken is cooked, take it out of the pot and coat it with sesame oil to maintain its original color. The stock for braising chicken is commonly known as the "aged soup". It is said that when Guo Zhiping came to Wugong County, he took a sealed ceramic pot with him, in which the aged chicken soup was stored. The soup contained codonopsis, ginseng, gastrodia, cloves and other ingredients.

The skill of cooking Puji braised chicken is mainly mastered by cooks in Puji Town of Wugong County. Now the authority of Wugong County has taken measures to protect this skill and tried to make it be inherited.

In 2009, the skill was included in the second batch of Shaanxi Provincial Intangible Cultural Heritage List.

咸阳琥珀糖制作技艺
Skill of Making Xianyang Amber Candy

陕西省咸阳市生产的琥珀糖是一种具有地方特色的著名食品。琥珀糖的历史悠久,相传秦时吕不韦制出琥珀糖为秦始皇之母治气管炎。琥珀糖在民间盛行于清末,曾一度成为最具代表性的咸阳特产,誉满三秦。

琥珀糖的制作十分讲究。首先要选用上等的小米和大麦芽熬制饴糖备用。制作琥珀糖时,要先将制好的饴糖化开。化糖是一项技术活,完全靠的是经验和感觉。在锅中熬制饴糖时,火候掌握不好易糊锅,做出的琥珀糖就会口味不佳,颜色发黑,没有光泽。搅糖是一道非常费体力的工序。随着糖逐渐化

The amber candy produced in Xianyang City is a famous and special food with local features. Legend has it that Lü Buwei, a famous politician in the end of the Warring States Period, made the amber candy to treat Qin Shihuang's (the first emperor of the Qin Dynasty) mother who suffered from bronchitis. The amber candy prevailed among the people in the late Qing Dynasty and once became the most representative specialty in Xianyang and well-known throughout Shaanxi.

The making of amber candy is very demanding. First, use the finest millet and barley malt to decoct malt sugar for later use. When making the amber candy, the prepared malt sugar should be melted, which is a skilled task requiring experience and sensation. If the heat is not well controlled, the malt sugar will probably be overcooked and the amber candy made from it will neither taste good nor look beautiful, the color being black with no luster. Stirring the malt sugar takes much labor. When the malt sugar gradually melts, it must be stirred continuously. Only when the stirring is enough, will the amber candy be bright, transparent and tasty. After the sugar melts, add walnut kernels, ginger

开，要不断地翻搅，只有搅的功夫到了，做出的琥珀糖才会晶亮、通透、口味纯正。糖化好以后将核桃仁、生姜粉、陈皮、桔梗、桂皮等配料按比例加入，迅速与糖拌匀，用板铲从锅中将拌好料的糖取出，放在案板上，趁热迅速拍打成3～4厘米厚的糖饼，然后用大铡刀切成薄片晾干，琥珀糖就做成了。

琥珀糖除有食用价值外，还有治疗咳嗽、气喘、多痰的药用价值。

2009年，咸阳琥珀糖制作技艺被列入陕西省第二批非物质文化遗产名录。

powder, tangerine peel, platycodon, cassia and other ingredients into the sugar in proportion, quickly mix them with sugar, remove the mixed sugar from the pot with a spatula and place it on the chopping board. While it is hot, quickly pat it into a sugar cake with a thickness of three to four centimeters, and then use a big knife to cut the sugar cake into thin slices and dry them. Through the above procedures, the amber candy is made.

In addition to its edible value, the amber candy also has the medicinal value for curing cough, asthma and phlegm.

In 2009, the skill of making Xianyang amber candy was included in the second batch of Shaanxi Provincial Intangible Cultural Heritage List.

陕北窑洞建造技艺
Architectural Craftsmanship of Cave Dwellings in Northern Shaanxi

陕北是华夏文明的发祥之地之一，深厚的黄土和丰富的砂石，造就了豪放粗犷的陕北人民，也造就了极具特色的黄土建筑——陕北窑洞。最早的窑洞距今已有4,500年的历史。陕北窑洞在周代是半地穴式，秦汉后发展为全地穴式，也就是现在的土窑，而窑洞建筑最辉煌的时期在明末清初。窑洞民居具有冬暖夏凉、节能节地、便于施工操作等特点，是陕北居民最主要的居所并沿用至今。

按照建筑选址与布局方式分类，陕北窑洞民居建筑有以下三种：

Northern Shaanxi is one of the birthplaces of Chinese civilization. The deep loess and abundant sandstones have not only bred the bold, unconstrained and rugged people of northern Shaanxi, but also the unique loess building—the cave dwellings. It has been 4,500 years since the earliest prototype of the cave dwellings came into being. Cave dwellings in northern Shaanxi were in semi-crypt style in the Zhou Dynasty, developed into full-crypt style (the present earthen cave dwelling style) since the Qin and Han dynasties, and entered its most glorious period in the late Ming Dynasty and early Qing Dynasty. Cave dwellings boast characteristics of keeping warm in winter and cool in summer, energy saving, land saving, convenient construction and so on. They used to be main residences for people in northern Shaanxi and are still in use today.

According to the site selection and layout, cave dwellings can be categorized into the following three types.

The first type is the cave dwellings built in a cliff. Horizontal caves are

第一种是靠崖窑，是在天然的黄土崖壁内开凿横洞，常常数洞相连，成排并列或上下相差。也有在土窑外接上一段石窑或砖窑，称为咬口窑。规模较大的则在崖外建房，组成院落，称为靠崖窑院。第二种是下沉式窑洞，或叫地下天井窑。该类窑洞多建于黄土塬上，星罗棋布。这种下沉式天井窑大都采取简单的地下四合院的形式，一户一院。第三种是土坯拱窑，即用土坯或砖石砌成拱形窑顶和墙身，上面用土加以覆盖筑成。这类土拱窑洞有半埋式的，也有筑在地上的，亦称独立式窑洞，又叫"四明头窑"，即前、后、左、右四头（即四面）都不利用自然土体而亮在明处，四面

dug in the natural loess cliff, and usually several caves are lined side by side or up and down. Sometimes a stone or brick cave is built outside the earthen cave, forming joint cave dwellings. Sometimes houses are built outside the earthen cave to form a courtyard, known as the cave dwelling courtyard. The second type is sunken cave dwellings or underground patio cave dwellings. Such cave dwellings are mostly built on and scattered around the Loess Plateau, most of which take the form of underground courtyards, and one household has one courtyard. The third type is the adobe arched cave dwellings. The walls and arched roofs of the cave dwellings are made of adobes, or bricks and stones, and the roofs are covered with soil. Some of this type of cave dwellings are semi-buried and others are built on

八、传统技艺　Traditional Craftsmanship

都得人工砌造。

陕北窑洞是我国黄土文化的重要象征，是原生态土生建筑的代表，更是我国建筑文化中不可多得的宝贵遗产，是陕北本源文化的最重要的组成部分之一。

2011年，陕北窑洞建造技艺被列入第三批国家级非物质文化遗产名录。

the ground, known as "free-standing cave dwellings" or "four-side bright cave dwellings", which means the front, back, left and right sides of the cave dwellings are artificially built instead of making use of the natural terrain.

The cave dwellings in northern Shaanxi are not only an important symbol of China's loess culture and the representative of Chinese original native architecture, but also rare and precious heritage of China's architectural culture. And they are also the most important part of the original culture of northern Shaanxi.

In 2011, the architectural craftsmanship of cave dwellings in northern Shaanxi was included in the third batch of China's National Intangible Cultural Heritage List.

岐山擀面皮制作技艺
Skill of Making Qishan *Ganmianpi*

岐山擀面皮，又叫御京粉，是用精白小麦面粉做成的冷食小吃，以"白、薄、光、筋、香"著称。

岐山擀面皮可追溯至清朝康熙年间，距今已有300余年历史。康熙初年，岐山县北郭乡八亩沟村王同江在皇宫御膳房当御厨，首创了这种美味的面食，深受后妃们的喜爱。由于它在京城仅作为御膳，秘不外传，故取名"御京粉"。康熙末年，王同江年老归乡，在八亩沟村收徒传艺，开设店铺经营"御京粉"。从此，这种宫廷食品传入民间。其中有道擀面的制作工艺，故而人们更喜欢称御京粉为"擀面皮"。

岐山擀面皮制作工艺独特，首先是放置好案板并抹上菜籽油，放上事先

Qishan *ganmianpi*, a kind of chewy wheat flour noodles, is also called *yujing* noodles. It is a cold snack made of refined wheat flour and is known for its "whiteness, thinness, smoothness, chewiness, and tastiness".

Qishan *ganmianpi* could be traced back to the Qing Dynasty when Emperor Kangxi ruled and has a history of more than 300 years. In the early years of Kangxi Period, Wang Tongjiang, who was from Bamugou Village, Beiguo Township of Qishan County, worked as an imperial cook in the royal kitchen. He created this delicious food that was loved by imperial concubines. Because at that time it was only a royal food and was kept a secret from the outsiders, it was named "*yujing* noodles" ("*yu*" means "royal", and "*jing*" means "capital"). In the last years of Kangxi Peirod, Wang Tongjiang returned to his hometown in his old age, took apprentices in Bamugou Village and opened a restaurant to sell *yujing* noodles. Since then, this kind of royal food has gained popularity among the masses. Due to the cooking step of rolling dough into a sheet, people prefer to call *yujing* noodles as *ganmianpi* ("*gan*" means "rolling", "*mianpi*" means "a dough

制好的面块，趁热稍作揉搓，盘光，摆放在案板的一端，用湿布盖上，保持温度。从发酵的面块中，揪取约125克的面块，用力揉搓成长约30厘米的条状，并拍压成厚约1.3厘米的面片，抹上一层菜籽油，然后用擀面杖在面片中间一压，就势两臂用力均匀地向前推擀面片至边缘，再向后回擀，一次擀成厚约0.33厘米的薄面皮，再抹上一层菜籽油，用刀把其四周边沿凸凹处划去，就有了33厘米见方的面皮片，如此反复制作，一张张摞起备用。面皮制作完成后，开始笼蒸，即把面皮每7～10张摞成一摞，每层

sheet").

Qishan *ganmianpi* features unique making procedures. First of all, place a chopping board and smear it with rapeseed oil, and then put the prepared dough on the board, knead the dough while it is a little warm until it becomes smooth, then place it on one end of the board and cover it with a piece of damp cloth to keep the temperature constant. Then take a small dough about 125 grams from the big dough, knead it into a strip with a length of about 30 centimeters, press and pat the strip into a dough sheet with a thickness of about 1.3 centimeters. Spread a layer of rapeseed oil on the dough sheet, and use a rolling pin to press the middle of the dough sheet, push with both arms forward and evenly roll the rolling pin to the edge of the dough sheet, and then roll back to form a thin dough sheet with a thickness of about 0.33 centimeters. Spread a layer of rapeseed oil again, and use a knife to cut the convex and concave edges to form a dough sheet about 33 square centimeters. Repeat the process of making dough sheets and pile the dough sheets up one by one for use. After making enough dough sheets, steam them in a steamer. Stack 7 to 10 pieces of the dough sheets together, coat each layer with rapeseed oil, put them in a steamer, steam them with hight heat for about 40 minutes, and then take them out. When they cool down, separate them one by one and cut them into noodles. In addition to making

涂上菜籽油，放在蒸笼里，上笼后即用旺火蒸约40分钟，下笼取出，待凉后一张一张分开，切成面条状，即成面皮。除笼蒸面皮外，还要制作辣子油、盐水、醋等调料和面筋等辅料。

近年来，在当地政府的支持下，岐山擀面皮制作技艺得到了进一步普及和提高，擀面皮的流传范围愈来愈广，正在向产业化的方向发展。

2011年，岐山擀面皮制作技艺被列入陕西省第三批非物质文化遗产名录。

ganmianpi, it is also important to prepare the seasonings including the chili oil, saline water, vinegar, etc., and side dishes like gluten, etc.

In recent years, with the support of the local government, the skill of making Qishan *ganmianpi* has been further popularized and improved. It is popular in more and more places, and its production is in the direction of industrialization.

In 2011, the skill of making Qishan *ganmianpi* was included in the third batch of Shaanxi Provincial Intangible Cultural Heritage List.

渭南时辰包子制作技艺
Skill of Making Weinan *Shichen* Steamed Stuffed Buns

时辰包子是陕西的一种名食，以渭南所制大油包子最为驰名。

相传清朝时，离渭南城三十里的一个村庄里住着一户人家，家里只有老母、儿子、儿媳三人。有一年秋天，老母病倒在床，小两口白天黑夜尽心服

Shichen baozi, a kind of steamed stuffed buns, is a famous food in Shaanxi, and the most famous *shichen baozi* is available in Weinan City.

According to the legend, in the Qing Dynasty, in a village 30 miles away from Weinan, there lived a family with only three persons: a mother, a son, and the son's wife. In an autumn, the old mother fell ill, and the young couple served her wholeheartedly day and night. The daughter-in-law asked the mother what she wanted to eat, and the mother replied she wanted to eat the best *baozi* in the city. Her son said, "I'll buy some for you tomorrow." However, he failed for the first three days. On the fourth day, when roosters crowed at the first time, he got up and started off. He sweated and panted heavily because he walked hurriedly on the whole way. This time, the effort has not failed his filial piety. He got to the *baozi* shop

侍。儿媳问老母想吃什么，老母回答说想吃城里最好吃的包子。儿子说："明天我就去买。"前三天都没买到，第四天，鸡叫头遍，他就起身赶路，一路连走带跑，累得汗流浃背，气喘吁吁。这一次功夫不负有心人，走到包子店正赶上辰时，包子刚刚下笼，他连忙买了十个。买到包子后，他心里高兴，就买了一张红纸，借店家的笔墨写了一首打油诗，贴在包子铺门口。这诗是："城里包子确实香，想买包子敬老娘。午时巳时都错过，正当辰时才赶上。"从此以后，人们就把这家店的包子称为"时辰包子"。

时辰包子经过百余年的传承和发展，形成了今天工艺独特、口味浓香、回味悠长、营养丰富的特点，是渭南饮食中的一绝。

时辰包子从选料到制作都有严格的规程。做皮的面要选上等小麦，用石器细磨，取其精粉。做馅的猪油要精心存贮一年后再用。猪油起沫后切成黄豆般的小粒，和上面粉，锅内加优质菜油，文火炒熟做馅。佐料用华县特产赤水大葱，配以韩城大红袍花椒和丁香、桂皮、豆蔻等制作的香料。每做六个油

before 9:00 a.m., and the cooked *baozi* had just been taken out from steamers. He bought ten *baozi*. He was so happy that he bought a piece of red paper, borrowed ink and a writing brush from the *baozi* shop, then wrote a doggerel on the red paper and pasted it on the door of the shop, which meant that the *baozi* was so popular that he could only manage to buy some by getting up hours earlier than usual. From then on, the *baozi* in this shop was called "*shichen baozi*" (*shichen* roughly means "hour" or "time").

After more than a hundred years of development, *shichen baozi* has become a unique food in Weinan, characterizing by its special workmanship, deliciousness, lingering aftertaste, and rich nutrition.

There are strict requirements concerning the selection of ingredients and making skills of *shichen baozi*. The refined flour made from the finest wheat is used to make wrappers. The lard used as the stuffing should be carefully stored for one year before use. While making the stuffing, the frothed lard should be cut into small granules, and then added into the flour. After the flour and the lard are mixed well, pour some high-quality rapeseed oil into a pot and stir-fry the flour with lard over mild heat until they are cooked. Then it will be used as the stuffing, into which the green onion and spices including Chinese red pepper, clove, cassia, cardamom, etc., are added. Every six *baozi* with lard stuffing

包子，搭配做四个素包子。素包子以豆腐、赤水大葱为馅。包子小巧玲珑，肥而不腻，香味悠长。人们常说，吃了时辰包子走十里路，口齿依然留香。

2011年，渭南时辰包子制作技艺被列入陕西省第三批非物质文化遗产名录。

will be matched with four vegetarian ones. The vegetarian *baozi* is stuffed with tofu and green onion. Small but exquisite, delicious but not greasy, the *baozi* has lasting aroma. It is often said that the yummy taste remains in the eater's mouth even he or she walks ten miles after eating *shichen baozi*.

In 2011, the making skill of Weinan *shichen baozi* was included in the third batch of Shaanxi Provincial Intangible Cultural Heritage List.

岐山农家醋制作技艺
Traditional Brewing Technology of Qishan Farmhouse Vinegar

岐山农家醋的酿造历史可追溯到西周。据传，当时人们普遍酿酒，用于饮宴和祭祀。岐山有一户人家因酿酒失误，酒浆变色，酒味变酸。周公视察民情来到这户人家，家主情急之下捧出此"酒"，周公尝后感到别有风味，加以褒奖。此后，人们纷纷仿效酿造这种带酸味的"酒"用于调味，一个酿造品种——岐山农家醋便产生了。

岐山农家醋的酿制配料以小麦、大麦、高粱、豌豆为主，辅料为麸皮。酿造工艺主要有拉曲、踩曲、捂曲、煮稞子、发醋、拌醋、纳醋、淋醋、放醋等9道工序，在酿造过程中不加任何添加剂。醋色黑红，酸中生香，香中微甜，

The brewing history of Qishan farmhouse vinegar can be traced back to the Western Zhou Dynasty. According to the legend, at that time people generally made wine for banquets and sacrifice, but a family in Qishan made the wine discolored and the wine tasted sour due to mistakes in the brewing process. Just then Zhou Gong (a great politician, strategist, thinker and educator in the early Zhou Dynasty) was inspecting people's living conditions and he happened to come to this family. The householder took out the "wine" in a hurry. After tasting it, Zhou Gong felt the "wine" special and praised it. Since then, people imitated the brewing of this sour "wine" for flavoring—in such a way Qishan farmhouse vinegar was produced.

The brewing ingredients of Qishan farmhouse vinegar are mainly wheat, barley, sorghum and peas, and the auxiliary material is bran. The brewing process mainly includes nine procedures and no additives are added in the whole brewing process. The vinegar is dark red in color, sour and slightly sweet in taste and fragrant in smell, and can be stored for a long time— the longer, the better. The vinegar has much nutrition and it helps digest, softens blood

久储不坏，愈老愈醇，营养丰富，有帮助消化、软化血管、强身健体等功效。岐山农家醋的品质独特，主要得益于以下几点：一是选用当地生产的粮食为原料；二是当地水质富含多种微量元素；三是使用农家特制的醋曲；四是酿制工艺复杂，成醋时间长达半年之久。

在酿制的过程中还有许多讲究：一是要敬奉"醋家婆"。传说"醋家婆"是姜子牙的夫人马氏，制醋人在配制的各个重要工序开始时，都要在"醋家婆"神位前上香祈祷，祈求"醋家婆"保佑，使自己酿的醋味道醇香。二是在制醋过程中要关好门窗，以免外人打扰。和同行交流时要小声细语，唯恐惊动了"醋家婆"。三是在煮醋（煮稞子）这天，主人家特地要做岐山臊子面，第一碗面要用来供奉"醋家婆"。

vessels, and strengthens the body. The unique quality of Qishan farmhouse vinegar is mainly due to the following reasons: first, the use of locally produced grains as raw materials; second, the use of local water which is rich in microelements; third, the use of special handmade vinegar yeast; fourth, the complex brewing process—the whole vinegar making process takes as long as half a year.

Many rituals are involved in the brewing process. The first one is to worship the "Vinegar Goddess". Legend has it that the Vinegar Goddess is the wife of Jiang Ziya (one of the founders of the Zhou Dynasty). When all the important procedures of preparation are started, the vinegar makers must pray in front of the memorial tablet of the Vinegar Goddess, and ask her to help them to brew high-quality vinegar. The second is to keep doors and windows closed during the vinegar making process so as not to be disturbed by outsiders. Vinegar makers should speak in a low voice when communicating with each other for fear that they might disturb the Vinegar Goddess. Third, on the day of cooking vinegar, Qishan noodles are specially made, and the first bowl of noodles is offered to the Vinegar Goddess.

In recent years, the production scale of Qishan farm vinegar has been expanding

近年来，岐山农家醋的生产规模日益扩大，占据了一定的市场份额，产生了较好的经济效益。

2011年，岐山农家醋制作技艺被列入陕西省第三批非物质文化遗产名录。

day by day, occupying certain market shares and generating good economic benefits.

In 2011, the traditional brewing technology of Qishan farmhouse vinegar was included in the third batch of Shaanxi Provincial Intangible Cultural Heritage List.

丹凤葡萄酒酿造技艺
Traditional Brewing Technology of Danfeng Wine

丹凤县位于陕西省东南部,地处秦岭东段南麓,是优质葡萄的适生地区之一。

丹凤葡萄酒酿造技艺已有百年历史。清宣统三年(1911年),意大利天主教传教士安西曼之徒华国文途经丹凤县龙驹寨时,得知这里盛产葡萄,不但产量大,而且果香味美,含糖量极高,遂产生了在此酿造葡萄酒的念头。他选择龙驹寨中心地段黄巷子十家院为厂址,采用安西曼传授的意大利酿造技术,生产"共和牌"葡萄酒,传承至

Danfeng County, which is located in the southeast of Shaanxi Province and at the southern foot of the eastern section of Qinling Mountains, is one of the good places for growing high-quality grapes.

The brewing technology of Danfeng wine has about one hundred years history. In 1911, Hua Guowen, the disciple of the Italian Catholic missionary Achima, came to Longjuzhai Town of Danfeng County, and saw that it was rich in grapes, which featured not only large output, but also fragrance, good flavor, and high sugar content. Therefore, he intended to make wine here. He chose the Shijia Courtyard in the Huang Alley located in central area of Longjuzhai as the factory site, and adopted the Italian brewing technology taught by Achiman to produce the "Republican Wine", which has been passed down to this day. The areas where grapes used for Danfeng wine are planted mainly include Dihua Town, Shangzhen Town, Longjuzhai Town, Yueri Town, Zhulinguan Town, etc., and it is in Longjuzhai Town that the wine is brewed.

The brewing of Danfeng wine includes 18 procedures, like selecting, fermenting, filtrating, aging, blending,

今。丹凤葡萄酒的原料产区主要分布在棣花镇、商镇、龙驹寨镇、月日乡、竹林关镇等，葡萄酒生产多在龙驹寨镇。

酿造丹凤葡萄酒的步骤有选料、发酵、过滤、陈酿、调制、装瓶等18道工序。调制的葡萄酒一般保质期为12个月。用红葡萄做的酒呈紫红色，白葡萄做的酒呈淡黄色。丹凤葡萄酒以家庭作坊的形式生产，完全是手工技艺，不用任何机械设备，不加任何添加剂，营养健康，所生产的葡萄酒主要供自己饮用和馈赠亲朋好友，极少量的会进入市场。

现在，丹凤虽然建成了大规模的现代化葡萄酒生产企业，但以传统手工酿造技艺生产葡萄酒从未间断。

2011年，丹凤葡萄酒酿造技艺被列入陕西省第三批非物质文化遗产名录。

bottling, etc. The general shelf life of the wine is 12 months. The wine made from red grapes is purplish red, and that made from white grapes is light yellow. Danfeng wine is traditionally produced in family workshops. It boasts high quality and nutrition for it is completely handmade, without the involvement of any machinery or additives. The wine produced in such a way is mainly for family drinking or serves as gifts to relatives and friends, and only a small amount enter into the marketplace.

Now, although a large-scale modern wine production enterprise has been built in Danfeng, the local people have never stopped producing wine in the traditional hand-brewing way.

In 2011, the traditional brewing technology of Danfeng wine was included in the third batch of Shaanxi Provincial Intangible Cultural Heritage List.

神仙豆腐制作技艺
Skill of Making Fairy Leaf Tofu

神仙豆腐是岚皋县的一种风味独特的食品。制作神仙豆腐的主要原料是生长在秦巴山区的一种特有的野生落叶灌木植物腐卑，又称神仙叶、凉粉叶树、豆腐叶。当地人大都称腐卑为神仙叶，神仙豆腐以此得名。

神仙豆腐的制作方法是：将采回的鲜叶洗净后放入盆内，倒入沸腾后温度已降至80℃左右的开水，水量为叶的

Fairy leaf tofu is a kind of food with unique flavor in Lan'gao County of Ankang City. The main raw material for making the tofu is a kind of unique wild suffruticosa plant named *fubei*, also called fairy leaf, bean jelly leaf, tofu leaf, etc., which mainly grows in the Qinling and Daba Mountains. Most of the locals call *fubei* as fairy leaf, hence the name fairy leaf tofu.

The procedures of making fairy leaf tofu are as follows. First, wash the fresh leaves and put them in a basin, pour into

the basin boiled water at the temperature of about 80°C (the amount of water is 5 to 6 times to that of the leaves). And stir them continuously with a wooden stick for about 10 minutes so that the leaves are fully broken and pasty. Then pour them onto a piece of gauze to filter. Knead with hands while filtering to press out the juice into the basin until no juice flows out. Then pour the residue into the original basin, add some boiled water, continue to stir and filter, and mix the filtered juice evenly. When the juice temperature drops to 50 °C to 60 °C, pour plant ash water into the juice according to the ratio of 1:1 (weight ratio of fresh leaves and plant ash), stir it by hand at the same time to make the two evenly mixed, then put it in a cool place for about two hours to cool and solidify. Generally, one kilogram of *fubei* fresh leaves can make five to six kilograms of tofu.

Shaped like gelatin, fairy leaf tofu looks as green as emerald, tastes soft and tender, and sends out unique fragrance of grass. It can be cooked in several ways. When served as cold dish, it can be directly seasoned with chili, pepper oil, salt, vinegar, etc.; when braised, it can be braised with cabbage, vermicelli, and meatballs; when fried, it can be stir-fried with pickled vegetables and lean meat. *Fubei*, the main raw material of fairy leaf tofu, contains 39.5% pectin, which is second to none in the domestic known fruits and vegetables. The finished product contains 21.7%

5～6倍，用木棒不断搅拌10分钟左右，叶子充分碎烂呈糊状为止，然后倒在豆腐布上过滤，边滤边用手揉搓，压出浆汁，直至无浆汁流出。然后将残渣倒入原盆，再加少许开水，继续搅拌过滤，将两次滤汁混合均匀，待汁液温度降至50℃～60℃时，按1:1的比例（鲜叶与草木灰的重量比）倒入灰水，同时用手稍加搅动，使二者混合均匀后，静置于阴凉处，约2小时即可冷却凝固。一般1千克腐卑的鲜叶可制作5～6千克神仙豆腐。

神仙豆腐绿若翡翠，状如凝脂，细软柔嫩，散发着一股特有的青草香味。食用时，既可凉调，也可烩、炒。凉吃时，可用辣椒、花椒油、盐、醋等调味；烩时，可与白菜、粉丝、肉丸同烩；炒时，可与酸泡菜、瘦肉爆炒。神仙豆腐的主要原料腐卑叶含39.5%果胶，在国内目前已知蔬果植物类中首屈一指。其成品含21.7%～34.8%粗蛋白质、13.1%可溶性蛋白质、21.6%食物纤维、4.3%灰分、0.3%叶绿素，还有丰富的淀粉、糖类、矿物质、维生素以及人体必需的17种氨基酸，尤以赖氨酸含量最高，有清热解暑、消脂凉血、强肾补阳、醒脑提神、降血脂血压的功效。

2011年，神仙豆腐制作技艺被列入陕西省第三批非物质文化遗产名录。

to 34.8% crude protein, 13.1% soluble protein, 21.6% dietary fiber, 4.3% ash, 0.3% chlorophyll, and it is rich in starch, sugar, minerals, vitamins and 17 kinds of amino acids, especially the highest content of lysine. The food has peculiar effects of clearing heat, reducing fat, cooling blood, strengthening kidney, refreshing mind, and lowering blood fat and blood pressure.

In 2011, the skill of making fairy leaf tofu was listed in the third batch of Shaanxi Provincial Intangible Cultural Heritage List.

紫阳毛尖传统手工制作技艺
Traditional Hand-Processing Skill of Ziyang *Maojian* Tea

紫阳毛尖生长在以紫阳县为中心的汉水中上游大巴山区。紫阳毛尖历史悠久,据《新唐书·地理志》记载,紫阳毛尖原名"金州茶牙",被列为贡品。清朝时期,紫阳毛尖被列为全国十大名茶之一。

紫阳毛尖的制作工艺精细。第一步是采摘鲜叶。每到春分后,紫阳茶农提篮背篓,上山采茶。采摘后用竹篮或背篓装鲜叶,因其透风、保鲜、不损

Ziyang *maojian* tea grows in the Daba mountainous areas on the upper and middle reaches of the Han River in Ziyang County. The tea has a long history. According to *A New Book of Tang History: Geography*, Ziyang *maojian* tea was originally named "Jinzhou Tea Shoot" and was listed as a tribute to imperial court. During the Qing Dynasty, the *maojian* tea was listed as one of the top ten famous kinds of tea in China.

It requires fine workmanship to process Ziyang *maojian* tea. The first step is to pick fresh leaves. After the Vernal Equinox, tea farmers in Ziyang County carry baskets and go up mountains to pick tea leaves. Then they use bamboo baskets to store fresh leaves in order to ventilate them, keep them fresh, and protect tender leaves. The second step is to ted tea leaves. The third step is to dehydrate (an essential step of green tea processing—high temperature can keep the tea leaves green, inhibit fermentation, soften the leaves, and meanwhile reduce the moisture in the leaves). The fourth step is kneading tea leaves for the first time. The tea leaves that have been dried in the third step are placed on clean stone slabs, and then tea farmers knead the leaves with their hands. The fifth

伤嫩叶。第二步是摊晾。第三步是杀青（绿茶加工制作的第一道工序，把摘下的嫩叶加高温，抑制其发酵，使茶叶保持固有的绿色，同时减少叶中水分，使叶片变软，便于进一步加工）。第四步是初揉。先将石板清洗干净，将杀青后晾凉的茶叶放在石板上，双手抱团似的旋转揉捻。第五步是晒干。第六步是渥堆发汗。渥堆发汗是紫阳毛尖制作过程中最为独特的环节，即将晾晒的茶叶堆积起来，盖上竹席或土布30~40分钟，使叶质再度变软，滋味更加醇和。第七步是紧条提毫。将半干的茶坯握在两掌中向不同方向旋转搓揉，使叶子翻卷成

step is to dry and air the leaves in the sun. The sixth step is to pile up tea leaves and make them moist again, which is the most unique step in the processing of Ziyang *maojian* tea making. The dried tea leaves are piled up and covered with bamboo mats or homespun cloth for about 30 to 40 minutes to make the leaves soft again and the taste more mellow. The seventh step is to knead tea leaves into the shape of needle. Hold the semi-dry tea leaves in two palms and rub them in different directions, so that the leaves are rolled into the shape of the needle, which is the key process of shaping *maojian* tea. The eighth step is to air and dry the tea leaves. The ninth step is to filter the dry tea leaves.

Ziyang *maojian* tea is famous both at

条，白毫显露出来。这是毛尖成型的关键工序。第八步是晾干。第九步是干茶过滤。

紫阳毛尖以"香高、味浓、耐冲泡、回味甘甜"蜚声海内外。紫阳也因盛产紫阳毛尖成为"中国名茶之乡"。

2011年，紫阳毛尖传统手工制作技艺被列入陕西省第三批非物质文化遗产名录。

home and abroad for its "fragrance, strong taste, and sweet aftertaste". Ziyang has also become the "hometown of China's famous tea" because of its abundance of *maojian* tea leaves.

In 2011, the traditional hand-processing skill of Ziyang *maojian* tea was included in the third batch of Shaanxi Provincial Intangible Cultural Heritage List.

商南草鞋制作技艺
Craftsmanship of Making Shangnan Hemp Shoes

商南草鞋由当地盛产的龙须草、葛麻编制而成。草鞋历史悠久，《诗经》中有"纠纠葛屦，可以履霜"之句。葛是一种藤本植物，茎可作纤维。葛屦就是用葛茎的纤维编制的草鞋。每年霜降

The hemp shoes of Shangnan County in Shangluo City are woven from the local abundance of Chinese alpine rush and kudzu hemp. Hemp shoes boast a long history, illustrated by relevant information in *The Book of Songs*. Kudzu is a kind of vine whose stem can be used for weaving shoes. After the annual Frost's Descent, the 18th Chinese solar term, local people collect Chinese alpine rush or kudzu that has grown on mountains for more than two years, and dry them for later use. Before being woven into shoes, the rush or hemp needs to be soaked thoroughly into water, and then softened with a wooden mallet. There are two kinds of hemp shoes. One is similar to sandals, and usually worn in summer and autumn or for wading through water; the other is similar to fabric shoes, and usually worn in spring and winter for cold protection.

The tool for making hemp shoes is called "straw shoe rake", which consists of a wooden plank and a wooden handle. The plank is about 40 centimeters long and 12 centimeters wide. Several wooden stakes that are as thick as fingers are installed on the vertical section of the plank and they are used for suspending the hemp strings or ropes. A wooden handle with a hook is

之后，将生长在山上的龙须草或生长两年以上的葛藤割回，晒干备用。编织之前，将干草（或麻）用水泡透，再用木棒槌捶软。草鞋有两种形式：一种叫偏耳鞋，类似凉鞋，一般在夏秋穿或蹚水时穿；另种叫满耳鞋，类似布鞋，一般在冬春防寒时穿。

打草鞋的工具叫"草鞋耙子"，由木板和木柄组成。木板长约40厘米，宽12厘米。在木板的竖剖面安装几根手指粗的木桩，作为挂绳的齿。木板后面安装一个带钩的木柄，以便使用时挂在板凳上，方便人骑在板凳上操作。

在漫长的历史时期，商南人乃至整个商洛人几乎家家会打草鞋，男人都穿草鞋。随着社会经济的发展，布鞋、胶鞋、皮鞋逐渐取代了草鞋，打草鞋工艺濒临失传。为此，商南县文化馆成立了专门的保护机构，使打草鞋技艺得以传承。

2011年，商南草鞋制作技艺被列入陕西省第三批非物质文化遗产名录。

installed behind the wooden plank so that it can be hooked on the bench when in use, and it is convenient for people to ride on the bench to make hemp shoes.

In a long period of history, almost every family in Shangnan County and even in the whole Shangluo City were able to make hemp shoes, and men here often wore hemp shoes. With the development of social economy, fabric shoes, rubber shoes and leather shoes have gradually replaced hemp shoes, and the craftsmanship of making hemp shoes is on the verge of being lost. Therefore, Shangnan County Cultural Center has established a special protection agency to pass on the skill of making hemp shoes.

In 2011, the craftsmanship of making Shangnan hemp shoes was included in the third batch of Shaanxi Provincial Intangible Cultural Heritage List.

传统乐器手工制作技艺
Craftsmanship of Making Traditional Musical Instruments

明清时期，梆子唱腔在陕西关中广大地区兴起，随之出现了以制作二胡、板胡等民族乐器为业的工匠。制作一件二胡、板胡需要经过选料、开料、加工、雕刻、蒙皮膜、做弓、成品出工、调试等九道工序。所用材料为木质坚硬的杂木，尤以紫檀、红木、乌木为佳。其制作技艺结合了造型、彩绘、镶嵌、雕刻等多种工艺手法，历史悠久，传承有序，至今依然保持着鲜明的原生态的手工技艺特征。

传统乐器手工制作技艺的制作工具有锯、凿子、锤、砂纸、抛光器、上皮器、刨子、手工钻、木刻刀等，共计九大类百余件。传统手工乐器制作技艺

During the Ming and Qing dynasties, due to the rise of *bangzi* singing tune in the vast areas of Guanzhong, the middle part of Shaanxi Province, artisans who made *erhu*, *banhu* (both are bowed, two-stringed vertical fiddles) and other national musical instruments appeared. The making of *erhu* or *banhu* requires nine procedures including selecting wood, cutting wood, processing, carving, making the bow, debugging, etc. The raw materials used to make *erhu* and *banhu* are hard wood, especially the red sandalwood, mahogany and ebony. The craftsmanship, which combines a variety of techniques such as modeling, color painting, inlaying, carving, has a long history and has been well inherited, still maintaining distinctive characteristics of manual skills.

There are more than one hundred pieces of nine categories of tools for making traditional musical instruments, such as saws, chisels, hammers, sandpaper, polishers, planes, hand drills, wood cutters. The craftsmanship of making traditional handmade musical instruments involves a wealth of practical experience and knowledge, including the knowledge of resonance relationship between *erhu* and

蕴含着丰富的实践经验和知识,其中包括对二胡、板胡共鸣关系的认识,对蟒皮、羊皮伸缩性和稳定性及其与音质关系的认识等。这些认识构成了民族乐器制作技艺的知识内核,使这一技艺具有系统性和科学性。数百年来,传统乐器手工制作技艺支撑着广大乡村自乐班和专业戏曲团体的演出,具有重要的文化价值。

目前,陕西完全掌握手工制作二胡、板胡等民族乐器的艺人仅有数人,且年事已高。此项优秀的传统技艺有濒临消失的危险,亟待保护。

2011年,传统乐器手工制作技艺被列入陕西省第三批非物质文化遗产名录。

banhu, the understanding of the elasticity and stability of python skin and sheep skin and their relationship with sound quality. Such cognition constitutes the fundamental knowledge for making national musical instruments, making this craftsmanship systematic and scientific. For hundreds of years, the craftsmanship with important cultural value has supported the performances of a large number of rural amateur troupes and professional opera troupes.

At present, there are only a few elderly artisans in Shaanxi who have fully mastered the hand-making skills of *erhu*, *banhu* and other national musical instruments. Therefore, this excellent traditional craftsmanship is in danger of extinction and needs being protected urgently.

In 2011, the craftsmanship was included in the third batch of Shaanxi Provincial Intangible Cultural Heritage List.

绥德石雕雕刻技艺
Craftsmanship of Suide Stone Carving

陕北绥德石雕艺术历史悠久，已出土的500多块东汉画像石以及至今保存的唐宋明清时期的石雕和摩崖石刻等都足以证明。

绥德石雕作品有的小巧可爱，有的高大威猛，有的雕刻精细，有的粗犷大气，真可谓千姿百态，栩栩如生。其种类繁多，用途各异。按照不同用途，绥德石雕可分为以下七大类别。

The stone carving art in Suide County of northern Shaanxi has a long history, which can be proved by the more than 500 pieces of unearthed stones reliefs of the Eastern Han Dynasty, as well as the well-preserved stone carvings and cliff inscriptions of the Tang, Song, Ming and Qing dynasties.

Some of the stone carvings are small and lovely, some tall and mighty, some finely carved, and some rough and majestic. They are truly lifelike and in various poses. There are a wide variety of Suide stone carvings with different purposes, which can be divided into the following seven categories according to the their functions.

The first category is stone utensils frequently used in people's lives, such as the guardian stone objects, stone gate piers, screen walls facing gates of houses, and stone beds, stone tables, stone benches, stone bowls, stone pestles, stone mills and so on. These stone objects have been used in the human society to this day, all showing Suide people's persistent pursuit of honesty, solemnity, generosity and plainness.

The second category is the stone reliefs of the Eastern Han Dynasty that can be called the essence of the cultural

一是与人民生活最为贴近的石器具。如护门石狮子、石门墩、迎门雕花照壁以及石床、石桌、石凳、石钵、石杵、石磨等。这些石器伴随人类社会延续至今，无不展示出世世代代绥德人所执着追求的浑厚、庄重、大方、纯朴之美。

二是堪称文物世界精粹的东汉画像石。绥德汉画像石的发掘、收藏始于1952年发掘的"王得元"墓藏。此后，又有许多墓藏被发掘。目前，绥德汉画像石展览馆等展馆收藏汉画像石500多块。这一批刻在石头上的历史画卷及其铭文墓志充分表现了绥德石雕工艺的精美和珍贵价值。

relics. The excavation and collection of the stone reliefs of the Han Dynasty began in 1952 when Wang Deyuan's tomb was unearthed in Suide County. Since then, more have been found in other tombs. So far, Suide Stone Relief Exhibition Hall and other exhibition halls have collected more than 500 pieces of stone reliefs of the Han Dynasty, which fully demonstrate the fineness and high value of Suide stone carving craftsmanship.

The third category is the most important and marvellous "lion culture" series represented by stone lions. Stone lion is a kind of mascot preferred by people in Suide. The local folks' worship for lions has a long history. There are stone lions placed on the head of beds to bless babies, majestic stone lions placed in temples on high

三是以石狮子为代表的最重要、最精彩的"狮"文化系列。"石狮子"是绥德民间的一种吉祥物,当地崇狮风尚久远。有珍藏炕头的"保锁"娃娃的炕头狮,有置于庙堂高山的威严的震山狮,有安放在公庭门前、广场、园林中高大威武的护神狮,有置放在家宅、墙头的震宅狮,有建于公园、桥梁、寺庙栏杆供人们观赏的千姿狮。

四是碑碣、亭塔石雕艺术。从古至今,无论在绥德城乡间的祖坟墓地、村镇大道,还是在高远山顶的寺观庙祠,人们多树碑碣来缅怀先祖、纪念要事或

mountains to protect the mountains, tall and mighty stone lions placed in front of the public halls, on squares and in gardens to guard the gods, stone lions placed in the house to protect people who live inside, as well as stone lions with various poses built in the parks, on bridges and temple railings for people to watch.

The fourth category is stone steles and pavilions. From ancient times to the present, in Suide, whether before the ancestral tombs, on the village roads, or in the temples on the top of high mountains, carved steles have been erected to honor ancestors, commemorate important events or pay homage to gods.

The fifth category includes all kinds of stone-carved birds, beasts (mainly the

祭奠神灵。

五是以石狮为主的各种飞禽走兽、花草人物、装饰品、工艺品。

六是石板画。由绥德工匠打造的永乐大道长廊上的365幅石板画充分展现了陕北黄土文化的厚重以及绥德石雕艺术的博大精深。

七是气势宏伟、集石雕工艺大成的牌楼、龙柱等。这些建筑物多建于广场、圣地、园林等地，设计精美，构图奇妙，雕刻精细，气势恢宏。

在中国的雕刻艺术中，常见的有木雕、砖雕、金雕等，但唯有陕北的石雕世代相传，经久不衰。因它源于生活，利于大众，不受拘泥，纯朴真实。它是一门独特的民间艺术，既具地方性，又具民族性，有极高的文史、艺术审美价值。

2014年，绥德石雕雕刻技艺被列入第四批国家级非物质文化遗产名录。

stone lions), plants, figures, ornaments and art crafts.

The sixth category is the stone-carved pictures. The 365 stone-carved pictures on the Long Corridor of Yongle Avenue created by craftsmen in Suide fully demonstrate the richness of the Loess culture in northern Shaanxi and the profoundness of Suide stone carving art.

The seventh category is the magnificent memorial archways and dragon pillars which are the epitome of stone carving craftsmanship. Such things are mostly built on the squares, holy sites, or in gardens and other places, which boast exquisite design, wonderful composition, fine carving and magnificent appearance.

In various Chinese carving arts like wood carving, brick carving, gold carving, etc., stone carving in northern Shaanxi shows its strong vitality and enduring appeal, and has been passed down from generation to generation. It comes from life, benefits the masses, and features simplicity and authenticity. It is a unique folk art that embodies both local and national characters, and has very high cultural, historical and aesthetic value.

In 2014, the craftsmanship of Suide stone carving was included in the fourth batch of China's National Intangible Cultural Heritage List.

九

传统医药

Traditional Medicine

孙思邈养生文化
Sun Simiao's Health-Preservation Thoughts

陕西省铜川市耀州区是我国古代伟大的医药学家孙思邈的诞生地。孙思邈医术精湛，医德高尚。他认为医生须以解除病人痛苦为唯一职责，其他则"无欲无求"，要求医生要替患者着想，尽量用便宜药治病，并要"博极医源，精勤不倦"。他去世后，百姓为他立祠建庙，神而祀之，后人尊称他为"药王"。

孙思邈创立了许多健身养生之道，他的至理名言为"人命至贵，贵于千

Sun Simiao, a famous Chinese traditional medicine doctor born in Yaozhou District of Tongchuan City in ancient China, is well known for his superb medical skills and noble medical ethics. He believed that doctors must be dedicated and diligent in treating patients, take the relief of patients' pain as their sole responsibility, think for patients, choose cheap medicines for patients, keep on learning medicine and improving their medical skills. After his death, people built temples to worship him and titled him as the "King of Medicine".

Sun Simiao found many ways to keep in good health. His most famous saying goes that "Human life is most valuable, which is worth more than one thousand taels of gold." Devoting his whole life to medicines and health care, he integrated prescriptions and health-preservation experience of different doctors before the Tang Dynasty, made breakthrough achievements in the field of health preservation, and his masterpiece *Qianjin-Yaofang* (*Important Prescriptions for Emergency*) is known as the encyclopedia of traditional medicine in ancient China.

金"。他穷其一生精力,博采众方,将历代医药经验的方药以及养生经验汇集在一起,集唐以前医学之大成,其著作《千金要方》被誉为古代医学的百科全书。

孙思邈在实践中总结出一套简单易行的科学养生方法,即"动以养身,静以养心",认为"流水不腐,户枢不蠹,以其运动故也"。衣着上,讲求简朴,适应气温变化,清洁干净,保护身体,免遭自然气候的不良影响。饮食上,反对膏粱厚味,淡素其食,倡导"常须少食肉,多食饭","常宜轻甜淡之物,大小麦面、粳米等为佳","食欲数而少,不欲顿而多",食勿过

Sun Simiao summed up a set of simple and feasible methods of health preservation in practice, that is, "movement to nourish the body, calmness to nourish the mind". He believed that "running water is never stale and a door-hinge never gets worm-eaten for they are not motionless". As for clothing, he thought it should be simple and clean, adaptable to the temperature, and protect the body from the adverse effects of climate. In terms of diets, he preferred food of light taste, less meat and more grain, more meals a day but less food at each instead of fewer meals a day but more food at each. As for sex life, he believed that people should master the principles and methods of intercourse in order to keep healthy. In regard to personal hygiene, he thought special attention should be paid to bathing, perfuming, gargling and teeth cleaning, etc.

Sun Simiao's thoughts on health preservation are based on the philosophic thinking of Confucianism, Buddhism and Taoism. His thoughts on health preservation cover rich contents, including morality and temperament cultivation, healthy and positive life attitude, balance between activity and stillness as well as work and rest, prevention first, fitness method of massage, medicine therapy, dietary therapy, sex culture, etc. In particular,

饱。性生活中,要人们掌握两性交合的原则和方法,以便得摄生保健之益。个人卫生方面,特别重视沐浴、熏香、漱口和洁齿等。

孙思邈养生文化思想以儒释道的哲学思想为依据,涵盖修德养性的养生思想,健康向上的生活态度,动静劳逸得宜、预防为主的保健意识,按摩导引的健体方法,以及药物养生、食疗文化和性文化诸多方面的内容。尤其是他的预防医学思想和养生保健学,更具有哲学科学意义和学术文化价值。

2009年,孙思邈养生文化被列入陕西省第二批非物质文化遗产名录。

his thoughts on preventive medicine and health preservation have philosophical and scientific significance as well as academic value.

In 2009, Sun Simiao's health-preservation thoughts were included in the second batch of Shaanxi Provincial Intangible Cultural Heritage List.

华县杏林许氏正骨技艺
Xu's Bone-Setting Technique in Xinglin of Huaxian

杏林许氏正骨术发源于西岳华山脚下。华山乃中华文明的发源地之一，也是上千年来佛、道、武、医云集之地。劳动人民在长期的生产生活中探索出许多针对跌打损伤及各种疾病的奇特而有效的骨伤康复治疗方法。其中一直散落在民间的医治骨伤病的技艺逐渐在华山脚下的华县杏林乡用于医疗实践，久而久之，这里便自然地成了治疗骨伤之地。

杏林正骨术秉承了道家的哲学思想，并将其融入脊椎相关疾病的治疗。

Xu's bone-setting technique originates from the foot of Huashan Mountain, which is one of the birthplaces of Chinese civilization and is also the place where Buddhists, Taoists, martial arts practitioners and doctors have gathered for thousands of years. Local people have explored and discovered many novel and effective rehabilitation treatment methods for traumatic injuries and various diseases in their long-term work and life. Among those treatment methods, the technique of treating bone injuries, which had been hidden among the folks, was gradually used for medical practice in Xinglin Township of Huaxian County. With time going on, this place becomes famous for treating bone injuries.

Xu's bone-setting technique adheres to the philosophical thinking of Taoism, which has been applied to the treatment of spine-related diseases by the doctors in

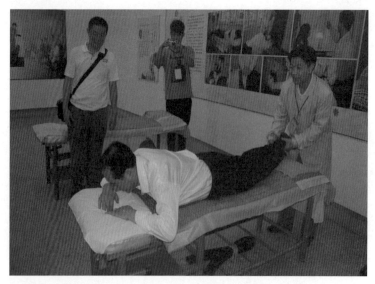

杏林正骨术在继承及发扬祖传切摸查病、提拿牵引、敲按复位等诊疗手法的基础上，以循经络、推穴道的方式矫正骨结构的平衡，调整肝脏腑功能，使人体的气血及经脉恢复通畅。

杏林正骨术的最大特点是诊断突出"切"字，通过手法切摸来观察患者病情。第二个特点是注重人体骨关节结构的整体平衡，调整施治，治疗能除根，预防再犯。第三个特点是遵循内病外治的原则，通过体表体内相通的原理，在体表找疼痛点。第四个特点是除经络推拿外，开展解剖推拿。解剖推拿的好处是对神经血管部位了然于心，清楚肌肉

Xu's clinic. On the basis of inheriting and developing the traditional diagnosis and treatment methods of feeling the pulse, traction therapy, restoration by massaging, etc., the doctors can restore patients' bone position and structure, improve the function of patients' internal organs and make *qi* and blood in patients' bodies circulate smoothly by massaging acupuncture points distributed along meridians and collaterals.

The biggest feature of Xu's bone-setting technique in Xinglin is the diagnosis of feeling the pulse. The doctors can judge patients' condition by feeling their pulse. The second feature is that doctors adjust their treatment on basis of the overall balance of patients' joint structure–the treatment is curative with sound effect. The third characteristic is that the doctors follow the principle of external treatment for internal disease. Following the principle of external symptoms are related to internal ailments, the doctors start their treatment from the external pains on the patients' bodies. The fourth feature is that the doctors not only carry out meridian massage, but also anatomy massage. The advantage of anatomy massage is that the doctors are quite clear about positions of the nerves, blood vessels and joints so that they can conduct accurate and effective treatment.

Xu's bone-setting technique is deeply affected by Taoist culture. It was first used only to treat fractures, joint dislocation and so on. Later, it gradually developed to treat

关节，治疗时能将位置找得更准，效果更好。

杏林许氏正骨术受道教文化影响深远，最早只用于整复骨折及关节脱臼等疾病，以后逐渐发展到在脊椎上通过正骨、拔筋治疗内脏病。发展到今天，用正脊推拿方法主要治疗因脊椎引起的常见病、多发病、现代病。

2009年，华县杏林许氏正骨技艺被列入陕西省第二批非物质文化遗产名录。

diseases of internal organs through bone-setting and massaging tendons. To this day, Xu's bone-setting technique of restoring spine by massaging is mainly applied to treat common diseases, frequent-occurring diseases and modern diseases caused by spondylodynia.

In 2009, Xu's bone-setting technique in Xinglin of Huaxian was included in the second batch of Shaanxi Provincial Intangible Cultural Heritage List.

杨氏一指诊脉技艺
Yang's Pulse-Feeling Diagnosis Technique

脉诊是中医独特的诊病方法，俗称"号脉"或"切脉"。战国时著名医学家扁鹊创立了中医"望、闻、问、切"的"四诊法"。

我国第一部脉学专著《脉经》诞生于晋朝，其中的诊脉方法和理论已相当完备。经历代医家在临床实践中不断完善，大量有关诊法的中医典籍形成了。杨氏一指诊脉技艺"独取寸口"的诊脉方法，在汉代成书的《八十一难经》中就有记载。杨氏将此技艺代代相传，杨凌一宁中医药研究所（现名陕西一旨门中医药研究所）的创办人杨宁是第四代传人。

一指诊脉技艺，是医家仅仅运用自

Pulse feeling, commonly called "haomai" or "qiemai", is a unique diagnosis method of traditional Chinese medicine. Bian Que, a famous physician in the Warring States Period, created the four-step diagnoses of "observation, auscultation and olfaction, interrogation, and pulse feeling and palpation". Observation refers to looking at the patient's complexion, eyes, tongue, skin, excretion, etc; auscultation and olfaction means listening to the patient's the voice, breath, sounds, coughs and smelling the patient's breath, body odor and excretions; interrogation is asking the patient or the patient's companion systematic and relevant questions about the disease; pulse feeling and palpation means pressing and feeling the patient's pulse, touching and pressing the skin, hands, feet, chest, abdomen and other parts of the patient's body.

The first book about pulse study in China, *Maijing* (*The Pulse Feeling Diagnosis Classic*), was written in the Jin Dynasty, and the pulse feeling diagnosis methods and theories in the book are quite comprehensive. Through continuous improvement in clinical practice, a large number of traditional Chinese medicine

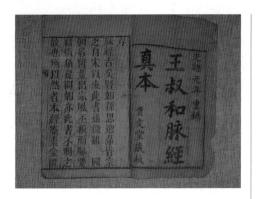

classics on pulse feeling diagnosis methods have been composed. Yang's method of pulse-feeling diagnosis with one finger, the technique of "feeling the *cunkou* pulse (pulse on the wrist)", was recorded in the book *Nanjing* (the full name is *The Yellow Emperor's Canon of Eighty-One Difficult Issues*, one of the classics of traditional Chinese medicine) which was compiled in the Han Dynasty. The Yang family passed on this technique from generation to generation, and Yang Ning, the founder of the Yining Institute of Traditional Chinese Medicine in Yangling (the present name is Shaanxi Yizhimen Institute of Traditional Chinese Medicine), is the fourth-generation successor.

己的一个小拇手指，切按在患者手腕的寸口之处，通过对寸口脉动的触摸及按压的触觉来体验患者体内脉象的变化，从而了解和判断患者病情的轻、重、缓、急的一种诊病方法。一指诊脉技艺诊断疾病的重要依据是脉象。这一决定性的特点与传统脉诊技艺如出一辙。

杨氏一指诊脉技艺是传统中医文化的结晶，在医疗实践中有重要价值。

2011年，杨氏一指诊脉技艺被列入陕西省第三批非物质文化遗产名录。

The technique of pulse-feeling diagnosis with one finger is that the doctor only uses the little finger to feel the changes of the pulse of the patient by touching and pressing the patient's *cunkou* pulse so as to understand and judge the patient's health condition. Doctors diagnose patients' diseases according to patients' pulse manifestation, which coincides the traditional pulse-feeling diagnosis technique.

Yang's pulse-feeling diagnosis technique is the crystallization of traditional Chinese medicine culture and has important value in medical practice.

In 2011, the technique was included in the third batch of Shaanxi Provincial Intangible Cultural Heritage List.

针挑治疗扁桃体炎
Acupuncture Therapy for Tonsillitis

很久以来，针挑治疗扁桃体炎的医术在渭南市大荔县、合阳县一带颇有影响。

针挑疗法是从传统的中医学砭刺术派生的一种古老的疗法，与针灸疗法中的针刺法同属中医外治法。简单地说，就是一种用针挑皮肤而达到治病目的的疗法。此法在医疗实践中不断改进，在选点取穴、针挑手法、中药配伍等方面都取得了明显的突破和进展，特别是不再使用传统的缝衣针、铜钱、剃须刀等陈旧器械，代之以特制钢针、刮痧板、手术刀、高压消毒设备等现代器械，其疗效和安全性大大提高。

针挑治疗扁桃体炎以其工具简单、手法独特、治疗彻底而著称。其手术要领是刮、刺、挑、割。刮是用刮痧板在

Acupuncture therapy for tonsillitis has been quite influential in Dali and Heyang counties of Weinan City for a long time.

It is an ancient external therapy developed from acupuncture in traditional Chinese medicine. In short, this therapy suggests that the surgeon uses a needle to pierce the skin to achieve the purpose of curing tonsillitis. This method has been continuously improved in medical practice, and obvious breakthroughs and progress have been made in selecting acupuncture points, needle piercing techniques and traditional Chinese medicine application. In the treatment, obsolete instruments like sewing needles, copper coins, razors have been replaced by specially-made steel needles, scraping plates, scalpels, sterilizer and other modern instruments, greatly improving the efficacy and safety of the treatment.

Acupuncture therapy for tonsillitis is famous for its simple medical instruments, unique treatment techniques, and sound cure effect. The essential process of the operation is as follows. Firstly, scrape the skin between the patient's rear hairline and the acupoint *dazhui* to make the skin congested. Secondly, puncture the skin with a special steel needle

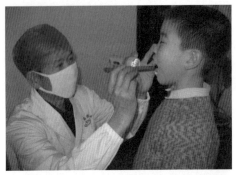

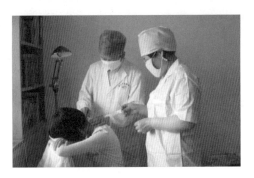

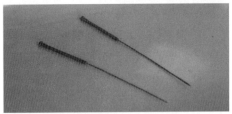

患者后发际与大椎穴之间进行刮痧,使皮肤充血;刺是根据选定的针挑穴点,将特制钢针快速刺入皮肤;挑是将针尖刺入皮肤后,用力向上挑起;割是将挑起的纤维用手术刀割断。其主要特点为不摘除扁桃体;痛苦少,术中不使用麻醉药物,患者易于接受;耗时短,见效快,手术过程不到10分钟,且无需住院,患者能较快恢复正常生活;手术操作不进入口腔,安全性高。针挑治疗扁桃体炎有极高的临床推广价值。

2011年,该疗法被列入陕西省第三批非物质文化遗产名录。

from certain acupoints. Then, lift up the needle vigorously. At last, cut the lifted tissue with a scalpel. The therapy features several advantages. First, the patient's tonsil needn't to be extirpated in the treatment. Second, the therapy doesn't causes too much pain on the patient, so anesthetic drugs are not used in the operation. Third, the therapy takes less time, produces quick and sound effect and patients can recover very soon. The whole treatment takes no more than ten minutes and patients do not need to stay in the hospital. They can return to normal life very soon. Fourth, as medical instruments do not go into the patient's mouth and throat, the therapy is much safer. Acupuncture therapy for tonsillitis has high promotional and application value.

In 2011, it was included in the third batch of Shaanxi Provincial Intangible Cultural Heritage List.

郭氏中医正骨技艺
Guo's Bone-Setting Technique

20世纪初，郭氏正骨创始人郭志祥为西安当地群众治疗骨骼上的病痛。郭氏正骨疗法传承至今。

郭氏中医正骨疗法的治疗过程分为诊断、整复、固定与后续护理四大部分。它改变了从前"手摸心意"的方式，参考现代检测方法的检测结果，能更加迅速、准确地判断患者骨骼的错位、断裂的具体位置及程度，能根据不同患者骨骼整复的需要，用触摸、拔伸、推按、扳提、捏挤等正骨手法，辨证施治，配合应用，纠正骨折所造成的成角、错位、重叠、旋转、侧方或分离移位等畸形，使患者的骨骼回到常态。骨骼完全修复后还需将患处固定，以促

Guo Zhixiang, the founder of Guo's bone-setting therapy, cured bone diseases for people in Xi'an City in the early 1900s. And the bone-setting technique was passed down to this day.

Guo's bone-setting treatment process is divided into four steps: diagnosis, restoration, fixation and follow-up care. The treatment is different from the traditional way of bone setting. The doctor determines the specific location and extent of the patient's bone dislocation and fracture more quickly and accurately by referring to the detection results of modern medical equipment. And various bone-setting methods like touching, pulling, pressing, lifting, pinching are adopted according to the needs of treatment to make the patient's malformed bones caused by fractures return to normal. After the bone is set, the

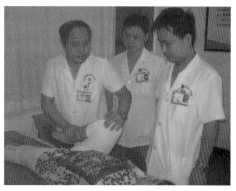

进骨骼的愈合。

郭氏中医正骨技艺的核心是准确的复位，有效的固定，合理的功能锻炼，外敷膏药消肿定痛，中药内服接骨续筋。郭氏中医正骨疗法的秘方膏药具有活血化瘀、消肿止痛、续筋接骨、祛风除湿、散寒消炎等功效。正骨后，必须敷上膏药，方能取得良好的治疗效果。同时，患者在后期康复中，还要根据骨折的不同程度，用配制的符合个人体质的外洗中草药进行药洗，以加快软化僵硬的关节，促进血液循环，达到骨折后期的消肿和功能恢复的目的。

在《医宗金鉴》一书提出的正骨八法（摸、接、端、提、推、拿、按、摩）的基础上，郭氏中医正骨技艺传人郭军胜提出了拨、展、扳、顶等手法，对颈肩腰腿痛治疗有奇效。

wounded part needs to be fixed to help the bone heal.

The core technique of Guo's bone-setting lies in accurate restoration, effective fixation, reasonable functional exercise, external application of plaster to reduce swelling and pain, and internal use of traditional Chinese medicine to promote reunion of fractured bones and tendons. The secret-prescription plaster of Guo's bone-setting therapy has effects of promoting blood circulation, removing blood stasis, reducing swelling and pain, renewing tendons and bones, dispelling wind and eliminating dampness, and reducing inflammation. After bone setting, plasters must be applied to achieve good therapeutic effect. At the same time, the external washing with Chinese herbal medicine is applied to the patient in the later rehabilitation period according to the degrees of the patient's bone fractures, so as to accelerate the softening of stiff joints, promote blood circulation, reduce swelling and help the bone to achieve functional recovery.

Guo Junsheng, the successor of Guo's bone-setting therapy, developed more bone-setting methods like poking, stretching, pulling, propping on the basis of the eight methods of bone setting (namely

2013年，郭氏中医正骨技艺被列入陕西省第四批非物质文化遗产名录。

touching, connecting, holding, lifting, pushing, massaging, pressing, and rubbing) written in the book *Traditional Chinese Medicinal Research*. His bone-setting technique has miraculous curative effects on pains on the neck, shoulder, waist and leg.

In 2013, Guo's bone-setting technique was included in the fourth batch of Shaanxi Provincial Intangible Cultural Heritage List.

马明仁膏药制作技艺
Technique of Making Mamingren Plaster

马明仁膏药制作技艺始创于清朝咸丰年间。始祖马六懿先生行医乡间，专注于风湿骨病的研究诊治，经多方探索和临床实践，熬制成"马钱风湿骨痛膏"。该风湿骨痛膏疗效确切，远近闻

Mamingren plaster (*gaoyao* in Chinese) is a drug for external use, the making technique of which dated back to the reign of Xianfeng in the Qing Dynasty. The founder of the plaster, Ma Liuyi, practiced medicine in the countryside and focused on the research and treatment of rheumatic bone diseases. Through various explorations and clinical practice, he produced a kind of *gaoyao* aiming to treat rheumatic bone diseases. The *gaoyao* has definite and obvious curative effect, and is well-known far and wide. For more than one hundred years, the Ma family developed the profession launched by Ma Liuyi. After six generations' inheritance, the ancient making technique of Ma's *gaoyao* has been completely inherited and preserved to this day. The technique has been developed over the past

名。一百多年来，马氏家族继承了马六懿先生创立的事业，经六代相传，将"马氏膏药"的古法工艺完整继承并保存至今。一个多世纪以来，马明仁膏药制作技艺历经岁月锤炼，最终沉淀为独树一帜的古方精品，在制作工艺上不仅完整继承了古法炼制的精髓，而且在不断的实践中丰富了传统技法，把膏药的药用价值和传统工艺很好地结合在一起。

century, and finally a unique and ancient prescription of *gaoyao* came into being. In *gaoyao* production practice, the essence of ancient refining technique has been inherited, the traditional techniques have been developed and enriched, and the

运用马明仁膏药制作技艺精心制作的膏药药性温和，药力持久，气味芳香，冬天不脆，夏天不流，外观黑如漆、明如镜，具有通行经络、活血散瘀、祛风除湿、消肿镇痛等疗效，对因风寒、湿邪、痹阻及慢性劳损引起的风湿、类风湿性关节炎、骨质增生、腰椎间盘突出、颈椎病、肩周炎、膝关节疾患等有十分显著的疗效。

2014年，马明仁膏药制作技艺被列入第四批国家级非物质文化遗产名录。

medicinal value of *gaoyao* has been well combined with traditional workmanship.

Mamingren plaster is mild in nature, durable in potency and fragrant in smell. It looks as dark as black lacquer and as bright as mirror, not brittle in winter, nor easy to melt in summer. With functions of promoting blood circulation and dissolving stasis, dispelling wind-evil and eliminating dampness, reducing swelling and pain, etc., it has very significant therapeutic effects on diseases caused by coldness, wetness as well as chronic strain, such as rheumatism, rheumatoid arthritis, bone hyperplasia, lumbar disc herniation, cervical spondylosis, periarthritis of shoulder, knee joint diseases and so on.

In 2014, the technique of making Mamingren plaster was included in the fourth batch of China's National Intangible Cultural Heritage List.

十

民俗

Folk Customs

黄帝陵祭典

Sacrificial Ceremonies at the Yellow Emperor's Mausoleum

黄帝陵是中华民族始祖轩辕黄帝的陵墓，位于陕西省延安市黄陵县的桥山之上。那里除黄帝陵外，还有轩辕庙、祭祀大殿、祭亭、黄帝手植柏等。

轩辕黄帝开创了中华文明之先河，被奉为"人文初祖"。为了纪念和缅怀黄帝，在黄帝"驭龙升天"之后，先民就开始了隆重的祭祀活动。据《绎史》记载："黄帝崩，其臣左彻取衣冠、几杖而庙祀之。"最早见诸史料的后世帝王祭祀黄帝的是周威烈王四年（公元前422年）秦灵公作吴阳上畤，专祭黄帝。汉代以后，祭祀黄帝成为朝廷定例。

1912年，孙中山先生就任中华民国临时大总统，派专人赴黄帝陵祭祖。抗日战争时期，国共两党多次共祭黄帝

The Yellow Emperor, also called as Xuanyuan *Huangdi*, is the ancestor of the Chinese nation. The Mausoleum of the Yellow Emperor is located on the Qiaoshan Mountain in Huangling County of Yan'an City. In addition to the Yellow Emperor's Mausoleum, there are also Xuanyuan Temple, the Sacrificial Hall, the Sacrificial Pavilion, Yellow Emperor's hand-planting cypress and other attractions.

The Yellow Emperor was considered as the founder of Chinese civilization and "the first ancestor of humanity". After his passing away, people held grand sacrificial activities to commemorate him. According to historical records, after the Yellow Emperor's death, one of his subjects took the emperor's clothes, chair and walking stick to the ancestral temple to worship him. It is recorded that the first emperor who worshiped the Yellow Emperor is Qin Linggong who did so in 422 BC. Since the Han Dynasty, worshiping Yellow Emperor has become a convention of the royal court.

In 1912, Mr. Sun Yat-sen became interim president of the Republic of China and he sent a delegation to pay homage to the Yellow Emperor. During the Anti-Japanese War period, the Kuomintang and

陵,毛泽东主席曾亲自撰写《祭黄帝陵文》。

在长期的实践中黄帝陵祭祀活动形成了一定的规模和祀典礼仪,大致可分为公(官)祭、民祭两种形式。

现在的清明公祭黄帝陵仪式庄严、肃穆。祭陵现场的布置是:在祭亭上悬挂一横额,上书"某某年清明公祭轩辕黄帝典礼",一般用农历纪年。祭桌上摆放祭器、香烛、时鲜水果、面花等。祭祀的仪程主要有奏古乐、跳古舞、献花篮花圈、行三鞠躬礼、主持人恭读祭文、鸣放鞭炮、绕陵一周、植纪念树等。

民间祭祀多在清明节前后和重阳节

the Communist Party members jointly worshiped the Yellow Emperor many times, and Chairman Mao wrote sacrificial oration for the worship.

The sacrificial activities held at the Yellow Emperor's Mausoleum are characterized by a large scale spectacle and certain ritual etiquette in long-term practice, which can be roughly divided into two forms: public (official) sacrificial ceremonies and folk sacrificial ceremonies.

The public sacrificial ceremonies at the Yellow Emperor Mausoleum are solemn and respectful, which are held during the Qingming Festival (the Tomb-sweeping Day). The site where sacrificial ceremonies are held is elaborately arranged: A banner is hung on the memorial pavilion, which reads "Worship Xuanyuan *Huangdi* on the Tomb-sweeping Day in ... year", generally

期间举行。民祭活动除了有公祭活动的一些内容外,更突出了民间性,增加了鼓乐队、唢呐队、仪仗队、三牲队。

改革开放以来,黄帝陵祭祀越来越受到海内外华夏儿女的关注,祭祀规模日渐宏大,祭祀礼仪日渐隆重。祭祀黄帝已成为开创美好生活、传承中华文明、凝聚华夏儿女、促进祖国统一的一项重大活动。

2006年,黄帝陵祭典被列入第一批国家级非物质文化遗产名录。

according to the lunar calendar; Sacrifice utensils, incenses, candles, fresh fruits, dough figurines, etc., are placed on the table. The sacrificial rituals include: playing ancient music, performing ancient dances, offering flower baskets and wreaths, bowing to the Yellow Emperor, reading sacrificial oration, lighting firecrackers, walking around the mausoleum, planting commemorative trees, etc.

Folk sacrificial ceremonies are mostly held around the Qingming Festival or on the Chongyang Festival (Double Ninth Festival). In addition to maintaining some of the rituals of the public sacrificial ceremonies, folk sacrificial activities highlight the folk characteristic featured by the drum band, *suona* horn band, honor guard, and sacrificial animal team.

Since China's reform and opening-up, sacrificial ceremonies at the Yellow Emperor's Mausoleum have attracted more and more attention of Chinese people home and abroad. Paying homage to the Yellow Emperor has become an important activity to inherit Chinese civilization and unify Chinese people to create a better life.

In 2006, sacrificial ceremonies at the Yellow Emperor's Mausoleum were included in the first batch of China's National Intangible Cultural Heritage List.

宝鸡民间社火
Baoji Folk *Shehuo* Performance

社火是由先民祭祀土神的社日和祭祀火神的迎神赛会活动逐渐演变而形成的一种民间巡游演艺活动。据史料记载和学者研究，中国社火发源于西秦宝鸡。宝鸡社火在其发展的历史长河中，由起初的集民间音乐、舞蹈、诗歌、杂耍、锣鼓为一体的戏剧形式逐渐发展为有固定表演形式的民间舞蹈艺术。

宝鸡社火按表演时间可分为昼社火和夜社火，按表演形式可分为造型社

Shehuo is a kind of folk parade performance which originated in ancient people's worship to land and fire. According to historical records and scholars' research, *shehuo* in China originated from Baoji City, Shaanxi Province. In the long history of its development, it has gradually developed from the original drama performance which combines folk music, dance, poetry, vaudeville as well as gong and drum performance into a kind of folk dance art with fixed performing form.

In terms of the performing time, Baoji *shehuo* can be divided into day *shehuo* and

火和表演社火两大类。造型社火有背社火、马社火、芯子社火、山社火、面具社火等，进行列队表演；表演社火有地台社火、高跷社火等，主要在场院进行表演。由于宝鸡社火的演员扮演的大多是古装历史剧和古典名著中的特型人物，所以服装、头帽、道具、枪棒把子全是以古装戏的形式出现。社火游演时一般是探马在前，后面跟着社火会旗、火铳队、旗队、社火队，最后是锣鼓队。社火游演队伍气势宏大，锣鼓喧天，热闹非凡，具有很高的民俗价值和审美价值。

宝鸡社火的脸谱与远古时期的图腾崇拜、原始歌舞有很深的关系，也与我国民间的祭祀活动密不可分，堪称我国最古老的脸谱之一。脸谱造型粗犷，纹样古朴，色彩浓烈。画脸谱的颜色早期只用青、赤、黄、白、黑五种。这是表现社火脸谱人物角色性格的基本色彩

night *shehuo*. In terms of performing form, it can be classified into various categories. For example, in the performance the performers usually dressed up as historical figures hold kids on their backs, or ride on horses, or wear masks, or stand on stilts, or have kids fastened aloft, marching ahead and doing different motions. Most of the roles played in Baoji *shehuo* are those special characters in ancient historical dramas and classical masterpieces, so the costumes, hats, props, spears and sticks are all in the form of those in ancient-costume dramas. During *shehuo* performance, horses usually take the lead, followed by the flag team, then *shehuo* team, and finally the gong and drum team. The whole parade team, to sonorous music of the gongs and drums, is lively and magnificent, boasting very high folk and esthetic value.

The facial makeup of Baoji *shehuo*, known as one of the oldest categories of facial makeups in China, not only has deep relationship with the totem worship and the songs and dances in ancient times, but also is inseparable from the folk ritual activities in China. The facial makeup

和语言。黑代表忠诚、铁面无私，白代表奸诈，赤代表侠义，青代表草莽，黄则代表残暴。经过漫长的时光雕琢，如今宝鸡社火脸谱已日臻精细和完美。其布局、设色、绘画、修整等已有一整套成熟的技艺和相对固定的程式，形成了鲜明的地域文化特点和独特的民间艺术风格。

改革开放以来，宝鸡民间社火艺术得到发扬光大，成为群众喜闻乐见的一种文化活动。社火队多次随国家民间艺术团体出国演出，受到国外观众的喜爱和欢迎。

2003年，宝鸡被陕西省文化厅命名为"民间社火艺术之乡"。2006年，宝鸡民间社火被列入第一批国家级非物质文化遗产名录。

features bold design, primitive patterns, and strong colors. At first, only five colors of green, red, yellow, white and black were used, which are the basic colors and markers of different characters in *shehuo* performance. Black facial makeup represents loyalty and selflessness, white represents treacherousness, red symbolizes righteousness, green represents roughness, and yellow means brutality. The designing, coloring, painting and polishing of the facial makeup have featured a set of mature skills and relatively fixed expression modes. Now the facial makeup of Baoji *shehuo*, after a long time development, is fine and exquisite and has developed into a kind of distinctive and unique folk art with regional cultural characteristics.

Since China's reform and opening-up, Baoji folk *shehuo* art has flourished and become a cultural activity enjoyed by the masses. It has been repeatedly shown in many foreign countries and has been warmly welcomed.

In 2003, Baoji was named as the "Hometown of Folk *Shehuo* Art" by Shaanxi Provincial Department of Culture. In 2006, Baoji folk *shehuo* performance was listed in the first batch of China's National Intangible Cultural Heritage List.

白云山庙会
Temple Fair in Baiyun Mountain

白云山地处陕西省榆林市佳县城南的崇山峻岭中，因山上建有道教名胜白云观而得名，是全国著名的道教名山和风景区。白云观是西北地区最大的明清古建筑群，观中供奉的神以道教系列神为主，儒、佛、道三教融合，可满足不同信仰者的需求。白云山庙会已有400多年的历史，是集宗教、文化、艺术、旅游等于一体的古老而传统的集会。

白云山在每年农历三月初三、四月初八和九月初九举行传统庙会，其中尤以四月初八庙会最为盛大。庙会期间有丰富多彩的迎贡、行香等道士科仪活动和许愿、酬神等信士活动，充满了神秘的宗教气氛。白云山庙会规模宏大，山

Baiyun Mountain, a famous Taoist mountain and scenic spot located in the south of Jiaxian County of Yulin City, is named after the Taoist scenic spot Baiyun Temple built on it. Baiyun Temple, originally built in the Ming and Qing dynasties, is the largest ancient building complex in northwestern China. The deities enshrined in the temple are mainly Taoist and Buddhist gods, and Confucian saints are also worshiped here, which can meet the needs of people of different beliefs. With a history of more than 400 years, the temple fair in Baiyun Mountain is an ancient and traditional gathering featuring religion, culture, art, and tourism.

Baiyun Temple holds traditional temple fairs on the third day of the third lunar month, the eighth day of the fourth lunar month and the ninth day of the ninth lunar month, among which the one on the eighth day of the fourth lunar month is the biggest. During the temple fair, rich and colorful Taoist religious activities are held, such as welcoming tribute, offering incense, making wishes and repaying gods, all of which feature mysterious religious atmosphere. The temple fair is of great scale and spectacularity, and people from Shanxi,

西、内蒙古、宁夏、甘肃等地群众也纷纷前来参加，场面壮观。

白云山道教属全真道龙门派。它在继承和发展中国土生土长传统道教的同时，又兼容了陕北黄土文化、黄河文化和大漠草原文化，形成了独具地方特色的白云山庙会文化。白云山庙会承载着陕北黄土高原上许多重大的历史文化信息，具有很高的历史价值、文化价值、学术价值和旅游价值。

2007年，白云山庙会被列入陕西省第一批非物质文化遗产名录。

Inner Mongolia, Ningxia, Gansu and other places have also come to participate in the temple fair.

The Taoist sect in Baiyun temple belongs to the Longmen sect of Quanzhen Taoism. While inheriting and developing Chinese native-born Taoism, it also integrates the cultures of northern Shaanxi, Yellow River basin and northwestern China, forming a unique temple fair culture. The temple fair carries much important historical and cultural information regarding the Loess Plateau in northern Shaanxi, hence it has high historical, cultural, academic and tourist value.

In 2007, the temple fair in Baiyun Mountain was included in the first batch of Shaanxi Provincial Intangible Cultural Heritage List.

谷雨祭祀文祖仓颉典礼
Ceremonies of Offering Sacrifices to Cangjie on the Day of Grain Rain

陕西省渭南市白水县自古就有清明祭黄帝、谷雨祭仓颉的民间习俗。仓颉是黄帝时期的史官，是中华象形文字的创始人，世人尊其为文字初祖。相传，仓颉创造了文字，结束了结绳记事的时代。此事感动了天帝，天帝便向人间洒下了一场谷雨。这就是我国二十四节气中谷雨的来历，也是后人在谷雨时节祭祀仓颉的缘由。

谷雨祭祀仓颉是中华民族汉字情结的具体表现。白水县建有仓颉庙，每年谷雨时节的仓颉庙会隆重热烈，世代沿袭，约定成俗。谷雨庙会以祭祀仓颉为主线，弘扬仓颉文化，融文化、经贸为一体，以书法展、唱对台戏、诗联赛、社火、锣鼓赛为主。祭礼大典主要以祭

Since ancient times, Baishui County of Weinan City has the custom of offering sacrifices to the Yellow Emperor on the Tomb Sweeping Day and to Cangjie on the day of Grain Rain. Cangjie, an official historian of the Yellow Emperor and the founder of Chinese pictographs, has been respected as the father of Chinese characters. Legend has it that Cangjie invented characters for writing and ended the practice of recording information and events by tying knots. This moved the Emperor of Heaven so that he poured grain rain to the earth, which is the origin of the Grain Rain (Chinese: *guyu*) in the twenty-four solar terms of the Chinese lunar calendar, and it is also the reason why later generations worship Cangjie on the day of Grain Rain.

Offering sacrifice to Cangjie on the day of the Grain Rain is the manifestation of Chinese people's love for Chinese characters. There is a Cangjie temple in Baishui County, where a grand temple fair featuring the integration of culture, economy and trade is held on the day of Grain Rain every year, during which sacrificial activities are held to promote the culture of Chinese characters. The

乐、祭器、祭品，恭读祭文，谒祖扫墓为主。

近年来，祭祀仓颉活动的规模更大，参与者更广，全国文化名流和海外侨胞纷纷来谒祖祭圣。当地逐渐形成了以仓颉文化为主导的区域特色文化，推动了渭北以古文化为主题的旅游事业，促进了区域社会经济的快速发展。

汉字的诞生是华夏文明的主要标志之一，而仓颉这位文化之神则是华夏文明的重要象征之一。保护和传承谷雨祭祀仓颉的礼仪，就是保护中华民族传统文化，其历史文化价值重大、意义深远。

2007年，谷雨祭祀文祖仓颉典礼被列入陕西省第一批非物质文化遗产名录。

main activities held during the temple fair include calligraphy exhibitions, operas, poetry contest, *shehuo* (a large scale folk performance), and gong and drum performance. The sacrificial ceremonies consist of playing sacrificial music, offering sacrificial vessels and oblation, reading memorial eulogy, and visiting Cangjie's tomb.

In recent years, the sacrificial activities have been on a larger scale and attracted more participants, overseas Chinese and cultural celebrities all over China included. As a result, a regional culture based on Cangjie culture has gradually formed through the sacrificial activities on the day of Grain Rain, which has promoted the ancient-culture-based tourism in Weibei area and the rapid development of regional economy.

Cangjie and the birth of Chinese characters are the main symbols of Chinese civilization. Protecting and inheriting the ceremonies of offering sacrifices to Cangjie is to protect traditional Chinese culture, which has great historical and cultural value and far-reaching significance.

In 2007, the sacrificial ceremonies were included in the first batch of Shaanxi Provincial Intangible Cultural Heritage List.

炎帝陵祭典
Sacrificial Ceremonies at the Yan Emperor's Mausoleum

陕西省宝鸡市是炎帝故里。据民间传说,宝鸡地区的炎帝祭祀活动可追溯至黄帝时期。约在5,000年前,炎帝因误尝火焰子(俗名"断肠草")而逝于宝鸡天台山,黄帝闻后急速赶往天台山祭奠。秦灵公三年(公元前422年),秦人开始祭祀炎帝、黄帝,开创了官方祭祀炎帝的先例。

20世纪80年代初,祭祀炎帝的活动开始在民间兴起。90年代初,在宝鸡市河滨公园(现"炎帝园")易地重修了炎帝祠,在常羊山重修了炎帝陵。自此,每年的清明节和炎帝忌日,炎帝祠、炎帝陵都会举行规模宏大的祭祀典礼。祭祀程序包括全体肃立、鸣钟、奏乐、敬献祭品、奠酒、敬献花篮、主祭人读祭文。仪式完毕后,全体肃立,向炎帝行

Baoji City is the hometown of Yan Emperor (Chinese: *Yandi*). According to the folklore, sacrificial activities for memorizing Yan Emperor in Baoji can be traced back to the reign of the Yellow Emperor. About 5,000 years ago, Yan Emperor passed away in Tiantai Mountain after he ate a kind of poisonous weed called gelsemium elegan. Upon hearing the news, the Yellow Emperor hurried to Tiantai Mountain for condolence. In 422 BC, people began offering sacrifices to Yan Emperor and the Yellow Emperor, which set a precedent for the official worship for Yan Emperor.

In the early 1980s, the activities of offering sacrifices to Yan Emperor began to rise among the people. In the early 1990s, Yan Emperor's memorial temple was rebuilt in the Hebin Park (now the "Yandi Park") in Baoji City, and Yan Emperor's mausoleum was rebuilt in Changyang Mountain. Since then, grand sacrificial ceremonies have been held in Yan Emperor's memorial temple and mausoleum every year on Qingming Festival as well as on his deathday. The sacrificial procedures include: standing solemnly, ringing the bell, playing music, offering sacrifices, pouring liquor, offering

礼。至此，礼毕。2005年10月3日，宝鸡市人民政府在常羊山炎帝陵举办了"全球华人省亲祭祖大典"，海内外一万多名华人参加了祭祀活动。

炎帝和黄帝同为中华民族的人文始祖，是中华文明的缔造者。炎帝陵祭典活动以一种文化的典礼"追中华文化之根，缅先祖功业之德"，传播全球华人同根同祖的民族观念。这对于宣传民族文化、弘扬爱国主义精神、促进祖国统一及世界各地中华儿女的情感交流起着重要的作用。

2008年，炎帝陵祭典被列入第二批国家级非物质文化遗产名录。

flower baskets, and the officiant's reading memorial eulogy. After the ceremonies, everyone stands up and pays homage to Yan Emperor. On October 3, 2005, Baoji Government held the Global Chinese Ancestor-Worshiping Ceremony at Yan Emperor's mausoleum. More than 10,000 Chinese at home and abroad participated in the activity.

Yan Emperor and Yellow Emperor are both ancestors of Chinese nation and founders of Chinese civilization. Sacrificial ceremonies at Yan Emperor's Mausoleum spread the concept that Chinese people all over the world are of the same origin and ancestors, which play an important role in promoting Chinese culture and patriotism, unifying the Chinese nation and enhancing communication between Chinese people all over the world.

In 2008, sacrificial ceremonies at Yan Emperor's Mausoleum were included in the second batch of China's National Intangible Cultural Heritage List.

药王山庙会
Temple Fair in Yaowang Mountain

药王山位于陕西省铜川市耀州区城东，为隋唐时期伟大的医药学家孙思邈的归隐之处。药王山庙会是古老的传统民俗及民间信仰活动，因纪念孙思邈忌辰而产生，其主要内容为朝山拜"药王"，以弘扬药王孙思邈的医德医风、发扬传统中医药文化为宗旨。

孙思邈系唐朝京兆华原（今陕西耀州）人，是我国医药学创新发展的开拓者和一代宗师。大约在唐代后期，人们就开始在这里为孙思邈立祠。北宋时，药王山庙会在青明宫举行。明嘉靖时，庙会规模开始变大，会期变长，经月余不绝。从清末至今，会期为农历二月初二至二月十一。数以万计的群众从四面八方云集而来，地方戏、歌舞、杂

Yaowang Mountain, located in the east of Yaozhou District of Tongchuan City, was the retreat of the great Chinese doctor Sun Simiao who was titled as China's *Yaowang* (King of Medicine) for his significant contributions to traditional Chinese medicine and tremendous care to his patients during the Sui and Tang dynasties. The temple fair in Yaowang Mountain is a traditional folk custom and folk religious practice in honor of Sun Simiao. The main activities at the fair are to worship Sun Simiao in order to promote his medical ethics as well as the traditional Chinese Medicine culture.

Sun Simiao, a native of Huayuan of Jingzhao (the present Yaozhou District of Tongchuan City) in the Tang Dynasty, is a pioneer and master of the innovation and development of traditional Chinese medicine. Around the late Tang Dynasty, people began to build memorial temples for him in Yaozhou. The temple fair in Yaowang Mountain can be dated back to the Northern Song Dynasty. During the reign of Emperor Jiajing in the Ming Dynasty, the temple fair developed into a larger scale one and lasted more than one month. Since the late Qing Dynasty,

技竞相表演，山上烟雾缭绕，钟磬齐鸣，鼓乐喧天，人声鼎沸。大殿内，人人虔诚叩首，个个恭敬上香，许下美好心愿，祈求长寿健康。古时还有"天明戏""路畔灯"及狮子、龙灯等大型社火活动。最后一天为庙会高潮，往往是万人空巷，非常热闹。

药王山庙会因纪念孙思邈忌辰而兴起，在表达人们对孙思邈的崇敬与怀念的同时，极大地弘扬了"药王"的高尚医德与精湛医术，对继承和发展中华民族的优秀传统文化、加强各行各业的职业道德建设具有积极的推动作用。

2008年，药王山庙会被列入第二批国家级非物质文化遗产名录。

the fair was held from the second day to the eleventh day of the second lunar month. Tens of thousands of people gather here, enjoying local operas, singing and dancing performances, acrobatics, etc. The mountain is overwhelmed by incense smoke as well as music of bell, drum and chime. In the hall, people bow devoutly, offer incense respectfully, and make good wishes for longevity and health. In the ancient days, there were also large-scale folk performances like lion and dragon dances, and the performances on the last day of the temple fair are most exciting and lively.

In addition to expressing people's respect and remembrance for him, the temple fair has also greatly promoted Sun Simiao's noble medical ethics and superb medical skills. It not only contributes to the inheritance and development of the excellent traditional culture of the Chinese nation, but also educates people from all walks of life to strengthen professional ethics.

In 2008, the temple fair in Yaowang Mountain was included in the second batch of China's National Intangible Cultural Heritage List.

楼观台祭祀老子礼仪
Ceremonies of Offering Sacrifices to Laozi in Louguantai

位于陕西省西安市周至县的楼观台被誉为"道教祖庭圣地"和"道文化发祥地"。春秋时期的大思想家、道家的创始人李聃（老子）写下了饮誉海内外的哲学巨著《道德经》。几千年来，基于《道德经》的重大影响，历代有60余位帝王下令在楼观台建造了数十处殿、亭、楼、塔祭祀老子，形成了具有特殊文化色彩的楼观台祭祀老子礼仪，并延续至今。

楼观台祭祀老子礼仪有皇家或国家祭祀、民间祭祀和宗教祭祀三种类型。皇家或国家祭祀的步骤依次是鸣奏黄钟大吕，表演国宾舞，主持人诵读祭文，全体祭祀人员行祭拜礼，在音乐的伴奏中列队绕场依次退散。民间祭祀的步骤

Louguantai, located in Zhouzhi County of Xi'an City, is known as the "Holy Land of Taoist Ancestral Temple" and the "Birthplace of Taoist Culture". Li Dan (Laozi), a great thinker in the Spring and Autumn Period and the founder of Taoism, wrote his philosophical masterpiece *Tao Te Cing*, which is well-known at home and abroad. For thousands of years, based on the significant influence of *Tao Te Cing*, more than 60 emperors in the past dynasties ordered to build halls, pavilions, towers and pagodas in Louguantai to worship Laozi, hence ceremonies of offering sacrifices to Laozi have formed and continued to this day.

The sacrificial ceremonies held in Louguantai fall into three categories: royal or national sacrifice, folk sacrifice and religious sacrifice. Royal or national sacrifice follows such steps: playing solemn music, presenting the state-guest dance, reading sacrificial oration, performing worship rituals, exiting the sacrificial venue in sequence to the accompaniment of music. The steps of folk sacrifice are beating gongs and drums, offering up big candles and sacrificial paper, chanting scriptures, offering incense to pray, performing dragon

依次是锣鼓及鼓乐演奏、献大蜡及纸活、诵经、进香祭拜、龙舞表演等。宗教祭祀的步骤是先选择黄道吉日，沐浴斋戒，设置祭坛，请主进位，道士立于其左右并上香，吉时升坛，俯拜上表，道众同拜，以表诚意，宣读礼赞老子的诗文，后参礼并依次上香行礼、诵咒。以上过程中均有道乐演奏。

近年来，国家对祭祀老子的活动非常重视，先后举办了多次"楼观台老子文化周"活动和"九九重阳节公祭老子"活动等，民间祭祀活动更是规模宏大。

2009年，楼观台祭祀老子礼仪被列入陕西省第二批非物质文化遗产名录。

dance, etc. Religious sacrifice goes through procedures of choosing auspicious days, bathing and fasting, setting up an altar, inviting the officiant to take his place (Taoist priests stand on both sides of the officiant and offer up incense), kneeling down before the altar to pray, reading poetic prose to extol Laozi, performing sacrificial rituals, offering incense and finally chanting scriptures. Throughout the above sacrificial ceremonies, Taoist music is played all the time.

In recent years, the state has attached great importance to offering sacrifices to Laozi, and has successively held activities like "Laozi Cultural Week at Louguantai" and "Public Sacrifice to Laozi on Double Ninth Festival", etc. The scale of folk sacrificial activities is much larger than that of the public sacrifice activities.

In 2009, the ceremonies of offering sacrifices to Laozi in Louguantai were included in the second batch of Shaanxi Provincial Intangible Cultural Heritage List.

西安都城隍庙民俗
Folk Customs in the City God Temple of Xi'an

西安是城隍信仰的发源地和传播地。西安都城隍庙，坐落于陕西省西安市西大街中段，始建于明洪武二十年（1387年），明宣德八年（1433年）由东门里移建于现址，迄今已有600多年历史。

西安都城隍庙民俗主要有祭祀仪式和城隍庙会。西安都城隍庙的道场祭祀分为阳事道场和阴事道场。阳事道场是为活着的人举行的消灾解难、祈福延寿等的仪式，一般安排为三天。阴事道场是为超度久处阴司的亡魂，使其超升仙界的仪式，一般亦安排为三天。道场安

Xi'an is the cradle and dissemination place of the belief in City God. The City God Temple of Xi'an is located in the middle section of the West Street of Xi'an City. Built in the twentieth year during the reign of Hongwu in the Ming Dynasty (1387 AD), and moved to the current site in the eighth year during the reign of Xuande in the Ming Dynasty (1433 AD), it has a history of more than 600 years.

The folk customs in the temple mainly include sacrificial rituals and temple fairs. The sacrificial rituals are mainly divided into two kinds, rituals for the living and rituals for the dead. Rituals for the living, which usually last for three days, are aimed at alleviating

排不是一成不变的，可根据法事内容的不同进行适当调整。

西安都城隍庙在每年农历正月初一、正月十五、四月初八、八月十五举办传统庙会，会期三天。六月十九日为圣诞、神诞节祭祖盛会。此外还定期举行酬神戏会。而新春祈福庙会盛况空前，动辄有数十万人参加。新春庙会上有许多民间传统活动，如送春联、祭城隍、迎财神、烧新年头炉香等等。也有秦腔、高跷、社火、民间绝活、鼓乐演奏等丰富多彩的民间艺术表演。

2009年，西安都城隍庙民俗被列入陕西省第二批非物质文化遗产名录。

disasters and praying for blessings and a long life for the living. Rituals for the dead, usually lasting for three days as well, are to release the souls of the dead from the nether world to the immortal world. The arrangement of the rituals is not fixed and can be adjusted appropriately according to the content of the religious rites.

Traditional temple fairs, lasting for three days, are held every year on the first and fifteenth day of the first lunar month, the eighth day of the fourth lunar month, and the Mid-Autumn Festival on the fifteenth day of the eighth lunar month. The nineteenth day of the sixth lunar month witnesses a grand worship ceremony for the birth of various gods. Besides, opera performances are held regularly to reward gods. The temple fair for Chinese New Year blessing is magnificent, with hundreds of thousands of people attending. There are many traditional folk activities at the New Year temple fair, such as handing out Spring Festival couplets, offering sacrifices to the City God, welcoming the God of Wealth, and burning incense. Various folk art performances are also put on, such as *qinqiang* opera, walking on stilts, *shehuo* performance, folk stunts, drum music and so on.

In 2009, the folk customs in the City God Temple of Xi'an were included in the second batch of Shaanxi Provincial Intangible Cultural Heritage List.

洛川婚俗
Luochuan Wedding Customs

洛川婚俗既保留了中国汉族传统婚俗的主要特征，又具有鲜明、独特的地方特征。

拜双雁是洛川婚礼中必不可少的一个重要仪式。洛川人用拜双雁代替了拜高堂。"双雁"一般是在红纸上用墨或金粉写出相向而对的两个"雁"字，衔首交尾。也有用整张红纸剪成两个相向而对的"雁"字，周围饰以"牡丹富贵""连生贵子"等求子求福的吉祥图

Wedding customs of Luochuan County retain not only the main characteristics of the traditional wedding customs of Chinese Han nationality, but also distinctive local features.

Bowing to *shuangyan* (*shuang* means double, *yan* means wild goose) is indispensable in the wedding ceremony in Luochuan. The people there replaced *gaotang* (the groom's parents) with *shuangyan* in the ceremony. Generally, the Chinese character *yan* ("雁") is written twice on a piece of red paper with ink or

案，挂于正堂，下置香案。新郎新娘对着双雁交拜，至此婚礼大成。拜双雁是古代婚礼用雁的遗风。《周礼》记载："纳采、问名、纳吉、请期、亲迎皆用雁。"这是说婚礼除纳征（俗称过彩礼）外的其余环节都要用雁。其实婚礼用雁，大约还有人们对鸟类旺盛的繁殖能力崇拜和对爱情忠贞不渝的寓意。大概由于大雁不易捕捉，有的地方代之以鹅，无鹅则用鸡代替。洛川一带订婚、商量话（即商定婚礼吉日）要用鸡，娶亲时亦须带一公一母两只活鸡。

在洛川婚俗中，要将一个枣树枝绑

gold powder: One is written in the normal way, and the other is inverted, so the two characters are facing each other. The pattern of the characters can also be cut out of a piece of red paper, then is decorated with auspicious patterns like peony and lotus flower (peony flowers symbolize wealth and honor, lotus flowers indicate having more children) and hung in the main hall. Below the *shuangyan* pattern, an incense burner is placed on the table. The bride and groom bow to *shuangyan* and the wedding ceremony is finished. Bowing to *shuangyan* is developed from the use of wild geese at weddings in ancient China. As is recorded in *The Rites of Zhou*, geese were used throughout the whole process of the wedding ceremony except for sending betrothal gifts from the bridegroom's family to the bride's family. In fact, the use of wild geese at weddings implies people's worship for the vigorous reproduction of birds and loyalty to love. Probably because wild geese are not easy to catch, geese are used as an alternative in some places. If geese are not available, chickens are used instead. A chicken is required for engagement and on the occasion of negotiating the auspicious date of the wedding, and one live hen and one rooster are musts on the wedding day.

During the wedding ceremony, a date tree branch should be tied to a broom, red dates, walnuts, rabbit figurines made of flour, etc., pierced on thorns of the branch. From the time when the bride and groom

在扫帚上，枣刺上要扎上红枣、核桃、面制的小兔子等，从新人下轿到拜双雁，直至新人入洞房，一般要由姐夫、姑父唱《拉枣枝歌》，表示对美满婚姻的祝福。洛川婚俗烦琐而隆重，尤其是男方家里，除婚礼以前的提亲、定亲外，在婚礼当日还有告祖、迎娶、闹洞房等礼仪。成婚后新娘新郎还要回门。洛川婚俗在民间代代相传，没有成文的规定，许多习俗都含有祝愿新人早生贵子、家庭和睦兴旺之义。

洛川婚俗从中国古代婚嫁"六礼"演变而来，蕴含着传统伦理思想和民族文化心理，具有重要的历史、文化和民俗价值。

2011年，洛川婚俗被列入陕西省第三批非物质文化遗产名录。

get off the sedan chair or wedding car to the time when they bow to *shuangyan* and then enter the bridal chamber, usually the brothers-in-law or uncles-in-law of the groom sing a song called *Song of Pulling Date Tree Branches* to express their blessings for a happy marriage. The wedding customs are elaborate and solemn, especially on the groom's side. In addition to the bringing up proposal and engagement before the wedding, there are also etiquettes such as worshiping ancestors, welcoming the bride, playing tricks on the bride and the bridegroom on wedding night. After the wedding ceremony, the newlyweds need to return to the home of the bride's parents on the third day after the wedding ceremony. Although the wedding customs of Luochuan are not kept in written form, they have been passed down from generation to generation, many of which have connotation such as praying for birth of children, and harmony and prosperity of the family.

Evolved from the "six rituals" of ancient Chinese weddings, Luochuan wedding customs contain traditional ethical thoughts and national cultural psychology, having important historical, cultural and folk values.

In 2011, Luochuan wedding customs were included in the third batch of Shaanxi Provincial Intangible Cultural Heritage List.

上巳节风俗
Shangsi Festival Customs

上巳节风俗主要流行于西安市。上巳节为三月上旬的巳日。曹魏之后定为三月初三。上巳节最早可以追溯到春秋时期。

据传，三月上巳这一天，郑国男女到溱、洧二水岸边举行祭祀，以消除灾害。年轻男女们也借春游的机会谈情说爱。《诗经》中《溱洧》一诗对这一民间风俗的盛况有生动的描写。秦汉以来，上巳节更是发展为全国性的大节日。据《汉书》记载："是月上巳，官民皆洁于东流水上，曰洗濯祓除，去宿垢疢（病）为大洁。"到了晋代始有曲水流觞之饮。除此以外，还有了上巳节

Shangsi Festival, on the third day of the third month of lunar calendar, can be traced back to the Spring and Autumn Period, and customs of *Shangsi* Festival are mainly circulated in Xi'an City.

It is said that on this day, people in the Zheng State held sacrificial ceremonies on the banks of Zhen and Wei Rivers to prevent disease and get rid of bad luck. Young men and women also took this opportunity of spring outing to court. The poem *Zhen Wei* in *The Book of Songs* vividly described the grand occasion of this festival. Since the Qin and Han dynasties, the *Shangsi* Festival has developed into a national festival. *The Book of Han* recorded how people celebrated it: "On this day, both officials and ordinary people bathed themselves in the river in hopes that water could wash away their illness." In the Jin Dynasty, an interesting game appeared: people took up wine cups to drink when the cups floating in the water move to them. In addition, people also played other games on

"曲水浮素卵"或"曲水浮绛枣"的游戏,即将鸡蛋或枣放在水中,漂到谁面前,谁就取食,以此为戏。盛唐时每逢上巳节,皇帝都会携妃子百官游览皇家园林芙蓉园。长安民众也纷纷前往曲江欢聚游宴。杜甫的《丽人行》中"三月三日天气新,长安水边多丽人"就描写了上巳节长安曲江禊饮踏青的盛况。

大唐芙蓉园建于唐代芙蓉园遗址之上,是中国第一个全方位展示盛唐皇家园林风貌的大型文化主题公园。目前,上巳节活动尚未在全社会范围内恢复。但是自2005年以来,大唐芙蓉园为传承上巳节这一盛唐极具代表性的节日做出了很大的努力,同时也得到了广大社会民众的积极配合、响应,以及专家学者的倡导和认可。比如,2007年,大唐芙蓉园举行了冠礼、祓禊、曲水流觞、踏青抛彩等"三月三·上巳节"精彩活动,让公众切身体验上巳古礼。

this day for amusement. For example, eggs or dates were put in the water to float away, and when they floated to a person, he or she should fetch and eat them. During *Shangsi* Festival in the Tang Dynasty, the emperor would take his concubines and officials to visit the royal garden Furongyuan (now called the Tang Paradise). The people in the capital city Chang'an (now Xi'an) also went to Qujiang Lake (the biggest scenic spot in Chang'an at that time) for a happy get-together. The famous poet Du Fu of Tang Dynasty described the spectacular outing in Qujiang area during the *Shangsi* Festival in his poem, which reads "the weather is nice on the day of *Shangsi*, beautiful ladies go for a walk around Qujiang Lake".

Built on the site of the original Furongyuan, Tang Paradise is the first large-scale cultural theme park in China to fully display the style and features of the royal gardens in the glorious age of Tang Dynasty. Currently, the activities to celebrate *Shangsi* Festival have not been fully resumed in the whole society. However, since 2005, the park has made great efforts to make the festival promoted.

2008年，大唐芙蓉园举办上巳踏青文化节，包含丰富多彩的古代游艺活动，如大唐斗鸡、蹴鞠、秋千等，让民众体验古人上巳节踏青游艺之趣。此外，大唐芙蓉园每年在庆祝开园周年的同时开展上巳节文化主题月活动，让上巳节深入人心。

2011年，上巳节风俗被列入陕西省第三批非物质文化遗产名录。

At the same time, it has received active cooperation and response from the general public as well as the advocacy of experts and scholars. For example, in 2007, wonderful activities like capping ceremony, spring outing, tossing colorful balls, etc., were held in the park so that the public could experience the ancient rituals of *Shangsi*. In 2008, *Shangsi* Outing Cultural Festival was held, which offered opportunities for the public to experience the fun of ancient people's outing at the festival through a variety of traditional recreational activities, such as cockfighting, *cuju* (an ancient Chinese ball game), playing on the swing. In addition, Tang Paradise holds activities themed on *Shangsi* Festival which last for a month while celebrating the opening anniversary of the park every year, which make the festival known to more people.

In 2011, *Shangsi* Festival customs were included in the third batch of Shaanxi Provincial Intangible Cultural Heritage List.

主要参考文献
Main References

[1] 陕西省文化厅,陕西省非物质文化遗产保护中心. 陕西省第一批非物质文化遗产名录图典[M]. 西安:陕西人民美术出版社,2008.

[2] 陕西省文化厅,陕西省非物质文化遗产保护中心. 陕西省第二批非物质文化遗产名录图典[M]. 西安:陕西师范大学出版社,2010.

[3] 陕西省文化厅,陕西省非物质文化遗产保护中心. 陕西省第三批非物质文化遗产名录图典[M]. 西安:陕西人民美术出版社,2012.

[4] 陕西省文化厅,陕西省非物质文化遗产保护中心. 陕西省第四批非物质文化遗产名录图典[M]. 西安:陕西人民美术出版社,2017.

[5] 《中国的非物质文化遗产》编写组. 中国的非物质文化遗产:汉、英[M]. 北京:北京语言大学出版社,2011.

[6] 中国非遗项目编写组. 非物质文化遗产在中国[M]. 北京:北京语言大学出版社,2017.

[7] 巴莫曲布嫫. 非物质文化遗产:从概念到实践[J]. 民俗艺术,2008(1):6-17.

[8] 陈芳蓉. 中国非物质文化遗产英译的难点与对策[J]. 中国科技翻译,2011,24(2):41-44.

[9] 陈芳蓉. 文化多样性与非物质文化遗产的译介[J]. 浙江师范大学学报(社会科学版),2013,38(3):64-69.

[10] 高昂之. 非物质文化遗产的外宣翻译与国际传播:现状与策略[J]. 浙江理工大学学报(社会科学版),2019,42(2):136-142.

[11] 田亚亚,孙雪娥. 生态翻译学对非物质文化遗产翻译的启示:陕西省非物质文化遗产翻译研究[J]. 渭南师范学院学报,2016,31(10):55-60.

[12] 田亚亚. 陕西省非物质文化遗产外宣文本中文化专有项英译探析[J]. 湖北第二师范学院学报,2018,35(7):120-123.